EVERYDAY MYSTICISM

ARIEL GLUCKLICH

Everyday Mysticism

A CONTEMPLATIVE COMMUNITY

AT WORK IN THE DESERT

Yale

UNIVERSITY PRESS

NEW HAVEN & LONDON

Published with assistance from the Mary Cady Tew Memorial Fund.

Yale University Press books may be purchased in quantity for
educational, business, or promotional use. For information, please e-mail
sales.press@yale.edu (U.S. office) or sales@yaleup.co.uk (U.K. office).

Set in Scala type by Integrated Publishing Solutions,
Grand Rapids, Michigan.
Printed in the United States of America.

Library of Congress Control Number: 2017934982

ISBN 978-0-300-21209-9 (hardcover : alk. paper)

A catalogue record for this book is available from the British Library.

This paper meets the requirements of ANSI/NISO Z39.48-1992
(Permanence of Paper).

10 9 8 7 6 5 4 3 2 1

All photographs are courtesy of the Neot Smadar Archive.

To all the residents of Neot Smadar

CONTENTS

Preface   ix

Introduction: What Is Neot Smadar?   1

1 A Search for Religious Experience   12

2 Washing Dishes   30

3 The Oasis of Neot Smadar: An Overview   45

4 A School for Self-Inquiry   64

5 The School after the Death of Yossef   82

6 The Art of Listening   104

7 Everyday Mysticism   121

8 Constructing the Art Center: Communal Project as
   Ascetic Practice   141

9 At Work in Neot Smadar: Making Wine, Milking Goats,
   Learning the Lesson of the Bolt   157

10 The Extended Family: Sociality in Neot Smadar   186

11   A Wedding Gift for Dani   206

     Conclusion: Looking Forward   219

     Notes   223

     Bibliography   241

     Index   251

PREFACE

NEOT SMADAR IS A REMOTE DESERT community that confounds easy judgments about the nature of religion, mysticism, and the monastic life. It is not a commune, a kibbutz, or even an intentional community. Its residents are mostly family people, and virtually all would fall under the fuzzy category of "secular" Jews. And yet the place is a special sort of school, which I call "spiritual" only at the risk of conveying a highly distorted meaning. The place first attracted my attention in 2010, and the relationship that developed continues to deepen.

I was very fortunate to study at Harvard when Professor Wilfrid Smith headed the Committee on the Study of Religion. Among the many substantive facts I learned from Smith was a major new way of thinking about religion. I came to see the concept "Religion" as a reified abstraction and a barrier to understanding my neighbors in this world. In his conversational writing style (as seen in *The Meaning and End of Religion*) and in person, Smith often repeated this insight: We "must leave behind the distraction of congealed concepts postulating entities different from the living person before" us. To study religion means to encounter persons—to enter into a conversation with them, to share an experience. In a century of constantly emerging theories borrowed from sociology, psychology, anthropology, literary criticism, and elsewhere, this was stunning in its simplicity, and it was quietly compelling.

As I approached the community of Neot Smadar in the remote Israeli desert, I wondered: what might such an approach look like in practice? How does one translate Smith's insight into a "method?" In the conversations I heard and read about in Neot Smadar were echoes of the Upanishads, *Bhagavad Gita, Yoga Sutras,* Shankara, and Buddhist texts as well. Members of the Neot Smadar community did not know this, and readers may also not realize this, unless they have studied Hindu and Buddhist thought, as I have. So it turns out that my experience in Neot Smadar was what Smith might mean by "encounter:" It is an encounter not between two or three religions but among persons. The story I tell, therefore, is not of Hinduism in Israel but of my encounter with the people who live and work in Neot Smadar, whom I regard as everyday mystics.

This is a special approach, one of many that Professor Smith has inspired. A related method can be seen in some of the work carried out by another student of Smith, Diana Eck, who has been the most consistent and fruitful in applying the idea of encounter to her work. She opens her important book *Encountering God: A Spiritual Journey from Bozeman to Banaras* by talking about a person, not a concept, and she writes about that person as would a novelist: "I grew up in Bozeman, Montana, in the Gallatin Valley, one of the most beautiful mountain valleys in the Rockies." Later she tells the reader that her book, about the encounter between her own Christian faith and the religious life of her Hindu, Buddhist, and Muslim friends, begins with "my own experience."

So what might I take away from Eck's encounter, from her detailed application of Smith's ideas to a pluralistic religious world? After all, the community of Neot Smadar avoids any reference to God and cannot be relegated to any of the familiar academic categories—including even "New Age."

The first and foremost lesson I adopt from Smith and Eck is this: The "fieldwork" is, more accurately, an encounter among persons, and it is a shared experience. There is no aspiration to know (understand) the members of the community in some objective fashion while bracketing myself. The totality of the shared experience must be the focus, and, honestly, I am a student and a novice among those who have had a greater say in how that experience has been shaped. The ethics of caring applies: the hospitality and generosity I have encountered can only be met with my reciprocal friendship. That is, not only must I remember Smith's insight that beyond the living person everything else can be somewhat misleading for understanding religion. I must also bear in mind Martin Buber's advice on how to regard another person, as a Thou.

But there is more. Other scholars who specialize in Hinduism, but did not study with Smith, work in a related manner. For example, Kirin Narayan wrote a wonderful book about folk narrative in India (*Storytellers, Saints, and Scoundrels: Folk Narrative in Hindu Religious Teaching*). She begins her book in the following way: "Swamiji lay in his deck chair. His legs, bare below the knee, were outstretched, but his eyes were alert." Needless to say, my attention was immediately riveted: the author had me as captive reader. But this is not about the pleasures of reading, however important that may be. I am commenting on the narrative approach. Much of scholarship seeks to achieve an atemporal mood, to set data firmly into a fixed form, like objects under a glass plate in a museum. But persons, and shared experiences among persons, are not museum objects or abstractions. Experience is essentially narrative in form, and persons live in time and, as Stephen Crites noted (in "The Narrative Quality of Experience"), even abstractions like death and eros must sometimes submit to the narrative form. That means that this book must describe not only where members of the community got their ideas and how they explain their practices. It must also describe what it is like for the author to work in the kitchen or in the goat pen and how shared experiences at work and elsewhere change his own worldview and working assumptions.

If I am to take Cantwell Smith seriously and write about persons and shared experiences, I need to integrate the narrative form into this work. And so half of *Everyday Mysticism* assumes a near-novelistic quality; the subject matter simply requires it. The other half is more conventional (in an academic sense) because every now and then I had to step back and reflect on the way I understand religious experience, mysticism, and other scholarly tools. Nonetheless, *Everyday Mysticism* is ultimately the report of an encounter, a sort of story. It tells about a shared experience in time, an experience that is unique and unreplicable.

This project attracted me for personal as well as academic reasons. It is a project about community and about individual quest—an odd hybrid that confounds religious categories. The point of departure was biographical. My maternal grandparents came from Greater Russia (Moldova and Belarus) to the land of Israel (Palestine) in the 1920s to form the perfect community. Their idea of perfection was a community that changes human consciousness—one that creates a new human being, a new Jew. They called this community "*kvutzah*," which may be translated as "commune" (literally, group). And, despite heroic efforts, their kvutzah—"Kvutzat Hasharon"—never approached perfection. In time they settled for the designation "kibbutz," and it is where I was born and spent the first seven years of my life.

On the academic side, I am deeply interested in Vedanta and Yoga philosophies and practice. I think of these methods of introspection as psychological tools for exploring states of consciousness. And as expressions not only of technical philosophical ideas but of committed practice, they tend to attract individuals who renounce social relationships. There seems to be a practical if not a conceptual chasm between contemplative discipline and social (and economic) actions in the world.

In Neot Smadar I believe I found people who have dedicated their lives to contemplation—a term I use for the array of practices associated with Yoga, Vedanta, early Buddhism, and monastic Christianity—without giving up on sociality and economic work. They call this practice "*limud*" (literally "study"), which I translate as "Self-inquiry" (systematic inquiry into the nature of the self). Their community centers on a school ("the school for Self-inquiry") where this discipline develops, and they have maintained a self-sustaining economy to support the school and their pursuit of limud. All of this takes place in one of the most challenging ecological environments imaginable: a remote desert plateau in the South of Israel, where annual rainfall averages about an inch.

I heard about the founding of this school in the early 1980s and about the desert community in 1989, when members of the school moved from Jerusalem to the desert. However, it was 2010 when I first visited and not until the summer of 2013 that I began to spend time and work in Neot Smadar for the research that went into this book. The physical work (fruit picking, food processing and packing, goat milking, winemaking, kitchen work, bricklaying, and much else) was both demanding and satisfying. It may have helped me build inroads into the hearts of the community members who had to welcome a different sort of volunteer, one who was far older than the others and who wished to write a book about the place. Very quickly I was embraced with great warmth and gradually felt the deepening of trust and confidence in me. Anat G. and Hanna were the first to share material about life and spiritual practices in Neot Smadar. Hanna shared with me her amazingly detailed and comprehensive diaries. These gave me my first glimpses of Yossef, the man who had founded the school in the 1970s and who refused to call himself a teacher. What I saw in those records was an unusually refined mind with an equally impressive gift for communication. I felt as though I had stumbled onto the text of some ancient Indian philosopher—a Vedantin or perhaps a Buddhist. It felt like finding a treasure, and I began to understand the magnetism of the place.

In time another resident, Alon, gave me access to the archive of the community, with its detailed transcripts of hundreds of conversations, reports, meetings, retreats, and so forth. Ilana (who was at that time secretary of Neot Smadar with Alon) provided me with transcripts of conversations that had taken place decades earlier when the school was in Jerusalem. There were thousands of pages of written material, but, just as important, there were men and women who were living and working in this community a decade and more after the death of Yossef. I kept a diary and recorded my experiences as a volunteer who went to work in the morning wherever I was told. Like other volunteers, I sensed that there was something unusual, deeply gratifying, about this place—but I had no clear understanding of it. I also recorded and wrote down my conversations with many of the community members and younger workers. I am under no illusion that I could have understood Neot Smadar today without patient guidance. More important, I am under no illusion that I fully understand Neot Smadar as it is today or the full meaning of the work of Yossef and the school for Self-inquiry as it evolved over the years.

The list of those in Neot Smadar to whom I owe my deep gratitude reprises the Neot Smadar phone list, which contains over a hundred names. I have thanked most of them in person, and besides, I know that they, too, think it superfluous to list dozens of names on this page. Not a single person in Neot Smadar would regard his or her patience and generosity as a currency awaiting a fair exchange via a book's acknowledgement. What they offered was a gift. For example, Dalit, Karen and Arturo, and Ehud allowed me to stay in their homes for the duration of my stay (they were all away for those three summers)—but none of them think of their homes in a proprietary manner (the residences rotate in Neot Smadar) and were delighted to share their space. The same applies (to so many other residents of the community) with regard to time they spent talking with me, showing me how to do things at work, and even spoiling me with snacks and sweets (Shlomit), books and other items (Isaac), and so forth. A number of Neot Smadar residents have also read over the manuscript once or twice and made invaluable suggestions and corrections. The book is far better for that editorial and substantive help. I have dedicated this book to all my friends in Neot Smadar because I share this work with them—it has been a shared project. I also thank Mark Juergensmeyer and Michal Palgi for their support and concrete suggestions, Jose Casanova and Benjamin Zablocki for their support of the project, Rony Oren and Avner Glucklich for ongoing intellectual exchanges, Kate Kelly for her valuable observations in Neot Smadar, Jennifer Banks at Yale for her trust, and Georgetown University—especially the Theology Department—for material support. I also thank Jennifer Hansen-Glucklich, the love for whom has made me grow in so many unexpected ways as this work has neared completion. Finally, this book is written with apologies to Karl Rahner, whose phrase I borrowed for the title despite the fact that Neot Smadar is a world apart.

EVERYDAY MYSTICISM

Introduction: What Is Neot Smadar?

CAN A PURELY CONTEMPLATIVE PRACTICE, something called "Self-inquiry" (or inquiry concerning the nature of the self), take place outside of standard religious institutions (monastery, ashram, Zen center) and form the basis of a self-sustaining householder community? This is the question that drives *Everyday Mysticism*. The question itself is complex and requires unpacking, while the answer must keep us waiting because it is still unclear what Neot Smadar—the community where I sought the answer—will become in time. For now, this community stands out as an extraordinary ongoing experiment in combining contemplation with communal life— and work—in one of the harshest places on earth.

In the spring of 1989 a number of young families and several bachelors from Jerusalem emptied out their apartments, loaded their furniture and other belongings on an old truck—piled high like the Dust Bowl trucks headed for California—and moved to one of the truly isolated spots in Israel. Deep in the Negev desert, about 60 kilometers north of Eilat but several kilometers west of the Arava (Afro-Syrian gap), was an old abandoned settlement that these city folks were able to secure on a trial basis. The new settlers, most of them in their thirties with young children, were students in a special school—a school for Self-inquiry founded and led by Yossef Safra in Jerusalem in the 1970s.

A documentary filmmaker, Aran Patenkin, recorded the move. In his film you can see the excitement and the chaos, the young and earnest faces ex-

Fig. 1. Yossef Safra

plaining to the camera why they had left the city for this austere location—what they were hoping to achieve and what worried them.[1] The backdrop shows sun-scorched hills and rocky mesas, and the viewer can't help wondering how these urbanites hoped to make a living there. You can also see Yossef Safra (Fig. 1), a small man with sharp features and intense eyes, sitting in the middle of a group in the shade of some trees. He explains to the camera in his remarkably expressive manner what they were all doing there: "We are pioneers," he says, "Zionists of human consciousness. The school for Self-inquiry is a place to alter human consciousness and human community. It will assume the external form of a kibbutz because it is the most expedient."

The camera shifts to the families moving into their modest dwellings, parents carrying children on their shoulders, furniture and bedding waiting for the dusting and mopping to end before being hauled inside. There are scenes of early farming, under a blazing sun of course. Everyone, except Yossef, is young and energetic. The whole thing has the look of early twentieth-century land settlement—the sort of thing my own grandparents undertook in the 1920s—videotaped here in color.

But let's not be deceived: these young folks did not come down to fight chronic aridity and intense heat in order to grow dates and raise goats. Nor did they come down to form the perfect community, to explore egalitarianism and communal work. Their goal was infinitely more subtle and elusive. They came because they had committed themselves wholeheartedly to Self-inquiry, and this commitment had led them to this isolated place. One could almost think of the ancient desert fathers (of early Christianity) or the Jewish Essenes or perhaps other unknown individuals who departed for the desert in order to practice unhindered introspection.[2]

All of this conjures an aura of mysticism, that elevated and exacting spiritual practice leading to direct knowledge of the divine. So were these people mystics? They wouldn't be the first mystics in religious history who refused to abandon family life for spiritual pursuit. Just think of Vimalakirti, Marpa, Kabir, Hassidim, Sufis, Kabbalists, and countless others who have pursued the mystical path as householders. You do not have to be a monk in order to practice mysticism. Most people in Neot Smadar, the eponymous name given to the new community, would today laugh at the suggestion that they were mystics.[3] "Mysticism," after all, carries such enormous associative baggage—most of which is vague and confusing. In fact, Neot Smadar residents today would deny that this is a religious community or that Self-inquiry is a "spiritual" pursuit. The need to define things, to label subtle and dynamic introspective practice with analytical categories of any kind, let alone these immense clichés, violates the very nature of Self-inquiry as pure process. So it is important to be clear (I can hear Yossef saying): the reigning position has been that the school in Neot Smadar is not "mystical" and the community is not "religious."

Here is how Yossef put the matter in a conversation with some of the students that took place on December 15, 1998: "I have been very careful all these years to avoid the 'element of mystery.' It's imaginary and it is too easy to stumble on it—this esotericism. But we know virtually nothing about the religious mind. As a result, we are either secular in an extreme fashion or we are slaves to images and traditions. Is there any connection between the two extremes?"[4]

The connection, elaborated later in that conversation, is that both extremes are modes of reifying the flow of existence into concepts that deceive. However, religion, in some undefined sense, was too important to just abandon. Yossef added rhetorically: "Is there any connection in my own mind between my attitude toward modesty or pride, integrity or dishonesty, and any possible religious dimension?" In other words, the deepest and most meaningful questions in life cannot be approached without some consideration for religion, once it is clarified and purified of preconceptions.

For sympathetic outsiders trying to understand Neot Smadar, this is a critical agenda, and it is complicated by the fuzziness of the "secular" and the "religious" as tools of understanding. Both the religious (including the sacred) and the secular are socially embedded constructions with particular histories. As Talal Asad notes, secularization first denoted "a legal transition from monastic life (*regularis*) to the life of canons (*saecularis*)—and then, after the Reformation, it signified the transfer of ecclesiastical real property to laypersons" and so forth.[5] In modernism, then, the secular represents liberation from the sacred and, in particular, liberation from the false consciousness of the religious mind.[6] A group that removes itself—at least initially—from its national context (Israeli secularism following a complex Western-Socialist hybrid) and disavows all discursive constructions cannot accept secularism as a meaningful category of self-understanding, not even in negation.[7] Hence, in trying to understand the facts that make Neot Smadar a self-aware community we are left without the usual analytical categories. We call it either religious or secular at our own risk. Furthermore, the same word of caution applies to its nature as a community: it is not a kibbutz, a *moshav* (semi–collective farm), a village, a town, or a club. And calling it an "intentional community" simply begs the question.[8]

Perhaps the most precise way of accounting for Neot Smadar's sociality —the coming together of urban professionals who abandoned the secularism of standard Israeli citizenship—is as what Philip Wexler has called "everyday mysticism." Wexler is talking about postmodernism, inducing "a variety of forms of non-institutional religion, of 'mysticism,' which are at least incipient antidotes to an intensified destruction of being" and which occur within social terms.[9] To summarize this in simple terms, in everyday mysticism the individual's pursuit of ultimately meaningful ("religious") questions takes on collective (communal) realization.

This does not make the researcher's life easy. But life is not easy in Neot Smadar, either. A constant tension plays out in practice between the impulse to continue undermining the discriminations that separate the secular from the religious, on the one hand, and the drive to satisfy the self's need for ultimate meaning, on the other hand.

An example will help illustrate this. The following is a song (translated) sung by the Shabbat kitchen crew on July 4, 2014. Someone in Neot Smadar, perhaps one of the singers, wrote it, and I obtained a copy.

> Lower my pride and raise my honor
> Lead me to my path and repair my thinking
> Inspire me with faith beyond doubt
> Remove my despair and strengthen my devotion.[10]

After the festive dinner, outside, the meaning was discussed with Bruria and Yoram, two veteran members of Neot Smadar and students of Yossef in Jerusalem. They are both strict in adhering to the way Yossef conducted Self-inquiry and have not accepted many of the changes that the place—particularly the school—has undergone. After the song ended, Bruria said: "I do not understand the value of such a song. We have always learned that you can only rely on yourself. We are not supplicants, and we do not require any assistance from God, whatever that is."

Yoram agreed: "Why search for strength, for anything actually, outside of yourself? If you can't find the Truth by looking into your own self, you are just engaged in delusion."

I was sitting at the table near them and listening to their discussion of self-sufficiency and psychological realism while Anat G. was sitting across from me. Anat is also one of the veterans in Neot Smadar, a woman who led the community and the school for seven years after the death of Yossef. She did not challenge their statements but rather responded in her own way. She said: "I recently joined a choir myself, a really good one. During the last rehearsal I cried from the thrill; the thrill of the music and the feeling of being together with these others singing along. The words of the song were just the vehicle to the main thing, they did not define the experience."

Anat was clearly but circumspectly saying that the others were getting hung up on the words of the song they had just heard, and in the process they were missing something more valuable. They were allowing the hymn to God to lead them in a chain of associations, in a dispute actually, about the path to meaning. The subtext I read in this was that the present moment—the singing and the listening—may have been sacred in some sense even if you ignored the explicit theology.

Later, Anat gave me the following song that she had written (in Hebrew):

> Cracks
> From within the cracks of fatigue
> And the skeleton of routine
> Thin breezes rise,
> Like small ants,
> Looking for passages.
> Like water in the soil,
> Looking for the openings.
> I am asking for the grace of the cracks,
> Let it appear between the words and the thoughts
> Cracks in the heart, cracks in the walls,
> In fog cracks—
> In order to see.[11]

I find Anat's song more appealing than the theological song I had heard at the Shabbat dinner, but I never heard it sung. I suspect that Yoram and Bruria would like it, too. But that is not the main point. Far more important is the longing expressed in Anat's song for something intangible, perhaps inexpressible. And that is what she felt in the choir rehearsal and perhaps in the singing of the Shabbat crew on July 4. There is nothing wrong with singing to God or about God as long as you realize that the truth of the song is not necessarily in its words but in the cracks the singing opens up in the aridity of immensely difficult daily routines, chores, habits of mind.

Still, the tension I identified between the two positions—the hardcore "emptiness" and self-sufficiency of Yoram and Bruria, on the one hand, and the spiritual feelings of others, on the other hand—is not only healthy; it is vital to the life of Neot Smadar. The real issue is not reliance on autonomous as opposed to external resources but rather sensitivity to and the vision of "presence" (in the language of P. D. Ouspensky) as opposed to acceptance of doctrine or ideology.[12] The ability to be fully present, fully awake, can be applied in any context and can express itself in diverse tropes. It transcends the distinction between religion and secularism.

In a sense, Neot Smadar appears typical of a widespread contemporary search for a communal solution to the tension between the religious and the secular on the practical level. There are many other types of community that have emerged to promote a powerful ideal with life-altering implications. These include communes or "intentional communities," eco villages, co-operatives, cohousing communities, and earlier types of community: kib-butzim and even Amish villages.[13] For example, Tamara in Portugal is a community that emphasizes natural and human environments as places of healing and love. Today in Portugal, the village is promoted as a place where cooperation and mutual reliance replace competition and war.[14]

However, even the best of these communities often exhibit their own inner tensions, especially the conflict between the communitarian and the individ-ualistic ideals. The first is the ideal of the community to which the individual subsumes herself through a strong commitment.[15] This idea ranges from softer communalistic versions to the hard identification (in Soviet psychol-ogy) of the individual mind with collective forces.[16] The individualistic ideal (with freedom and justice at its core) is associated with liberal political principles and is currently identified philosophically with the work of John Rawls.[17] The group is the fair society of individuals who negotiate often conflicting interests. I believe that there is no permanent way of resolving or balancing out the pull of the two modes of sociality in contemporary communities.

Neot Smadar appears to exist on this spectrum, too. It exhibits the values of communalism, such as tolerance, reciprocity, trust, altruism, compan-ionship, and others. But it is also individualistic in the sense that the overriding agenda is Self-inquiry in a school and the community flows from that. But the situation in Neot Smadar is more complicated. Self-inquiry is not, properly speaking, individualistic, either: it seeks to unmake the individual self as a social value and empirical fact. And the community does not arise from an explicit ideology, values, or principles of any kind; it is merely the set of "conditions" in which Self-inquiry can take place.[18] And so neither the communitarian nor the individualistic models (or the spectrum they represent) appear adequate for understanding Neot Smadar. Are there additional types of community that may illuminate this unique arrangement?

The concept of community is rather elusive, but the baseline is something like this: "a group of people, larger than a household, interacting among themselves who refer to each other in terms of 'us' and who share some norms and values."[19] If this is accepted, can we regard monastic groups, sectarian groups, devotional groups, and even ritual groups (e.g., pilgrims) as examples of (intentional) religious community? Naturally, these include nonreproductive groups such as all Dominican or Franciscan monks, members of a specific monastery, or members of a Buddhist monastery or Hindu ashram.[20] They could also apply to Hasidic courts and the families of followers of a specific rebbe, followers of a Sufi shaykh or a Hindu swami, and so forth. Such groups have often been studied as "charismatic," with charisma (of God or a human representative of God) offered as an alternative to both individual and communal ideals.[21] At the extreme end of the charismatic spectrum is the community that is dubbed a "cult," but that is a notoriously difficult term to define and identify in practice.[22]

Neot Smadar is none of these, either. The person who led the move to Neot Smadar did not regard himself as a teacher (transmitter of information), and the practice that dominates the study in the school is not the internalization of some teaching, doctrine, or object of faith; nor is it veneration, devotion, or any of the other religious attitudes that characterize the devotional group, the sect, and so forth.

Neot Smadar is unique, and it must be understood on its own terms before it can take its place in the academic spectrum of sociality.[23] Furthermore, today, fourteen years after the death of Yossef, it is undergoing substantial changes. As Neot Smadar evolves it searches for new modes of self-understanding and ways to keep vibrant the connection between Self-inquiry and communal life and work. Whatever picture of this community emerges in this book will have to be revised in a few years.

This draws us back to the concept of everyday mysticism, where the emphasis is on the daily. That is, the Self-inquiry at the heart of this place must radiate to daily life in a way that bridges the individual self (which is always challenged) and the community. Hence, to give one example, work is not just instrumental activity geared toward economic survival. Work—physical labor and otherwise—is the place where the self meets the other and sociality develops organically from spiritual practice (driving the concept of the "extended family" model of sociality). To put this in Christian terms, a "theology of work" links daily action to ultimate concern and deep psychological practice—as we shall see throughout the book.[24] But there is nothing theological about any of this, no higher power, no esoteric truth. Work is not even symbolic in the (Zen) sense that it points to the absurdity of distinguishing between the mundane and the ultimately meaningful. Work is work, and the objects used are tools, raw materials, or supplies. You fix a car because you need to go somewhere, and its stubborn mechanical glitch is a condition that you must confront as a matter of both transportation and Self-inquiry.

This imposes a distinct methodology for historians of religion who wish to understand the ways that contemplation translates into everyday living. I approached Neot Smadar as a "participant observer," and I was interested in the self-understanding of its members rather than in a quantitative and causal analysis of some "deeper" principle that accounts for their actions. However, the reality of the community dictates an approach that differs from the work of the cultural anthropologist, who seeks the meaning of symbolic acts and objects, or the historian of religion, who observes and participates in the annual festival and liturgical cycle of a religious community in India or Israel. The world of Neot Smadar—including objects and work with those objects—do not signify in a standard religious sense. There is nothing to decode. Instead, I have had to work with other workers and try to understand how the work and how working together create (or describe) the conditions in which Self-inquiry takes place: How do they intentionally confront the reality of their world? Hence, if I describe a junkyard in great detail (behind the garage) or take the reader to a day on the goat farm, it is because those are facts of life in Neot Smadar, and that is the context in which contemplation and mindfulness take place. Junk and goats symbolize nothing; the former needs to be removed and the latter milked—no less and no more. What may constitute a religious moment and what I must understand is how these tasks are met as the conditions in which the school of Neot Smadar operates.

The key to the project, then, is linking the rigorous practice of Self-inquiry to everything else that takes place in Neot Smadar. That is the substantive agenda. It requires that I answer several questions, including these: What is religious experience? What is mysticism? What is a religious community? How does asceticism contribute to both mystical practice and community? How does everyday mysticism translate into humane farming and a work environment? However, I am also obligated to show how I came to the answers I provide, both because it reveals an aspect of the school's methodology and perhaps also because it replicates to some extent the epistemological journey that I took, like that of other novices in Neot Smadar.

The chapters of this book include the narrative of my encounter with the community and my increasing familiarity with its members and core practices, as well as the more analytical reflections by means of which I have interpreted what I saw, heard, and read. The first, fourth, and seventh chapters discuss the nature of religious experience and mysticism, examining in detail the ways in which Self-inquiry can be understood in a nuanced manner. The eighth, ninth (opening sections), and tenth chapters discuss the way that contemplative practices translate into the important areas of work and community. A great deal of the material in those chapters comes from the archive of Neot Smadar, where conversations dating back to the community's early years in Jerusalem are recorded. I have quoted (in translation) substantial portions of this material so the reader will have a fuller sense of the style with which refined observations have been made about human consciousness. Despite the extended quotes in this book, only a small percentage (no more than 2–3 percent) of the actual material referenced is included. I have also interviewed dozens of community members and worked with them on a routine basis over three summers, and these conversations, along with personal observations, constitute the foundation for my writing about Neot Smadar in the present.

The remaining chapters (2, 3, 5, most of 9, and 11) record my arrival at Neot Smadar and my deepening relationship with it and its people. Some of this material will read like a diary—a topic that will be discussed in Chapter 1—but all of it is framed in a broader hermeneutic context. For example, the description of the ritual that preceded the wedding in 2013 (Chapter 11), which is highly personal, must be understood in the context of postmodern and secular transformations of rites of passage into aesthetic experiences, sometimes tinged with irony. However, in these descriptive chapters I seek to inform my readers about how I understood the encounters that took place before theorizing began. The reader's enjoyment is also something that I take into account. At no point do I pretend that my observation and analysis of Neot Smadar are objective in the sense of being detached from the cultural constructions that define me (as an American scholar of religion, as an Israeli émigré, and so forth). The reader will be invited throughout the book to engage in the same sort of reflection; Neot Smadar excels at making people do that sort of thing.

1

A Search for Religious Experience

ISRAEL IS A TINY COUNTRY WITH A huge desert—the Negev—and Route 40 meanders down its spine from Beer-Sheva to just north of Eilat. The traveler makes his way south slowly, beyond the last patches of vegetation and the crater town of Mitzpe Ramon. It's a spectacular geological location and a shabby town of North African and Russian immigrants on the lip of the crater Machtesh Ramon, the largest of its kind in the world. The car slowly zigzags down the switchbacks of Route 40, hugging the shelf of steep limestone, toward the soft sandstone and gypsum surface below, where the Tetis Sea once deposited its minerals. Nothing grows there— or anywhere in sight. The sun, off to the right, animates broken geological strata in shades of violet and gold and darker browns set against the near-pink of the distant Moav Mountains. This is an old place and an empty one in the late afternoon of mid-May. It feels vaguely threatening, and one proceeds in low gear. The final destination, at this speed, is almost two hours away. There is no rush; the magnetic desert landscape beckons for a slower pace; it forces the traveler to ruminate in a car today, as it must have in the past, when traders on camel or mystics on foot understood that rushing served no purpose.

Perhaps the emptiness simply stifles the hyperactive brain and overburdened senses of the modern traveler. Like the silence that precedes a thunderclap, it is as shocking as the explosion that came after. You slow down now because you want your mind to slow down. If you choose the eastern

Fig. 2. The desert

route to Neot Smadar, the journey leads past Qumran, where two millennia ago other city dwellers opted out in order to live in this Martian landscape. And it is not too far from the places where early Church fathers also settled.

Indeed, you can easily see why the desert (Fig. 2) is such a powerful trope for the spiritual quest, why Jesus simply had to go to the desert for his forty-day isolation, and why early Church fathers had to follow. Where else are the senses so deprived of stimulation that the mind begins to hallucinate before it settles into the silence? True, in India this is as likely to have taken place in a high mountain cave or in the impenetrable depths of a forest, but in the Middle East it has to be in the desert. This is where the seeker leaves everything behind, isolates himself from social interaction, tests his resolve against the harshest conditions, and confronts emptiness.

Below the cliff of Machtesh Ramon the road straightens out in what looks like a wide flood plain, then begins its soft curves around low table-land rises, down multiple washes, and past screes deposited by ancient events. By the time one turns south at the isolated intersection with Route 13, the sun will be kissing the western hills and then the expanses of the Sinai desert. The new road runs straight and flat. The desert is no longer pristine here; its topsoil has been churned into dirty talcum by the spin-ning chains of maneuvering tanks, and the wind plays with dust devils that somehow appear much bigger at a distance than they really are. A mile to the east, on a slight rise, stand distant targets that look like miniature tanks, and closer to the road one sees several real tanks parked. Soldiers wearing dusty green fatigues mill about the tanks. The road runs straight south and then dips between two hills and away from the high plane, swooping left between a harsh empty landscape and a soft oasis, which is Neot Smadar.

After miles of nothing but abstract forms and vivid colors, with little for the mind's eye to latch onto, suddenly one sees irrigated fields, olive and date trees behind them, orchards of deciduous fruit trees beyond that, and then the gate. As one enters, off to the right against the darkening sky is a tower that looks like a cross between a drunken Orientalist's idea of an old Iranian minaret and a huge penis. Straight ahead is a lotus pond in the center of a surprising traffic circle. Up the dusty road a little way is a thatch-covered round hut, or a building that closely resembles one; it is hard to tell in the shadows. One finally arrives at the office of Neot Smadar, the end of the physical journey and the start of a far more challenging quest.

The people who live in Neot Smadar, those who settled here in 1989, knew a great deal about the New Age—some of it as manifested from the 1960s into the 1980s in the United States but mostly in its Israeli varieties, mostly in Jerusalem. To be sure, few among these Jerusalem individuals read Jack Kerouac or Ken Kesey. But a subtle mix of philosophy, mysticism, and literature made its way into that Jerusalem culture via numerous other writers. The best known included Gurdjieff, Ouspensky, Krishnamurti, Buber, Bucke, Castaneda, Lilly (and Leary), Isherwood, A. Huxley, R. Dau-mal, and even Robert Pirsig and David Bohm. There was little drug use, but there was a hyper-self-aware spirituality tempered by hard-nosed Israeli realism. Despite a few stabs at Judaic learning, they were wary of orthodoxy, including even the more existentially oriented Hasidic versions and that of the hip Jerusalem yeshivas, which were run by maverick young rabbis who catered to lost sheep in the 1970s, 1980s, and still.

These are people who, in more academic settings, read Gershom Scholem, Mircea Eliade, and D. T. Suzuki, mid-twentieth-century scholars who appeared to successfully disentangle the sacred from the mundane roots that kept mystical religious experience grounded in local traditions—seemingly irrational, convoluted, and insistent. For those studying the "History of Religions" in the 1960s and 1970s it was clear that religious experience could be studied as some sui generis topic in a protected enclosure, conceptually distinct from everything else. As Rudolph Otto (the godfather of the religion program at Harvard) had put it, religion is about something wholly other, mysterious, and awe-inspiring—the "Holy." There was an element of the quest for ultimate meaning in such studies, something that could find little nourishment in sociology, psychology, or other reductions of religious experience.

The people of Neot Smadar, with one exception (Meir, who grew up in Seattle), did not study religion in such settings, but they matured in a culture of spiritual quest, or questioning, outside of any traditional milieu. This could mean Zen in the streets of San Francisco or Yoga and Vipassana in India before they became mainstream.[1] It is important to keep in mind that in coming to this remote desert location they were not trying to reenact the cliché of desert mysticism. They did not follow the model of the Jewish, Christian, or Muslim mystics who had sought union with God in the emptiness of arid spaces. In fact, they came here like pioneers (*halutzim*) to build something: a school (*beit-sefer*) for the pursuit of "Self-inquiry." The concept of Self-inquiry may remind some readers of Ramana Maharshi (the twentieth-century Indian mystic from Arunachala), but the emphasis in the desert is more on "building a school," which means that work and living together (not meditative introspection) is the location for Self-inquiry. In fact, in coming to the desert and building a school and around it an agricultural oasis, the people of Neot Smadar acted more like the early Zionists who had founded the first communal farming settlements in Israel and looked for spiritual rebirth through labor.[2] And so, if the remote desert is to act as a metaphor for the spiritual quest, one must complicate the trope, because the desert here, while awe-inspiring in its vast emptiness, has also been mastered by human will and collective effort. That is to say, Neot Smadar forces us to recognize that religious experience is both uniquely empty and inseparable from all other human endeavors. The following section analyzes the nature of religious experience in a technical manner. Readers who are so inclined may skip the next several pages.

The Emptiness of Religious Experience

In his work on South Indian religion, *Fluid Signs,* E. Valentine Daniel described a group of pilgrims on a trek to Sabari Malai following in the (mythical) footsteps of the god Lord Ayyapan, son of Shiva, as he struggled against a beautiful demoness.[3] The pilgrims had committed themselves to celibacy, going barefoot, sleeping on the hard ground, suffering hunger, and other forms of self-deprivation. Hardest of all was the long barefoot walk on hot surfaces, causing pain from blisters, sore muscles, and burns. Daniel demonstrated how all of this discomfort actually contributed to the feelings of devotion displayed by the pilgrims toward God. He noted: "Several pilgrims seemed to believe, however, that after a while, pain, having become so intense, began to disappear. In the words of one pilgrim from my village, 'At one moment everything is pain. But the next moment everything is love (*anpu*). Everything is love for the Lord.' "[4] Daniel explained that this was the experiential goal of the difficult pilgrimage: for their love for Ayyappan to become so intense that all other thoughts and feelings would dissolve.

Pilgrims are usually householders and not fully committed mystics, but the ritual, with its discomforts and pains, seems to produce states of consciousness that block out everything but love for God. This is highly suggestive for researchers who seek other ritual subjects undergoing dysmorphic performances elsewhere in the world: perhaps various embodied rituals yield a singular state of consciousness—one that is both entirely personal and at the same time universal.[5] Would this constitute a religious experience, and would it be, in fact, universal and entirely distinct from nonreligious experiences? Perhaps a less dramatic example would help clarify the matter further.

In *Becoming Religious,* Susan Kwilecki interviewed several women in Virginia who had undergone significant religious conversion or who otherwise displayed strong religious feelings and views.[6] Kwilecki conducted a careful psychological and sociological analysis of the factors that brought these women to possess their religious feelings, but the subjects themselves, like

Daniel's pilgrims, have no doubts about the authentic (sacred) nature of their encounters with the divine.

Kate, born in 1941, was a mother of four when interviewed by Kwilecki. Her appearance suggested a sweet disposition. "However," Kwilecki wrote, "beneath that soft mien, I quickly learned, lurked an intense, uncompromising attachment to God. Poised on the edge of the sofa, she launched into a testimony before I could ask the first interview question: 'I serve a risen Savior, Jesus Christ. And God planned for him to come into the world and to suffer so that man might be saved.'"[7] The personal circumstances that led Kate to her intense convictions were complex, if not unusual. They included family and domestic stress, social turmoil, the ups and downs of marriage—nothing truly out of the ordinary. However, in 1987, in the wake of several years of family crises, she looked again at John 3:16 and saw it in a new way. This time, she explained that faith, "believing in" is "the attitude toward Christ required for salvation"—as a translation of the term "*pisteuon,*" in the scripture. This meant, she said, total surrender of oneself to another. "Now I know that I'm his, and I know that he's inside me," she announced to her interviewer. "If he's inside me—and he is—and I walk out that door, he walks out that door. . . . There's never a place that I'll go that he's not there. He's with me. And so I just commune with him like, all the time."[8]

Regardless of how Daniel's pilgrims or Kwilecki's subjects might feel about the circumstances that brought them "nearer to God" or produced their religious experience, one thing is reasonably clear: They would deny that their inner experience was the product of either physical hardships or a family crisis. They would certainly refuse to acknowledge that they were expressing social or psychological facts in an intensely personal idiom. If they could articulate this, they would argue that their experience is immediate and genuine, that it is different from all other experiences they have had—it is sui generis—and that it is about something sacred: God.

I regard their reflection on their own state of mind as a "folk theory" (an informal and semiexplicit conception of one's situation). This is broader than either attribution or ascription, which in general terms are, respectively, conscious and nonconscious modes of interpreting personal experience. As we shall see, "Self-inquiry" (in Neot Smadar) undermines the mechanics of both attribution and ascription.[9] For religious individuals this is hardly an academic matter, but the folk-theoretical interpretation of their own experience resonates with Otto and Eliade; in fact, this emphasis on the intentional experience of the Holy was a major position in much of twentieth-century religion scholarship (in the United States, at both Harvard and Chicago, with journals like *History of Religions* and *Numen*) and continues to do battle in academia today against a vast array of reductive forces: interpretive anthropology, cultural psychology, feminism, postcolonialism, postmodernism, social and cultural constructivism, scientific reductionism, and numerous other enemies of the sacred. To repeat what has been mentioned already (following Rudolph Otto): there is a distinct sacred experience of something altogether different, which is holy and cannot be explained away. Religious experience is an apperception of the Holy, and it is authenticated by its phenomenal intentionality—no other tool required.[10]

This is most striking when the experience of the Holy is ostensibly unmediated by other religious practices, when it is mystical. By definition, all mystical experiences must be about that common core—whether this is described in theological terms or in terms of pure consciousness. The many differences in mystical reports can be accounted for in terms of the ineffability of the experience itself. This position (the so-called perennialist or essentialist) has been as influential in the field of mysticism as the work of Eliade has been in the study of myth and ritual during most decades of the twentieth century. It is associated, again, with Rudolph Otto's study of Meister Eckhart and Shankara (*Mysticism East and West*) and with the work of a long list of other scholars and popular writers.[11]

In recent years the essentialist position has been undermined, not only by philosophers and social scientists but within the study of religion itself. As Russell McCutcheon argues, in a Nietzschean vein: "There is no territory, no original, and thus no direct experience of a real world, without the application of a prior, constructed map that not only exists at a distance from that which it eventually represents, but more importantly perhaps, whose use actually transforms the generic, chaotic and thus unknowable limitless background."[12] McCutcheon correctly notes that "the essentialist approach has, for the past few hundred years, settled on private experience as the true essence of all religion."[13] And indeed, the turn by so many twentieth-century religion writers to the experiential dimension of the sacred mirrors the glow of a Romantic epiphany. This is brilliantly analyzed by Charles Taylor in the works of artists, poets, and even theorists like Adorno, who "still held in some way to the original Romantic ideal of a full reconciliation of reason and sensibility, a pleroma of happiness in which the sensual desire and the search for meaning would be fulfilled in perfect alignment."[14]

This emphasis on experience, a neo-Kantian one for religious writers, stands in marked tension with the Nietzschean emphasis on the "utter lack of order in original raw experience," the "formless unformable world of the chaos of sensations," and the realization that "reality" is the imposition of order on chaos. In literature, in all of human communication, a tension plays out here between the allegedly particular and the overly general or abstract—a pitched battle, actually, over the meaning of the symbol and the reality that it supposedly represents.[15] For the religion essentialists, the symbol is never merely a map; it is a special container, the actual territory or place where the sacred becomes revealed as "hierophany" or the "Holy," and is directly accessible to unmediated experience.[16]

The distinction between the essentialist and the constructive interpretation of religious experience is not simply a matter of theory when you take into account the sort of discourse we encountered in South India (Daniel) or Virginia (Kwilecki). Consider three distinct possibilities: the actors are undergoing some extraordinary, indeed revelatory, experience that they accurately report; the actors are undergoing some powerful but unspecified ("chaotic") experience that they interpret by means of some preconceived "map"—their religious folk theory; or the actors are experiencing a culturally and socially overdetermined constellation of values and feelings that is neither universal (essential) nor uniquely individual. Ann Taves has argued that "the experience of religion cannot be separated from the communities of discourse and practice that gave rise to it without becoming something else: an experience considered "mesmeric" in one context (late nineteenth century) might have been regarded in an earlier setting as a visionary journey to heaven.[17] In removing the narrated experience from its embedded cultural context in order to fit it into a theoretical discourse (including mystical theology) we lose what is genuine about it—the entire setting. The experience becomes, as Taves says, quoting William James, "decomposed." The context, be it a Hindu pilgrimage, a difficult American family, work, or a psychiatrist's couch, does not occlude any "genuine" experience but rather constitutes it.[18]

On this theory, the narrating experience of pain-turns-to-love (in Daniel) and such theoretical discourses as either hierophany (Eliade) or neuro-dynamics (Glucklich) are not mutually validating.[19] They involve fragmentation, both theological and scientific reductions to which religious persons are likely to passionately object. But regardless, according to "map" theorists like Taves, McCutcheon, Desjarlais, and others, nothing meaningful (sacred) is left over beyond the speaker's "markings and soundings"—her mastery over the language rules that constitute her cultural world.[20] There is nothing primordial or universal about the religious person's claims, nothing that language translates into a meaningful narrative. Rather, the medium is the message.

This is a persuasive and widely held view today, but as presented here it still does not account for the way that individual consciousness develops —that is, for the way, in the language of Peter Berger, that cultural products are "internalized" before they become "objectivated" again.[21] This is the domain, cognitive theorists argue, in which the objectivist fallacy lurks. The objectivist fallacy refers to taking the world and our experience of it as consisting of objects, properties, and relationships that exist independent of our interpretation of them.[22] The map theorists (social and cultural constructivists) are perhaps less likely to commit the objectivist fallacy than the essentialists, who attribute the content of consciousness to some transcendent or at least objective reality.[23] But the threat remains real in strictly epistemological terms. From a psychological point of view, replacing ostensibly objective reality ("the sacred") with cultural facts ("the highly valued") does not solve the problem of how the individual can come to accept (in a cognitive manner) any fact as though it were objective, thereby generating the phenomenal impression of the objective world.

The argument of McCutcheon and others against essentialism is consistent with the view that language does not express concepts that map onto objects, properties, and relationships in a literal, univocal, and context-independent fashion. In psychology this view belongs in a long-running sociocultural response, most famously associated with Vygotski, to Neo-Kantian schema theorists like Piaget and others who have argued that thought and knowledge emerge when we integrate raw information into pre-existing schemas.[24] Where constructivist theorists fall short—they may not be wrong, but they fall short—is in failing to acknowledge the role of the body in the formation of so-called (pre-conscious) schemas on which cultural idioms depend. The familiar work of Mark Johnson and George Lakoff on embodied schemas mediates between the twin poles of socio-cultural theory and the cognitive theory of schema. On their understanding: "Meaning includes patterns of embodied experience and preconceptual structures of our sensibility (i.e., our mode of perception, or orienting ourselves, and of interacting with other objects, events, or persons). These embodied patterns do not remain private or peculiar to the person who experiences them. Our community helps us interpret and codify many of our felt patterns. They become shared cultural modes of experience and help to determine the nature of our meaningful coherent understanding of our 'world.' "[25]

This view requires both the movement of the body in space and the mediating interpretation of culture in turning these movements into metaphors. Consciousness itself (the awareness of awareness) can be regarded as such a metaphor—a map, if you will—consisting of both objects and the subject.[26] And from "object" as a schema one derives subsidiary schemas such as link, goal-path, center-periphery, part-whole, and a variety of others that come to define the way that the "subject" may interact with the object.[27]

However, the concept of maps as the cultural scripts for mental contents is too neat, too fixed. In fact, maps can be volatile, unsteady, vulnerable to disruption via trauma, illness, physical strain, or, for that matter, religious rituals. These can produce disorientation, gaps, reversal of values, and other fissures, which have been the subjects of fascinating psychological and cultural studies.[28] But that does not mean that the breakdown of the map is sheer chaos or meaninglessness.

The dynamic nature of maps is also the reason they can work in a constructive fashion under traumatic conditions. For example, because of the way the body functions in ostensibly traumatic contexts, pain signals to the brain (nociception) can actually be overridden by powerful information coming out of the brain: emotions, beliefs, attention to significant distractions, and so forth. This is a universal neurophysiological aspect of the human organism, but it has vast cultural implications. Hence, we see with the pilgrims in South India that strong motivation and distraction mask the feeling of foot pain as a matter of physiology. Thus, from a psychological point of view, pain "becomes" love due to the way their culture construes this cybernetic nature of nociception—and the entire experience is imagined along the goal-path schema as a means of relating to God.[29]

In more elaborate psychological processes the embodied nature of the construction of consciousness can translate into the subject's awareness of possessing a discrete and embodied self that is a "recipient" of cultural influences. Some of these, in ritual contexts, feel as though they enable the subject to internalize cultural values while enabling others to voluntarily become disembodied, and hence experience ecstasy, self-transcendence, self-surrender, love, and so forth.[30] In other words, as far as individual consciousness is concerned, the relationship between the cultural and the embodied is bi-directional, each informing the other, depending on each other, neither entirely primordial.

The pilgrim's feeling of love for God is a complex combination of embodied presence—a neuropsychological process—and learned evaluations for interpreting these, and so is Kate's feeling that God is inside her wherever she goes. The universal here is not an essential experience or an objective idea but rather the complex and systemic relationship between body-self and culture.[31]

The study of religious ideas, consequently, must sometimes go beyond disembodied texts (maps). It does so not in order to find an essential core (either mystical or biological) but to examine the way that experience reveals the binary and dynamic play between culture and embodied schemas or how maps come to define (both make and unmake) territory. It's how any individual's phenomenal being-in-the-world emerges creatively as she moves about and works and how such a world can emerge even while the subject is trying to bypass ideological constructions. This is where the impression of something ultimately meaningful may be found, even when the concept of the sacred is absent. It's a different sort of mysticism, an everyday mysticism, so to speak.[32] In such a context, to give an example, members of a religious community may come to regard language and thought as obstacles to the realization of Truth but may then characterize the essential quality of this truth as empty, that is, consisting of nothing truly extraordinary.

This may be the case of Neot Smadar, where the dominant cultural value calls for disentangling oneself from the bonds of thought (and the thinking self) and at the same time insists on collective work and ongoing dialogue. If my understanding of religious experience is correct, we can see in Neot Smadar a new way of thinking about mysticism as an experience of transcendence and a new mystical heuristic—namely work and conversations. And yet, at the same time, members of this community deny the concept of "religious experience," acknowledge no myths, no significant rituals, and certainly no metaphysical claims. The creative interplay of embodied schemas and cultural maps takes place below the level of ideology or even language, but the everyday life of these desert farmers acts like the mystical poetry that tries to grasp that which constantly eludes it.

Conversations on the Emptiness of Experience

The material included in this section comes from two conversations that took place between Yossef and several of his students. The first occurred on April 3, 1986, and the second on July 7, 1995.[33] As noted in the introduction to this book, conversation between two or more persons is the primary mode of Self-inquiry and, for the researcher, one of the best ways to gather information on the ideas and practices that underlie the school at Neot Smadar. These two conversations, greatly edited (abbreviated) and translated from Hebrew, provide two snapshots—nine years apart—of what lies at the heart of the self, of what is experience, the role of thinking, and other important themes.

"Group and Self"

This conversation took place in a large living room with a kitchen at one end and a corridor to the bedrooms at the other.[34] Participants sat along the walls on couches and pillows, while Yossef sat closest to the kitchen end of the room. Yossef was still sporting his enormous Gurdjieff-style moustache and, like everyone else, was simply dressed. As usual, Yossef asked what was on people's minds; there was no set agenda, and anything might come up. Alon, a philosophy student at Hebrew University and a retired army officer, spoke first: Given that the conscious mind is preoccupied with the self, and given the suffering that this causes, why do people persist once they realize this fact through Self-inquiry?

Yossef did not immediately respond, and others spoke—raised questions —in turn until Ruth, echoing Alon's question, noted that she feels truer to herself when surrounded by others. She described a sharpness and clarity to her state of consciousness when she exists for the sake of others.

It was then that Yossef began to speak or, more precisely, to ask a series of questions for the group to contemplate. He said: "So, let's look at it. Does my life have any value without the other?" And "Can we truly exist without the other?" He then explained that the relationship with the other relies on thought, which is an isolating activity of the ego. Therefore, Yossef asked, "Can the existence of the other accompany me even beyond my thoughts about him?" Yossef's conception of "thought" included the full range of mechanical mental processes, among them feelings, perceptions, and desires. He was asking whether a domain of consciousness existed in which the other and the self are one, or at least intimately related.

The matter touched on psychology, not ethics. People do not come together because of some obligation to cooperate or because they recognize this as a desirable state of affairs. On the contrary, such thinking leads to isolation because it posits a duality. One must realize that the individual is naturally one aspect or manifestation of a greater totality—but only implicitly so. The realization of this state of affairs, and working together with such a mindset, leads to "living joy." Yossef told the group: "Self-inquiry is the study of dysfunction, it is a study of my situation as it is." He meant suffering. He emphasized that this was a difficult practice that demanded discipline and being careful to avoid a wasteful life: "Am I aware of the fact that I am causing suffering to myself?"

In recognizing the cause of isolation and suffering in patterns of habitual thinking and feeling, one may obtain authentic existence. True unity with others comes from removing the obstacles to clarity and freedom. This is the source of joy.

"Experience Is Empty"

Six years after the arrival of the residents of Neot Smadar in the desert, the conversations were continuing, in that remote setting, late into the night. One such Wednesday, the day of the first group, Shimon, who is an accomplished carpenter, opened the conversation by mentioning those who had recently passed away. Pressed by Yossef, he acknowledged that the death of others brings to mind his own death, the brevity of his life. Yossef immediately steered the conversation in the direction of Self-inquiry: "What can I accomplish as myself, for myself, including my own death? Whose 'my' is this anyway, my body?"[35]

As the members of the group listened, he then noted that we behave as though there is such a one as the subject of "I" or "my"—failing to see how false that is. There is no such one: "Usually I rely on 'I' as some sort of collection of 'mind.' This includes my memory . . . but these things do not exist." Instead, "The 'I' that I depend on, my entire inside, is a material movement." It is the product of thought (broadly understood), and often the product of the plans we design in order to avoid seeing what we are right now. That is one way thought perpetuates the illusion of the self's existence. "The thinking 'I' and the thought come from the same place: the observer and the observed are both conditioned thought."[36]

One of the men sitting and listening, Yehezkel, asked how he could avoid the trap of thought. Yossef assured the group that if the matter was of sufficient interest, it was actually very simple: "I can be aware of this entire dynamic; it is so simple. It depends only on energy and attentiveness" in order to avoid the automatic responses of thought. There is no secret discipline, no formula for changing oneself, just awareness and steadfastness, and the illusion dissolves of itself.

Commentary

The raw text of Yossef's conversations suffers from the problems that plague all translations. The terminology of the participants, who are not professional philosophers or scholars, shifts, and it is difficult to determine which English word to use for each usage. Furthermore, the speakers share many implicit assumptions that account for conversational shortcuts and for jargon. Speech patterns (speed, intonation, volume) and body behavior figure in the communication that takes place and is particularly significant in the person of the teacher. Because the conversation is a momentary collective phenomenology, it is important to avoid overinterpreting the conversation and certainly to avoid judging the philosophical validity of the points being made.[37]

With these warnings in mind, the reader may discern the following general themes: What we normally take to be experience is empty because it depends entirely on the presence of an "I" and a "my" (constructed agency) who does the experiencing. Because the ego (subject) is constructed and is a false entity, its products are false. For example, the observer and the observed in any given experience are distinct products of thought that represent the work of the ego. However, in another sense authentic experience does exist, but it is collective and perhaps even universal. It is not gained by thought, and the major block to attaining it is our sense of individuality, which breeds desire and error—along with suffering and wastefulness.

The role of "society" (the group) here is ambiguous and will be clarified later. For the time being, we see that society accounts for the cognitive way in which the individual thinks about his experience (and the reason he is always carrying others along, wherever he goes). This is a negative function. And yet authentic experience transcends the individual person and organism and can be validated—paradoxically—only by means of others.

Because the members of Neot Smadar eschew any kind of generality or label, as far as they are concerned there is nothing religious, let alone mystical, about attaining authentic experience—it is available at all times and in every mundane situation. But authentic experience is not ordinary, either: it depends on suspending the primacy of thought, which is deeply implicated in the structure of the ego (agent) and in the ego's conception of time and causality.[38] Many other conversations will demonstrate that in order to obtain genuine experience we must be "mirrored" honestly and sharply by others, we must be perfectly "naïve" (precise in describing the simple present state of consciousness), and we have to abandon the past (avoid "telling stories"), which is a product of thought and social accumulation. Surprisingly, these disciplines generate broad moral obligations: hard work, volunteerism, caring, honesty, patience, and others. All of this is what a "school for Self-inquiry" means, which is essential to understanding Neot Smadar.

Translated into the terms that are widely used in religious studies (from Jonathan Z. Smith and others): the residents of this community-school not only recognize a categorical distinction between territory and map but also insist that the map (the way they speak about experience) is an obstacle to experience. They set up a paradox in their hyper-self-aware manner of being in the world and reflecting on it. They use a map to undo the map. But they do so without deploying any ruse of a sacred state of mind or some occult excuse for ineffability.[39]

In practical terms, what this means is not just the pursuit of a qualitative research method by taping long interviews and recording the narrative of the residents of Neot Smadar, which is bound to be paradoxical anyway. It means, rather, becoming their colleague and acting and writing as their friend. It means sharing, as far as possible, their narratives, getting close to the meaning of their lives.[40]

Consequently, the record that I put together as I search for the meaning of Neot Smadar has to be a narrative of work—conversations, too, but mostly work—with those who rely on work to pursue Self-inquiry. However, it is important to avoid what Bourdieu called narcissistic or "egological" reflexivity and what Clifford Geertz called, following Roland Barthes, "the diary disease" in narrating my encounter with the people of Neot Smadar. These conditions imply an overly impressionistic hermeneutic of the encounter without due attention to the social conditions that define my own situation.[41] Bourdieu's solution to this is what he calls "participant objectivation," which is an awareness not of my "lived experience" but of the limits and effects of that experience as underscored by the social conditions that make them possible.[42] In another way of putting the matter, one needs to think of such a study as an encounter. I echo Robert Tyler on this: "To encounter religion, as I understand it, is to undertake a 'disciplined suspension,' to use Robert Orsi's phrase, of one's own locative impulses and thus allow the difference between the scholar's own world and the world of the religious other to emerge in as much detail as is possible."[43] In Neot Smadar such occasions arise every time interlocutors remind me of how badly I am misconstruing them and how blindly I sometimes project my own social practices onto the way I interpret what they are saying or doing. But then we get back to work together, and try again later.

All of this is unusually tricky in the case of Neot Smadar because, as the conversations reveal, the task becomes not an accumulation of knowledge but the elimination of obstacles to absolute simplicity. This I can do only by joining in their work and in their powerful conversations. My "research" must become a narrative of a journey toward the core of their practice, until I can fully join in seeing the "emptiness of experience" in the same complicated (or simple) manner that they do. That is how I shall see their world as meaningful and manage to communicate this.

I follow here in the footsteps of Charles Taylor, who acknowledged his own indebtedness to M. Heidegger, P. Ricoeur, A. MacIntyre, and J. Bruner when he wrote: "I have been arguing that in order to make minimal sense of our lives, in order to have an identity, we need an orientation to the good, which means some sense of qualitative discrimination, of the incomparably higher. Now we see that this sense of the good has to be woven into my understanding of my life as an unfolding story. But this is to state another basic condition of making sense of ourselves, that we grasp our lives in a *narrative*."[44]

There are three dimensions to the narrative that emerges. The first includes the events, experiences, or speeches that are selected for consideration. Second, this narrative unfolds in a temporal manner in which the reader, too, learns to situate herself. Finally, the narrative is no mere stringing together of discrete events, even when mutually caused, but is subject to a moral ordering. Some overarching theme must organize these events in a meaningful way, that which Taylor called "orientation to the good."[45]

This is an unusually difficult task for the students of Neot Smadar. Their own narratives (maps in time) emerge with great reluctance because of the injunction against "storytelling" and because the ultimate telos is empty— in the Buddhist sense of "empty." And yet the life and work of the residents of Neot Smadar reveal a genuine struggle with meaning and much hard work that enfolds an abundance of meaning. It is possible, though perhaps a bit early, to state that the work itself is the locus of meaning, however implicitly. To put this in abstract terms, the "map" is play—it is the tracing of movement in space, of work, and it dissolves in the next instant. Just as "washing dishes" means so little and so much in Zen discourse, hard work in Neot Smadar may be carrying an immense, yet silent, conceptual load. If this is so, the narrating has to be done by the author who needs to join the group and work there to the best of his abilities. That is what I did. And my friends in Neot Smadar helped me chart the topography of the map in time and validate its reading, assigning a mostly moral correspondence between the map and its terrain of daily action.

2

Washing Dishes

THE MORNING AFTER MY ARRIVAL AT Neot Smadar, a loud phone ring jarred me awake. A man's voice said with crisp formality: "Good morning Ariel, I'd like to invite you to the kitchen."

I looked at my watch: it was 5:45. I had missed the morning meditation by 30 minutes, and the kitchen crew was gathering for the day's work.

The man on the phone had not identified himself, or, if he had, I had missed it. In my fatigue I could not tell if his exaggerated politeness was ironic or patronizing.

"I'll be there in five minutes," I said, trying to sound fully awake.

I had slept right through the alarm, set for 5:00; that was my best sleep of the night. There was no air conditioning in the room, no fan, and I had gone to bed with an open window above my head. A gentle breeze rustling the acacia pods outside lulled me to sleep. Hot as it was in the tiny room, I floated joyfully on images of my first workday in Neot Smadar. I was thrilled to finally be there, in the desert, working on a new project.

Suddenly, or maybe an hour later, I found myself on the floor, my heart racing. Something immense had exploded nearby, rattling the open window, thumping on my eardrums. The boom was followed by two seconds of silence, then an immense and ludicrous honk—like a broken clarinet—just outside my window.

I climbed back on the bed and waited for the adrenaline to dissipate. Then another explosion rocked the room, followed, two seconds later, by that idiotic horn. I was already awake, so this second round failed to startle me. And then I remembered: "The damn tanks! They're doing target practice . . . " I checked my watch ". . . at 12:30, for God's sake!" Those tank crews I had seen on my drive were preparing for drills, not shutting down for the night. But what was the honk? I had not realized this previously, but Neot Smadar was home to peacocks, about twenty males and females. Someone would later tell me that Meir was responsible for bringing the birds to this place, and, knowing this, it became difficult for me to treat the elderly man with equanimity. A few of the birds had tucked themselves away for the night right under my window and were just as startled by the boom as I had been.

So that was my night: a hot room with an open window that exposed me to explosions and honks—I couldn't say when the commotion ended or whom I hated worse, the Israeli army or the outrageously overdecorated and hysterical birds. I began to visualize myself wringing their necks, and that settled me down until the next explosion. I had no visual pacifiers to help with my aggression against the tanks. They won.

It took me about ten minutes to shuffle over to the dining room. The sun was just reaching the point where you had to squint when looking directly to the east; it had not yet dissolved the dawn's slight chill. I roomed in the area reserved for volunteers, most of whom were in their twenties, and they doubled up in rooms the size of my own, men and women separately. This was a desert campus, with heroic grass struggling through the sandy soil, scraggly, dusty vines hugging the walls of the low-slung three-room dormitories. Each room had its own entry, and the volunteers slung laundry on wooden pegs above their sandals or flip-flops, which they left behind when they laced their work boots before dawn. The path, covered with sand and broken here and there, meandered between the prefab dorms. A sprinkler to my left kicked up desert petrichor, making me feel oddly at home. I had no boots but thought, incorrectly as it turned out, that sandals would be fine for working in the dining room and kitchen.

Around the northern side of the dining hall I arrived on a scene of men and women milling about in twos and threes, talking about work or just whispering, sipping warm herbal tea in glasses they held between thumb and forefinger. They were standing on a semicircular patio about ninety feet across, inlaid with large, dusty cement tiles in a complicated pattern. I saw a long table with plastic jugs containing light green tea, a basket with bread slices, and, next to it, two small containers with jam. No one spoke loudly, but the feeling of a workday already begun made me feel inadequate and rushed. And I had no idea where to go. The dining room was a carry-over from the abandoned kibbutz that had gone bust decades earlier, and it was a simple rectangular cement structure with two black-framed doors at the front. Both were open. Inside the dining room a woman I did not know looked at me directly, unnervingly, then pointed outside. "If you're in the kitchen today, they're meeting outside right now," she said.

The eight or so people assigned to work in the kitchen and dining room that day were sitting in a circle on the stone wall out front and listening to a young woman with anthracite-colored hair and a pale round face as she described what needed to be done. Anat was in that group, and she nodded and smiled when I sat down, but all the others were lost in their own world. I tried to guess who the caller had been, but none of the men fit the image I had in mind of an ironic prick. The group consisted of permanent community members and a few volunteers. The young woman who was explaining the work, Natalia, spoke with a thick Russian accent: "We need two or three people to prepare the dining hall for breakfast, and we need the same number or more to wash and prepare the vegetables and prepare the eggs. And we need someone to wash dishes and pots."

Only the volunteers showed any interest in one job over the other; the veterans took whatever task they were assigned. No healthy adult in Neot Smadar avoided kitchen work. On average, everyone worked there once or twice a week or, in total, dozens of times a year. The work hardly varied because, as I would discover over time, the kitchen and dining room routines and menu were kept uniform. Each day of the week had its own unchanged lunch and dinner (a rotation of seven days), and breakfast was always the same, as far as possible—vegetables, cheese, hardboiled eggs, and tahini. In the course of many years, even varying the job one performed each day in the kitchen, one would have sliced the same vegetables over and over again, mashed the same potatoes, served the same platters with rice and poured the same servings of goat-milk yogurt. There was really no point in choosing one task over another, in clinging to favorite jobs.

I ended up on the team that set up the dining room with Avi and Noam. Naturally I had no idea what to do—there had to have been some procedure I was not yet familiar with. Avi was my guide, my "leader." He was an introspective twenty-five-year-old volunteer who had arrived early for a construction seminar that was to take place that summer. I later discovered that he was an accomplished guitar player who performed all summer long, accompanying singers and leading the children in their various performances, including a play, *The Wizard of Oz*, which they put on when the school year ended. Like everyone else in Neot Smadar, he barely spoke at work, and if I wanted instructions I had to ask or just follow his example.

The dining hall was large for a small community of about two hundred people, at around fifteen hundred square feet. Twenty long tables stood along three walls and down the center of the room. The sidewalls had long dirty windows and, above them, rickety air conditioners that had to be turned off during meetings because they drowned out speakers in deafening clatter. On the rear wall hung a bizarre-looking wooden art piece of no discernible aesthetic value—what I later found out was the first communal art project created by Yossef's students in Jerusalem and was called *The Flutes* as homage to the modest wooden wind instrument. A year after my first day in the dining room, work would begin on the construction of a new dining hall, which would replace the drab functionality of the old one with one befitting Neot Smadar's inventive style.

Work began with lifting the chairs onto the tables, each chair atop another, then pouring buckets of sudsy water on the tiled floor and spraying it with a pressure hose. We each grabbed a push broom and scrubbed the entire surface of the floor—under the tables and at every corner. I was wearing my old sandals, and now wished I had a pair of boots—Avi and Noam were wearing the same brand of pull-on boots I saw on everyone in the kibbutz—and my feet were quickly soaked. It wasn't a cold morning, but I found myself slipping inside my sandals. Then we used the most Israeli of all cleaning tools, floor wipers, to move the water into a single drainage hole at the corner of the room, under the coffee and tea apparatus. I could smell the coffee and thought about making a cup, perhaps hot tea. I needed the jolt, especially this morning. I found myself wondering about the tank gunners—when they went to bed and when they got up that morning. I hoped they were as tired as I was. The remaining wet spots we dried with floor mops, that is, rough towels with holes in the middle with which to drape them around the wipers—also an Israeli invention. Then the chairs came down, the tables were wiped clean, and we began to set the tables with plates (simple white ceramic) and utensils that came off the same cart where they were stored after being washed following the previous meal.

The work was mostly silent, and I saw no wasted motions. Every act pointed to a specific and efficient purpose. That's what I thought, anyway, until Alon—the reluctant doryphore—came and pointed out a few wet spots we had missed, which I felt would dry in ten minutes on their own. I did not tell him this, but in my mind a conversation with Alon began. Later he pointed out that the plates were not precisely lined up across from each other and that the edges of the knives—all of them so dull they could barely cut through cucumber peel—had to be turned inward. My inner conversation with Alon became louder and took derisive tones. Alon was one of the toughest men in the community. He was small, around sixty years old, with long, thick hair swept back, and he was severe looking. He expected perfection and full effort from himself and those who worked with him. He had a way of quietly but quickly insinuating himself into people's mental slot of where a "commander" or "master" belonged. At least that is where he was lodged in my own head.

As Avi and I set the plates—six to a table—and the cutlery (following Alon's instructions), Noam finished cleaning the toilets, which were two unisex rooms behind the space where workers washed their hands before dining. He then set up the corner where people prepared coffee or tea after their meals. This was basically a large aluminum water heater with two faucets for hot water. There was coffee powder that one spooned into a glass (stacked in a crate below) before pouring in hot water. The tea was available both as a concentrate in a small metal pot and as several types of herbs (mint, lemongrass, sage, Louisa, lavender, calendula) for those who avoided caffeine. A small sugar bowl with a couple of teaspoons was off to the side.

I couldn't believe Noam had not assigned the toilets to me, the newest person there. That's what you'd get in another kibbutz, I thought, not to mention a restaurant. He now scrubbed the aluminum surfaces clean, set out the fresh herbs, added za'atar (Syrian oregano) to a small bowl, added fresh tea leaves to the teapot that sat atop the hot water machine, topped off the two bowls of coffee powder and sugar, and made sure there were clean mixing spoons. Noam was a small and powerful-looking man in his fifties. Even his tanned, shaved head looked powerful. He ran the agriculture branch of Neot Smadar, leading community members, volunteers, and a few paid laborers (Thai and Sudanese) in fruit picking, weeding, and soil preparation in the sun. Here he worked like all the rest of us, just getting the place ready for breakfast; he rarely spoke and said nothing to me. The kitchen and dining hall turn was the great equalizer in Neot Smadar, and there was little satisfaction in doing that work. Or maybe there was, but I failed to see it. People just got through it. For me it was a novelty and therefore interesting—I especially enjoyed watching the others carry out their tasks.

The work was simple, but everything had to be done just so, which meant that I was mostly helpless on my own. And yet there was no feeling of being at the bottom of a workplace hierarchy—like being new at a pizzeria or a garage. There was no tone of authority, and the procedures one had to follow did not feel like commandments or even rules. One did not follow instructions, let alone commands, but observed others and asked for help when necessary. None of the others appeared to have internalized or mastered a code that made them somehow better than those who had not. It was more like learning to speak a language, with some doing better and others less well; few people get a swollen head from being fluent in their own native language. It was also strangely reassuring that everyone, even Noam and the other veterans, had to ask a question at one point or another. Natalia, a relative newcomer to Neot Smadar, was the one who had all the answers on that day. But she, too, just happened to be running the kitchen; in two or three years she might be starting out as a novice at the dairy or the Pundak (restaurant).

After setting the tables, while the kitchen crew was preparing platters of washed and trimmed vegetables (tomatoes, cucumbers, onions, lettuce, and garlic as well as bean sprouts, herbs, and lemons) and while Bill—an American volunteer—was noisily washing dishes and trays, I followed Noam and Avi as they continued to set the tables. A glass accompanied each plate—not above it but just off to the right side (Alon came and showed me)—to make room for the items that followed. There were glass bowls into which we scooped tahini, smaller bowls of the same design for olives, and tiny ones for something called "schug," which is a Yemenite condiment made of coriander or cilantro, garlic, and spices. We cut goat-milk "Bulgarian cheese" onto rectangular aluminum trays and used small aluminum bowls for jam. All of these items had to be placed at the correct end of the table, reserving the other end for a pitcher of water and a bread basket with both whole-grain and white bread—five slices of each. The white bread almost always remained uneaten and ended up on the dinner table, where it tended to be eaten because there was no other bread. The center of the table was reserved for the vegetable platter and a bowl of hard-boiled eggs.

The food at breakfast seldom varied—we ate the same exact items every day of the year. We could vary the proportions of vegetables in our own salads; we could mix them with tahini or yogurt or could slice hard-boiled eggs into them. But it was always the same food, the same breakfast. That morning, as I watched the vegetables being cut and the bread sliced (with an electric machine placed in the corridor between the dining room and the kitchen) and as I poured tahini into glass bowls—it seemed like the best food in the world. My stomach ached for it—I suddenly recalled that I had not eaten dinner the previous evening; I had had nothing since lunch the previous day. My hunger felt like a desire for everything I saw in the bustling kitchen that morning—even the nondescript white bread that surely came from a third-rate industrial bakery.

Then there was the matter of the salad oil. In addition to a napkin dispenser and salt and pepper shakers, each table had a small glass bottle of oil, which was essential for the salad dressing. I got the job of emptying out these bottles, all of them nearly full of canola oil. Avi told me where to find the pitcher marked "canola oil" but didn't know where I might find the pitcher marked "olive oil," out of which I would refill the bottles. Natalia sent me to her office in the back of the long kitchen, where a four-gallon container and the pitcher sat side by side. This was Thursday, I was told, and Thursday was olive oil day—it was an alternating pattern with only enough bottles for one day at a time. By the end of breakfast, virtually all the olive oil was gone. The next day the same bottles would be filled up again with canola oil, and so on. Weeks went by before I brought up my thoughts about this with other people, but when I did it became clear that everyone, at one point or another, goes through his "oil absurdity" moment, and then drops it and moves on. That's what I did, too.

Breakfast was at 8:00, and by 7:40 the preparations were completed, so Natalia called for another meeting outside in order to plan the continuing work and discuss whatever was on our minds. We met in the "smoking shed," an eight-posted octagon with a thatched roof of dry palm branches just outside the dining hall. We sat around a table where someone had placed a pitcher of herbal tea, dates, and glasses. It was a golden morning; the barren hills reflected the warm morning light, and the sound of sipping framing the silence. I was the only one looking around, at the desert and at the others, but then I caught Bill watching me and we nodded. Everyone else was lost in some sort of reverie, drinking tea. Bill was a college teacher from Arizona who had previously volunteered in a number of Israeli kibbutzim. He told me he loved this place best and was seriously considering it for possible retirement. I began to suspect that he was secretly studying the place for unauthorized research on religious cults—he was so inquisitive and he could not possibly have believed they would take an American retiree. Then I realized that I was probably projecting my own fantasies on that innocent man, whom I grew to like and respect despite his naïveté about Neot Smadar.

Finally Natalia asked if anyone had a subject they wished to raise for discussion, which I assumed referred to the work in the kitchen. I was thinking about the foolishness of replacing the oil every day instead of buying a few more bottles, but kept that to myself. Instead of offering a response, the workers reached for dates and the tea jug, and the long silence grew longer. I finally had my morning snack, two dates and tea. Meanwhile, no one seemed to mind the absence of response, least of all Natalia, who appeared to be daydreaming. Natalia was married to a man, Doron, who had been in this place a long time but still looked different from all the other men, who wore light cottons, faded khaki, gray, or grubby white. Doron appeared meticulous in an urban sort of way. They had a baby that Natalia would sometimes nurse during these meetings—as did all the other young mothers. She may have been thinking of the baby just then. The silence was now five minutes old, and I began to feel a need to fill the void but had nothing to say. I was equally tired and curious.

Then Rony M., one of the veteran school members, a tall man with smiling eyes and deeply grooved features under thick, curly hair, spoke: "I'd like to talk about the inner perception that takes place during work—the different ways I perceive being alone as I work with people around me, as opposed to the feeling of being connected to those people. Both of these perceptions happen at the same time, or rather I alternate between one and the other in rapid succession."

It seemed as if Rony stopped mid-thought, and I had no idea what he was trying to say. No one interrupted or responded. I suddenly realized he was the one who had awakened me, but it didn't matter. I looked at Natalia. Was this what she had in mind with her question, that is, an abstract observation about introspection? Is that what people discussed during work breaks here? No one picked up the thread or said a word, but they hadn't exactly ignored him either. They just let his comment hang in the air until someone would decide to do something with it. Then Natalia paraphrased Rony and confirmed that she had the same feeling—and that she often made the choice of moving from one feeling to the other: from isolation to connection and back, according to need.

To this statement Iris L. responded immediately: "No, you don't. You can't control it. The feeling is completely conditioned, and you can only become aware of it. Thinking you can move from feeling isolated to connected at will is just an illusion."

I couldn't tell how Natalia felt about being told what she could or could not do in her own head because she said nothing. But Anat spoke, making another point: "I don't think I would call this 'isolation' or 'separation.' I think 'singularity' or 'particularity' is better, and certainly it is less judgmental. This is not about cutting off people to be alone but about being somehow more of what you are as such." Again I was taken aback by the presumption of refining the words that described what another was feeling. How could Anat know whether Natalia's (or Rony's) "isolation" was actually "singularity"—whatever that meant?

Rony also sounded put off, but not by the presumption: "Anat, I don't understand what you're saying. What's your point? What's the difference between isolation and singularity? What is singularity anyway?"

I found this conversation both surprising and a bit disturbing. Expecting a discussion of kitchen procedures, I found myself listening to workers talking about stream of consciousness, about mind control, and about the semantics of isolation and connectedness. What was this, a graduate seminar in psychology? Of course graduate students may correct each other's ideas or thinking, but would they presume to evaluate what another was feeling? I was surprised that Natalia said nothing.

Anat began to respond to Rony, but Natalia cut her off—gently—saying it was time to stop and plan the next stage of the work. She assigned the jobs of serving the food ("server" and "waiter" were two different jobs in the dining hall), the dishwasher, the lunch preparers, and so forth. My job was to wait on the tables for the first twenty minutes of breakfast, see what needed replenishing (tomatoes, bread, tahini, and schug were the common items), and pour goat-milk yogurt for anyone who raised his glass in the air. After that I could sit down to eat.

At 8:00 people began to arrive, individually and in pairs. I sat behind a table at the front of the room, where waiters watched for raised hands, and observed the arrivals. The tables filled up in neat sequence, beginning at the front left of the room. Newcomers always took the next available seat on either side of the table, and everyone immediately got busy preparing their meal—mostly in silence. A few sat quietly in meditation for a few moments. The following year a new policy would be instituted; no one was to begin eating until the table filled up and the last person was seated and fully centered. Now hands reached across neighbors to the center of the table for vegetables. Diners usually started with a large leaf of lettuce, which would be cut to thin slivers. This was followed by exquisite slicing and dicing of cucumbers, tomatoes, onions, and even garlic. The salads were piled high on the plates, topped by squeezed lemon and olive oil. Some added tahini, herbs, and bean sprouts on top of their salads, and, likewise, some diners sliced the hard-boiled eggs onto their salads, while others saved the eggs for a second course. Those who did not top their salads with tahini just poured it next to the salads to be scooped with slices of whole-grain bread that were spread with the spicy green schug. An empty aluminum bowl at the center of each table quickly filled up with eggshells and the detritus of cut-up veg-etables. The room resonated with the sounds of salad making—the click clack of metal hitting ceramic—and with the soft pulling and pushing of chairs.

As this was my first turn at this job, I missed some of the subtleties that later would become self-evident. For example, veterans never wasted words. Making a request, they grunted, "Olives" or "Cheese"—no verb, no please. The last person to finish at a table made sure it was cleared, then grabbed a cloth from the counter and wiped the table clean.

The veterans generally arrived later. I immediately noticed that they moved insouciantly, unlike the volunteers. They placed their body weight on their heels, feet slightly apart as they moved forward, hips thrust out. Their shoulders were raised, but their arms hung down heavily. It was a loafer's display of lassitude that gave the overall impression of a person who feels at home, shows confidence, but is exhausted beyond repair. The young people, especially the women, were dressed with a carefully executed casualness, with elements of Indian clothing (pajama bottoms, kurtas, Shiva and Krishna scarves around their necks) or with combinations of these with cargo pants. Most wore heavy pull-on *chukkas*, or scruffy san-dals. The general theme was "Avoid the sun at all cost." Everyone kept their shirts untucked—everyone except Alon, Doron, and Ilana—and those who worked outside wore long sleeves despite the heat.

I was noticed by almost everyone who passed by, but only a few of the veterans nodded, and no one said a word. It was only later that I realized that speechless greetings were customary here. Shlomit, the former wife of my oldest and best friend, later explained this to me: "Yossef believed that the usual greetings, "Hello," "How are you?" "What's going on?" are like dogs wagging their tails."

"What's wrong with dogs wagging their tails?" I asked. "They're showing affection."

"He thought it was wasted energy. . . . And when you run into the same people over and over again on the same day, are you going to repeat the entire ritual every time?" This was not a bad point, and so they dispensed with greetings, or rather they concentrated a greeting into a meeting of the eyes and—for some—a nod or even a dipping of the head. Shlomit, or perhaps someone else, told me that some residents of Neot Smadar use casual meetings as a sort of spiritual laboratory, experimenting with gesture, emotion, and self-examination.

The power of group gestures is remarkable, I thought. After Shlomit's explanation I silently vowed to greet people with an extra helping of words in order to test their response: "How is your day going, it's great to see you," but I noticed how hard that was to keep up when the response was always a smile that I read as dismissive. Meanwhile "the walk" (as I started to think of it) would take a few more days to confirm, and then I became determined to maintain my natural gait, that is, walking on the balls of my feet and alert. This makes me sound juvenile perhaps, but it allowed me to focus on my body in relation to theirs, which I regarded as useful in a study on culture and embodiment. The American volunteer, Bill, remained unaware of the walk. A slight man in his 50s, he barely spoke Hebrew, and yet, despite his obvious otherness, three weeks after arriving he started to move like the community veterans. There he was, shuffling with his hips thrust forward and his arms hanging down in a gesture of endless fatigue. I was stunned by this trivial but concrete example of the power that courses silently through this community and saturates the periphery (newcomers) with behavior that springs from the center. I wondered if ideas about the self—the heart of Neot Smadar's world—also flowed like that and whether the conversation I had witnessed was an example of that.

The work after breakfast continued to be hectic. I helped Iris with the dishes. Food had been scrubbed from them into garbage containers, and they had then been dropped into large water tanks. The tanks also held bowls, trays, and platters but not the cutlery and water pitchers. Dishes were piled up on a cart, then moved to special plastic trays, which rolled into a powerful dishwasher that took about two minutes to finish a single tray. From there I moved the dishes to another cart that would be used to set the tables for lunch. Iris said nothing as she worked. She sported a 1970s-style auburn Afro, like a Brandeis University professor on a summer research stint. I later discovered that she was extremely articulate and erudite, but here she remained silent. Meanwhile, the kitchen was buzzing with lunch and dinner preparations. Lunch on Thursdays means vegetable masala (*alu ghobi*), rice, sliced tomatoes and onion, and the ever-present tahini. After finishing the dishes I was directed by Natalia to help with the antipasto for dinner: slicing squash and spicing it with a paste of garlic, salt, and olive oil, then placing trays of this into the oven. The kitchen was a mess, of course, and after lunch the cleaning—which was called *hissul,* or "elimination"—would be just as hectic. I helped (imitating others or getting guidance) in sudsing and scrubbing the floor, doing the same with the food preparation tables, washing the drainage filters, cleaning the food-processing machines, putting everything away, and getting things ready for dinner.

Shortly before lunch, Natalia called for another meeting in the smoking shed, this time with an assortment of fruit—including apricots. Natalia asked if anyone wished to continue the topic from the previous meeting, and a red-haired woman whose name I had not heard immediately said: "I've been having a problem, no, just a minor issue, a conflict if you will, with Noam. I didn't say anything, and he doesn't even know about it, so my 'inner dialogue' has been repeating to me how I should have behaved. What I should have done. The longer I kept quiet, the louder spoke this inner voice—I think it's some sort of protective mechanism." Anat responded: "I know what you're saying. I do the same thing, but I think it's a way of avoiding my true feelings—nothing protective about it." I wanted to get involved and ask Anat if she meant that it helped her avoid resentment or fear of confrontation, but the red-haired woman spoke quickly. "Yes, but this inner dialogue doesn't have to be about avoiding a conflict. It can take place anytime, and be about anything; I was just giving one example." I wondered why she chose that particular example—her issue with Noam—to illustrate a general point about the inner dialogue we all have. The inner dialogue is ubiquitous, of course and had followed me around all day—just as it does everyone else—like a loyal but annoying dog. I recalled my thoughts about the gorgeous morning, regretting working in sandals, feeling embarrassed about showing up late, thinking that Alon should get lost and that my back hurt, critiquing the man who translated the Hebrew for Bill, and God knows what else. On and on went the inner voice, the white noise of mechanical thinking and unregulated feeling, running all morning long, protesting, contradicting, whining, with the occasional self-congratulation dissipating quickly into noisy distraction. This is what she was undoubtedly referring to.

Noam, who was the object of this woman's internal conflict, listened with interest, but it didn't appear that he was going to speak. No one showed any interest in the original conflict or demonstrated that gossipy social habit most of us have of wanting to know who offended whom and how. I have to admit that I was curious: what had he done to annoy her, intentionally or not? But I was just as fascinated by their self-control, which appeared effortless. The talk turned to the inner dialogue as a general phenomenon and what sort of purpose it possibly served. Two or three people offered opinions in turn, but none of the points developed earlier ones. I saw no "progress" in the discussion, only turn-taking. Then I lost the thread of the conversation as I began to wonder why I was looking for progress. I thought about being a professor and the way I normally directed class discussion toward a general classroom understanding, if not a consensus. Here things seemed random and rather dispersed in comparison. There was no goal and perhaps not even a direction to the conversation. One person spoke her mind, everyone listened attentively, then someone else spoke. People listened closely but responded—when they did—in ways that carried the conversation in unpredictable directions. In time I began to refer to this as "crab-walk conversation," but I had mixed feelings about it. I was not entirely sure there was anything wrong with it. Not only that; people made sharp observations about the internal lives of others, and no one seemed to mind. Well, at least no one said anything that sounded defensive. It was as though they shared a single brain.

I began to notice this and became curious. It would be weeks before I began to understand where this pattern originated and the purpose that it served. No, not the purpose—rather why and how it was perpetuated. It wasn't like in a family, where people can "read" each other's minds, the way my brother and I often do. This was a community of individuals who agreed to share thoughts and feelings because they considered it important to do so. What they were sharing was each person's vision—a holistic form of illuminating introspection that was designed to reveal the present state of affairs in one's mind. The vision was seldom contradicted, but the words could be refined, their meanings sharpened, and that is what I mistook for invasive comments about others' states of mind.

There was no true disagreement unless the speaker appeared to be putting on airs, lying (to himself or others), or merely being chatty. If you can imagine a "group think" in which the participants constantly appear to disagree but are perfectly content to hear another perspective, you have an early glimpse of Neot Smadar conversations. I believe this type of conversation originated in the way the teacher, Yossef, conducted his meetings, beginning in the 1970s and 1980s in Jerusalem. He must have assumed that this form of communication can lead to Self-inquiry. It was endlessly fascinating to observe how the pattern trickled down from the now-dead teacher to his former students, who were now running the place. And, unlike "the walk," this was far more difficult to pass on to the newcomers.

3

The Oasis of Neot Smadar: An Overview

I WOKE UP ON THE FIRST SATURDAY morning confused about where I was. The peacocks had roosted elsewhere that night and I had not set my alarm, so at 7:00 I snapped awake convinced I was missing something important. Breakfast on Shabbat is at 10:00, a sort of brunch actually, featuring omelets and toasted garlic bread. It's a festive affair, with families arriving together, dressed in white, the servers greeting each person entering the dining room, and the tables covered in white linen. The place pulsates with a pleasant commotion and children's laughter—a sharp contrast to the silent weekday breakfasts when one hears little but the muted sound of vegetable chopping.

I washed and left my room, though the meal was still three hours away and the dawn dissipated silently but for some mourning doves. The volunteers in the rooms around mine slept off whatever it was that single men and women in their twenties do late into Friday nights. The last hints of night chill clung to the shadows of the creepers near my door, and I decided to explore the grounds of Neot Smadar without being seen. I headed toward the craggy hills to the west and watched them losing the early coral blush to a golden hue as the sun gained height behind my back.

I passed between the run-down huts of a neighborhood known as "the project," hearing the muffled sounds of early morning inside the tiny homes. The tall grass inside the circle of huts and the low-hanging bougainvillea gave the area a lush feel, which quickly yielded to the rocky terrain

Fig. 3. Olive harvest above lake

of the desert behind the neighborhood. The barren hills, as I got nearer, became obscured by increasingly dense vegetation of pomegranate, date, eucalyptus, and poplar trees, with the thick undergrowth of bougainvillea and other creepers clinging to the fence that surrounded something entirely unexpected: a lake of brackish water surrounded by a tall ring of reeds and water grasses (Fig. 3). The lake was oval shaped, about two hundred meters by one hundred and twenty, with an island at the center—a cluster of rocks with trees and bushes. This stunning teardrop in the middle of a vast desert was clearly man-made: up close one could see the moss-covered black plastic tarp that prevented water saturation into the thirsty limey soil. But on this fresh morning the lake felt anything but artificial. The reeds swayed lightly in the breeze, and I spotted a few plovers and a couple of ducks. Coming from the poplars behind my back I could hear the cooing of mourning doves, and I suspected that the water's edge concealed frogs and there were probably scorpions under those rocks near the small dock to which two canoes were tied.

A streamlet of clear water fed the lake on its northern end—a trickle, actually, coming down a narrow channel in a green arroyo—all of this man-made. It was part of an elaborate watering system that provided desalinated drinking water, irrigation, and bathing water, which relied on a number of sources—mainly deep subterranean water of high saline content.[1] It was this water, and the ingenious purification and recycling system constructed by members of Neot Smadar, including Uri Moran and the late Gil, that made it possible to turn one of the driest corners of the world into a human oasis and a riotous resting spot for migratory birds in the spring and fall seasons.

Like other projects in Neot Smadar, the lake and the stream serve an important function in the ecology and economy of the place—swimming and splashing for the children not least—but the construction work was largely its own purpose, a demanding project for the disciples in the school for Self-inquiry.[2] Like visitors who are blown away by the beautiful incongruity of the desert lake, on that day I was simply delighted, and it took some time and a great deal of work to figure out the true motivation for digging a lake in the fierce desert or, for that matter, building a huge art center with a phallic-looking tower, or cooling stack, at the front end of the community, near the gate.

I headed north, up the narrow stream, with a wall of limestone boulders on my left and a row of pomegranate trees on my right. These yielded soon to the darker foliage of apricot and apple trees—I reached up and snapped off a couple of apricots of the few remaining. The path angled upward, then veered to the right, where I was now climbing a steep, barren hill. At the top, behind a lonely date tree, was a pool, crystal clear and surrounded by a wall of rocks cemented with smooth masonry and about fifteen meters in diameter (Fig. 4). I scanned the area—no one there at 7:40 on a Saturday morning—then took off my shirt and pants. The water was cold and the steps slippery as I pushed off. The bottom was slick but solid, and standing with the water just below my chest I spun and took in the vast panorama of the desert in every direction, with Neot Smadar below me in a southeasterly direction. The pool was known as the Pool of Wolves, and, like the lake, it performed a variety of functions in the life of the community—some of them spiritual. Because it stood at the peak of a hill with a panoramic desert

Fig. 4. The Pool of Wolves

view, the cool water and the arid landscape clashed in the imagination and reminded me of mornings in Banaras, India, when ritual bathers observed the rising sun from the coolness of the Ganges waters.

The sun dried me in no time as I planned the rest of my stroll before breakfast. My eyes followed the unfenced perimeter along the dry wash that separates the vineyards from the table-rock northern mountain range. Sweeping past green rows of Shiraz and Sauvignon Blanc (pulled out a year later) in the far distance, I could see olive groves and, far beyond them, a solar-panel farm and the houses of Ye'elon. The entire area of Neot Smadar is about one by one and a half miles (over one thousand acres), not including Ye'elon, the solar-panel fields, and the date groves in the distant Arava (Afro-Syrian rift). From the altitude of a breezy hill, sitting on a stone wall as I dried and stared east into the light, Neot Smadar looked like a rich place. I could see the "neighborhood," a cluster of eighteen villas—two- and three-bedroom homes—with their cooling stacks. All were painted Rajasthani blue, all surrounded by colorful gardens of roses, dahlias, sunflowers, marigolds, snapdragons, gaillardias, Mexican egerton, and dozens of other flowers with which I was not familiar. The gardens were watered by timer-operated drip and sprinkler systems that ran in the early morning and late afternoon. From this distance and with the sunlight in my eyes, I was staring at a scumbled Monet landscape against the canvas of an austere desert. Shielding my eyes from the glare, I was able to see people moving in the distance, peacefully.

In fact, in 2013 Neot Smadar was anything but well off. The big money-makers—if one could call them that—were the dates (mejool and deglet noor) that grow on a thousand date palms several miles away, in the world's lowest farmland—the Afro-Syrian rift, known in Israel as the Arava. Working there just after dawn, as I would discover soon, was pure joy and highly favored by the young volunteers and older community members alike. It meant a dawn van ride, with breakfast supplies boxed in the back, down the stunning switchbacks of Route 40 as it descends twelve hundred feet to below sea level. The work (trimming bunches, tying them, covering them against bird damage) often takes place on forty-foot ramps atop swaying trees interrupted by a sumptuous breakfast in the cover of low-lying trees, all of this less than one kilometer from the border with Jordan.

The goat farm and dairy also make some money, and the work there is intense and dusty, but for those who love goats—there are about two hundred on the farm—and do not mind the occasional kick or the 4:00 a.m. milking, this was a great place to work. The dairy (white, silent, and antiseptic) processed goat milk into a variety of cheese products, including feta and Bulgarian and an exquisite brie—all of them marketed to the finest and most expensive health-food boutiques in Israel.

Aside from these profitable (but labor-intensive) branches of the community's economy there were less lucrative but equally valued enterprises. The farming operation, run by Noam, who had shared my day in the kitchen, varied according to the season and included growing deciduous fruits like apples, pears, apricots, plums, and peaches, as well as olives and grapes. The growth seasons, in which each fruit had its own schedule, ranged from sleepy to intense during picking season, when the entire community would sometimes be recruited. For example, if a certain type of grape was right for winemaking at a specific time, the vintage required all hands at once. Picking fruit, like apricots (Fig. 5), was more gradual but still called for more pickers than Noam had on a regular basis. These fruit-picking days had the feel of a special project; they brought new workers and veterans together and were cheerful and almost celebratory. The fruit-processing plant, run (in 2013) by Guy (the young one), formed a triangle with the winery (run

Fig. 5. Apricot harvest

by Shmuel) and the dairy (run by Gadi, later Maya), with a shady gazebo surrounded by a garden at the center with base mint, lavender, desert sage, calendulas, ginger, and other herbs and tubers, each marked with a small sign. From the hills north of the community—I was walking in the shade of date palms planted in two rows along the pathway surrounded by vineyards (Shiraz, Merlot, Sauvignon Blanc)—you could almost reach out and touch that cluster of buildings. In front of them was the goat pen—the goats, I could see about 60, were currently enclosed within a two-acre alfalfa field, waiting to be let out on their morning trot. A young man with deep brown skin, Idan from a northern kibbutz, who was doing his national service here instead of serving in the army, was watching the goats. The animals ignored Shabbat, and Idan, too, worked on this day, as he does all week long.

On the roof of the fruit-processing plant was the tiny room, a work station actually, where Tessa brought the herbs and flowers she had gathered to be sorted out and prepared for spices and perfume. Like Amnon, who tended to the community gardens and landscaping, Tessa spent most of her days under the fierce sun, bent over some plant or another, concealed in her white fabrics and wide-brimmed hat. My one day with her, planting young seedlings in the field behind the goat pen, was perhaps the hardest I would spend in a period of several years while trying out most of the other jobs: 110 degrees without a hint of shade, bending over or crawling on my knees row after row. Somehow Tessa, who was small and leathered brown, with radiant black eyes, seemed one of the happiest persons in the community and rarely spoke in public forums.

At the far west end of Neot Smadar, just across Route 40 where it intersects with Route 12, is the Pundak, which means "Inn." This is a restaurant and shop enclosing an unexpected oasis in the back, refreshed by a cool-water spring with a small pond stocked with goldfish. Here travelers can buy cheeses, wines, olives, dates, and other community products or eat breakfast (an omelet laced with herbs and a salad on the side) or lunch (a grilled-cheese bagel, salad on the side) and top this off with a double espresso and a date pastry. Neot Smadar does not serve or consume meat, but fish (such as tilapia in mustard sauce) is offered on Friday nights. This allows the place to meet the minimum kosher standards without actually observing the laws of Jewish *kashrut* (purity). The Pundak is strictly vegetarian. Unfortunately, it was not attracting as many visitors as it should have; Israeli tourists on their way to the seaport city of Eilat prefer the faster Arava road (Route 90) or shopping at the more commercial rest stop in Yodfata, about twenty miles farther south.[3]

Neot Smadar also generates income by selling arts and crafts made in the metal and wood workshops and in the studios located inside the art center. There is a shop there, on the first floor, with highly individualistic work, such as Meir's inventions made of polished driftwood, Shimon's exquisite wood pieces, detailed stained-glass works, pottery, Hanukkah lanterns, toys, fabrics, and lighting fixtures—many in shockingly vivid colors.

The heart of Neot Smadar's busy day is the kitchen and the dining hall, as I discovered on my first day. A new dining room is slowly rising a few feet away, where the "smoking shed" had previously stood. West of the dining room, in the shade of tall trees, is a bomb shelter that houses the library and music room. South of the shelter is the clinic, where, a couple of years later, I would lie on the treatment table and have Chinese needles stuck into my body by an Israeli nurse from Yodfata. The same dusty brick path that runs between the shelter and the clinic leads to a communal laundry, a storage room for the maintenance crew, and, down from there, the office complex, which includes the office of the two secretaries (Alon and Ilana, later Omri and Galit), the accountant, the farm CEO (*merakez meshek*), and the treasurer. Adjacent to these is a large meeting room in a stand-alone structure where the heads of the various economy sections meet once a week to report on their work. The path then leads to an elementary school of tiny proportions—the classes are largely blended. The children in Neot Smadar do not engage in limud in the sense of Self-inquiry. However, as we shall see in Chapter 10 on sociality, they reap the fruit of their parents' Self-inquiry. They live and study in a noncompetitive and nonjudgmental environment, one in which attentiveness is more highly prized than demonstrating one's excellence. Beyond are the nursery and kindergarten. Most of these structures remain from the old deserted kibbutz and were assembled of prefabricated cement walls bolted together in the manner of remote Israeli military bases of the 1950s and 1960s. The landscaping in this part of the community was nondescript in 2013, with the vegetation (faded bougainvillea, mimosa, flimsy eucalyptus) gathering dust. During the following years the entire area would undergo a massive landscape upgrading in another strenuous community project in which I participated (see Chapter 10).

Two hundred meters farther south, past the cluster of "family trailers," was the long structure—previously an immense chicken coop—that housed the garage and the metal workshop. In 2013 a young immigrant from the United States, Samuel, ran the garage accompanied by a resourceful and reticent Ofer, neither one of whom possessed much automotive or mechanical experience. A year later a paid worker from Thailand took over running the garage—this was no place to learn automotive mechanics on the run.[4]

It was hard to prosper in this remote desert location. The community ran innovative and transformative seminars on desert construction, farming, and winemaking and also rented guest rooms for overnight stays in the structures that the seminar members constructed in Ye'elon, but the income from all of that added up to little. There would be some financial benefit deriving from the solar plant a couple of miles east of the main gate,

Fig. 6. Two-generation Shavuot celebration

but it was not yet operating in 2013. By 2016 the plant was slated to become a major source of income—a great boon to the community. A few members, like David and Anat, worked outside the kibbutz, at least part-time, and their salaries belonged to the community.

It is difficult to assess the exact number of Neot Smadar residents. Volunteers come and go, spending between one month and a year, with a few of them, like Bettina—originally a volunteer from Germany—residing and working there for years. The children of the founding members of Neot Smadar get drafted into the military, then study in universities, colleges, and art schools. Some of these individuals are close to thirty years of age now, but, like others of their cohort, they remain unlikely to return to this distant and isolated community. They do return for periodic stays, to see their parents or take a breather from the breakneck pace of Israeli life (Fig. 6).

At any one time the community may include about 230 to 250 people ranging in age from newborn to nearly eighty. Approximately 50 adults (in their fifties and sixties) count among the founders who moved in 1989; the others are younger arrivals and families. From the very start, members of this community, including Yossef, called it an "extended family" (*mishpaha murhevet*). In principle and formally, as the school charter declares, this means "the necessary basis for maintaining a community of people for whom Self-inquiry is the essence of their life together. Deep cooperation, mutual support, respect, trust and friendship are the foundation of such a community's existence." The most easily observable aspect of this extended family is the treatment of children. Several couples in Neot Smadar have young children, even infants, who relish being handled by any willing adult. Older kids move between members of the community as within an extended family of aunts, uncles, and miscellaneous surrogate parents. However, the concept of "extended family" signifies something far subtler and explains the sociality of a school for Self-inquiry. I devote an entire chapter to this later (Chapter 10).

Demographically the question of continuity plays a central role in the community's future but does not figure in the spiritual discipline to which the school is committed. The more urgent question—a subterranean one —is whether the vision of Neot Smadar can be passed on to younger members and survive. That is, can the school's mission, the Self-inquiry that brought its founders to the desert, the hidden challenge of coming to "see" oneself through introspective conversation and shared work, illuminate the lives of the younger generation of residents, at least those who are committed to staying?

One senses a tangible but subtle tension between life in a communal economy—nominally a kibbutz—and a school for inquiry into the nature of the self. The former is a formal necessity driven by regional and national institutions, such as the national kibbutz movement, with its funds, licensing, information, and other forms of support.[5] And so—to give one example—the community collectively owns about ten cars, so individuals running errands must rely on shared rides or public transportation, or they may hitchhike with visitors or stick out their thumbs on the open road. Although most kibbutzim in Israel have now privatized their economies, leading to family ownership of homes, vehicles, and income, Neot Smadar adheres more than most kibbutzim to the original vision of shared labor and communal ownership—even as it rejects communal ideology.

On the flip side, the school in Neot Smadar is highly individualistic—you pursue your own course at your own pace; no two people look at the school (or at life) in quite the same way. One of the first students in this school, a soft-spoken woman with warm eyes—Dalit—likened the school to the tower at the art center, with its circular balcony high above the ground. "Depending on where you stand," she said, "you can only see a sliver of this place. Each person facing a different direction sees a partial truth but all are valid. That is the school here." The school does not tell you how much or how often to eat, how hard to work, how to raise your children, or what you should be getting out of life in close proximity with other people. And yet the school requires, or inspires, other-oriented acts that far transcend the expectations of kibbutz communalism. As Yossef put it when the original members moved from Jerusalem to the desert, "This community should be governed by the dynamics of the inner life, not by external rules." And so, ironically, the community (the physical embodiment of the school) resembles the original vision of the *kvutzah,* which was a revolutionary communalistic idea.[6] It is in observance of some inner principle, not a conventional rule (like majority vote or equality), for instance, that members of Neot Smadar pack up all their belongings and rotate homes every seven years, change work stations every three years or so, and, above all, participate in remarkably difficult work projects after their day jobs are finished.

According to Alon, who was the secretary of Neot Smadar when I first came, the key difference between a kibbutz and a school is the nature of the "togetherness." While a kibbutz attracts people due to its ideology, institutions, economy, and perhaps psychological benefits, the school attracts individuals who share an interest in Self-inquiry. The school can take any form; it is merely a set of conditions in which Self-inquiry can take place. Yossef had often stated that he did not know what a school was, and Alon came to understand this as I have just explained it: as a set of conditions for Self-inquiry. A school can take many other forms besides that of a kibbutz.[7]

The inner principle that drives this community is hidden, and it would be hard to reach a consensus that explains it. To me it seemed that attachment to property and to the status of one job above another is a threat to honest Self-inquiry. It calcifies the self around key markers and makes it hard to become perfectly "naïve," as Yossef put it. Of course, this is just one point of view, not yet fully informed.

I reflected on the other communities in this part of the country: kibbutzim and private settlements. Each had its own character and reputation. Collectively they have all been praised for innovative water usage and sustainability, humane farming, desert tourism, the adoption of solar energy, and other achievements. Neot Smadar shared some of this, with the excellence of its goat-farming practices and organic products at the forefront. But the finest aspect of the place, its "treasure," lay hidden from the outside world. And that was the school for the inquiry into the nature of the self and the unexpected ways that such a school transformed the lives and work of those who lived in the community. In fact, this school and the man who led it for many years were responsible for generating media and online reports of a dark nature about Neot Smadar. Whispers and shouts about a "cult" and "brain washing" appeared both in mainstream publications and in blogs, and these have naturally forced members of the community to erect walls of privacy.

Collective communities in Israel, kibbutzim, are tightly structured. It seems that the more egalitarian they seek to be, the more binding the authority of the institutions.[8] And so the typical kibbutz would be run by a secretary (*mazkir*), merakez meshek, budget director (*gizbar*), and accountant (*menahel heshbonot*), the deceptively powerful and hyperanxious job coordinator (*sadran avodah*), and then all the heads of the different branches of the economy, ranging from field farming to the goat or cow pen, the dairy, the kitchen, the garden, the factory, and others—depending on the size and complexity of the community. There is no mystery about the purpose of this system: running an economy and managing power flow according to the values upheld by the community. Neot Smadar, at first glance, differs little in principle from other kibbutzim, but it also has educational institutions, including seminars for adults; water management, restaurant, marketing, security, transportation, garage, and other operations; as well as a committee for social affairs (*yahid ve-hevrah*).

As in any democracy, such kibbutz positions are filled by election and by appointment, all of this under some type of charter that states both general principles (equality, fairness, transparency, and so on) and specific mechanisms or procedures (majority vote, open or secret ballot, and so forth). None of these positions are permanent unless they require a high degree of specialization—and these are not leadership roles. Given the dramatic changes that Israeli kibbutzim have undergone in the past thirty years, it is difficult to generalize about governing—just as it would be difficult to generalize about the governing bodies of American homeowner associations (HOAs). However, due to the fact that Neot Smadar is first of all a school and only externally a kibbutz, a number of radical differences apply.

The community was established in 1989 as a school (couched in the form of a kibbutz) under the leadership of one person, Yossef. It would be inaccurate to describe him as a "guru" and absolutely false to characterize him as a cult leader. The community consisted of both men and women, many of whom possessed dominant personalities and strong wills. Impressed by qualities they identified in Yossef as an advanced and highly perceptive Self-inquiry practitioner, each made a decision—and constantly re-examined it—to join a school in the desert. However, one of the primary features of learning to inquire about the nature of the self was the will to renounce ways of life that many of them had taken for granted: comfort, attachment to things and to relationships, the ego-driven exercise of decision making. And so Yossef—who called himself "*sharat*" and not "teacher," was the one who appointed individuals to fill the positions of the new community.[9] To give one example, for the first ten years there was just one school "principal" or manager (*menahel beit-sefer*), and that was Ruth B. However, a year later Arnon became the merakez meshek and modeled the community as a kibbutz. A year later the position of mazkir was created, and Alon occupied it. From that point on, all of these positions ran concurrently with the school principal. Ruth was an excellent choice given her skills with people and her mild manner, but her appointment was predictably troublesome for some of the dominant men, who felt more highly qualified to run the place. There were no elections at that time, and decisions were arrived at by means of lengthy discussions. The authoritative hierarchy (in the school) was as simple as they come: a leader who decides who runs what. Yossef (like Ruth) was ignorant of all things pertaining to management and running an economy—especially a farming economy—while others were far more highly qualified. His reasons for appointing Ruth and other individuals, which will be discussed in later chapters, owed little to economics and government and much to Self-inquiry. They were based on the way he had always run his study groups and on the methods he used for problematizing customary notions of agency.

I heard this from several members of the community; it is a narrow path a sharat treads between pointing out painful truths honestly and openly to individuals and their taking offence or perceiving some slight. Here, too, is where rumors of a cult and of brainwashing took root (see Chapter 5). But the evidence from the participants is far more nuanced and interesting. For example, a year after my first arrival (ten years after the death of Yossef) I heard the following anecdote from Dalit, the veteran student. Dalit had been the merakez meshek when, along with others, she handled planning for the construction of a new chicken coop. In a stormy meeting that Yossef ran it was finally decided to cancel the project—a painful decision for members of that planning team. Dalit said to me: "I am not angry at him. . . . The difficulty, the friction, was part of the process of acquiring self-knowledge. . . . Yossef punctured the bubble of my self-importance."[10]

I learned of this incident in a conversation that took place after a summertime dinner, sitting on the lawn in front of the dining hall. There were conversations everywhere, some people nursing cups of tea, others smoking, a light breeze playing at the tops of the trees, and children chasing each other and laughing out loud. The evening was pleasant, and Dalit kept smiling as she reminisced about Yossef. I asked her what she meant by "piercing the bubble of self-importance," and she spoke about being trapped in a prison of self-importance, about decades of chaining herself to norms and succumbing to the expectations of other people—as she saw it—and finally, in her early sixties, achieving freedom, particularly giving herself permission to become happy. Looking back, she said, she could understand how breaking those bonds required cutting something inside, even if that meant letting someone else, either the sharat or co-learners, point out your faults. And she added that she believed that the function of Neot Smadar today was to pass on that understanding to other people who are interested in learning for themselves.

Other individuals, mostly former members who had left the community, did not see Yossef's motives so nobly, and a few even spoke to me about lasting harm. But for those who stayed, strong and insightful individuals, the logic behind the governing by leader appointment served the goals of a school for Self-inquiry. Whether it was always so and whether it was always successful is open to debate—by universal admission—but the guiding spirit was and remains positive.

And so, while the standard community institutions remain, they are motivated by the idea of the school even today, twelve years after the death of the "sharat," Yossef. One afternoon in July 2014, the secretary of Neot Smadar, Alon, invited me to his house to explain how leadership functioned in the community—how governing a kibbutz was related to the ideas behind the school after the death of Yossef. Alon began by being very clear that the school at Neot Smadar has no connection to the ideological sources of a kibbutz—the kibbutz was a useful external form.

There were two leaders of the school at Neot Smadar in 2013—two secretaries (*mazkirim*): Alon and Ilana. In the report she wrote upon ending her tenure, Ilana reflects that the secretary—as head of the school—needs to discover her true role. She writes: "In this job it is important to sense, as far as possible, the pulse of the times." She quotes Galit, who served in an advisory committee, as saying: "Our role is to make sure the secretaries will be able to succeed and find satisfaction in this sensitive and responsible position. And in order for that to happen, we must be supportive and joyful. Let's not hold on to the past and let's not hold on to what cannot be."[11] Alon and Ilana are radically different personalities, and what could have become a paralyzing clash of leadership styles (and emotional turmoil) became another moment of Self-inquiry leading to insight.

You may diagram Neot Smadar on a page as a triangle consisting of three key terms: school, community (*kehilah*), and economy (*meshek*). But the three are not equal: school is at the top of a pyramid, with the other two as its base; it is a sort of "canopy" that overhangs everything in the place. In other words, in order to understand the place, one needs to understand the school. However, a basic sketch of the school community can also be diagrammed with the people of the *sukkah* (tabernacle, the octagonal meeting structure) and its membership at the top. A variety of other groups, some led by members of the sukkah group, others not, operate under the auspices of the first group. These include groups of veterans, young women, young men, mothers, workers (such as date grove workers), those attending seminars, volunteers, and retreat groups. Informally this structure, too, can be sketched as a sort of pyramid: the higher up the group in the scheme, the more intensive and introspective does the work become—not economically but as far as Self-inquiry is concerned.[12]

As I listened to Alon, it occurred to me that the entire community can also be conceived as concentric circles, with volunteers (myself included) in the outer circle, then young men and young women (separate groups), and so forth. The farther outside the circle in which you move, the less you know what it means to live within the inner circles and what Self-inquiry means or that it is even there (see Chapter 5). During my first few weeks I worked with many such volunteers, all of them in their twenties, and none had any clear idea about the school or the real work that takes place in Neot Smadar. This sort of knowledge does develop, inceptively to be sure, in the members of the seminar groups (also young people in their twenties and thirties), who come for three months or so.

Those in the inner circle understand that the economy is secondary or subservient to the work that takes place at the school and to the principles that guide self-study. Those in the circles outside the sukkah can see this only in a partial manner, and the newcomers have no idea. What they do perceive—this I found out immediately—is that Neot Smadar is an extraordinary place to work. The work environment is like no other: egalitarian, gentle, contemplative, and responsive.

Running the place is tricky, with the danger of calcification ever-present. The school had to be a place that ran on inner dynamics—organization following the dictates of Self-inquiry. But institutions were necessary, even for a school, and that meant that power could come to rest in those institutions and the people who ran them. There were ways of avoiding this situation—in principle—and such solutions defined the difference between Neot Smadar as a school in the form of a kibbutz for other communalistic societies.

"Can you give me an example?" I asked.

Alon responded, "Let me tell you a bit about leadership today." In the absence of Yossef and his dictates, major decisions are ideally made in the sukkah. None of this is democratic in the formal political sense—there is no majority voting. Instead, the members of the appropriate committee look at the candidates and discuss each one of them in great detail, in successive rounds as the field is narrowed. The decision that is finally reached, after considering more than one candidate, is unanimous.

The discussion—in time I would witness several—is not something that can be communicated here easily. It does not resemble anything I had ever seen elsewhere: parliamentary debate, jury deliberation, faculty discussion, or HOA jaw-flapping. Chapter 5 illustrates the conversation that takes place among two dozen men and women, or even more, where no one wields power, no one carries more authority than the others and claims greater insight or can set the agenda or the direction that the conversation will take, and where active listening is a gift. The goal of unanimity, unlike jury deliberation, is not total justice or eliminating the appearance of dissent (and the desire to appeal) but the product of what a school tries to achieve: deepening human awareness or consciousness beyond the limitation of individual agendas—regardless of the subject at hand.

The appointment of lesser personnel obeys similar school dynamics. So, to give yet another example, when someone is appointed to run a work crew (huli'ya)—such as that in the date grove or the food-processing operation— the individual is not selected on the basis of seniority, experience, or expertise but on the basis of the Self-inquiry trajectory of that individual and consideration of how that role would further the inquiry dynamics. In time I would work with Guy in food processing, with Yuval in the date grove, with Adva in the goat pen, with Samuel in the garage, and so on. All are young individuals whose Self-inquiry would be deepened and perhaps enhanced by their roles in the economy. A veteran would be assigned to support them in their economic functions and leadership roles. Power struggles, which are natural, were not to be avoided as taboo but rather were aired out in the way that all inner processes are to become transparent and subject to group feedback in Neot Smadar. There was no hierarchy within the work groups, Alon emphasized. The person who leads the group is not superior to or more powerful than anyone else, even the newcomer.

"What about the community, the kehilah?" I asked. "How is that influenced by standing under the umbrella of the school?"

Alon responded, "A school is a set of conditions that facilitate Self-

Fig. 7. Date work

inquiry. It is not an agenda, and it is not ideology. The same is true for the community." He then gave me the example of the dining hall, which he considered the public or communal face of the school. While virtually every other kibbutz allows free sitting and the dining hall is a chaotic riot of loud voices, shuffling furniture, and clanging utensils, the dining hall in Neot Smadar is almost monastically austere. As noted earlier, one takes the next available chair in a proper sequence. There is no talking, and those at a table (at lunch) do not commence eating, or even serving, until the last chair is occupied. In the meantime, as Alon emphasized repeatedly, one sits quietly and gathers oneself in the present moment: letting go of what came before, emptying the mind of unnecessary distractions.

"We are not trying to be controlling or arbitrary," he said. "I believe that the meditative moments before eating are valuable and beneficial to the individual." And because everyone comes to the dining room at least twice a day, he implied, that is the best chance for even the newest person in Neot Smadar to put the idea of Self-inquiry into practice. Alon explained that he was not interested in "enlightenment." And, unlike some members of the community, he was never disappointed when no transcendent illumination had broken into his life. He had spent some time studying Zen and was captive to no salvific imaginings. But he valued self-understanding and thought the school a great—if vulnerable—achievement. I understood in time that it was people like Alon who hold the key to understanding everyday mysticism (Fig. 7).

This view of the relationship between the school, the community, and the economy is still preliminary. It needs to be deepened by a more detailed understanding of what a school truly means (Yossef often claimed he had no idea what a school was!)—and that is the topic of the next chapter. But government and community were not the only domains that were ideally served by or saturated with Self-inquiry. So was morality—a term I rarely heard used. Like any community, Neot Smadar has an unwritten code of conduct, with mutual obligations and implicitly recognized norms. One does not take someone else's bicycle or hat, one shows up to work, and when asked a question, one is expected to answer truthfully. Life together in a close community imposes such codes; they are basic and unexceptional. However, the school both imposes more stringent expectations and, at the same time, provides an entirely different way of thinking about the reasons for being moral.

4

A School for Self-Inquiry

LIVING AND WORKING IN NEOT SMADAR as a researcher—or as a volunteer—it is too easy to mistake the place for a kibbutz with its labor arrangements and communal dining hall. I was often corrected, patiently but with persistence: "This is not a kibbutz, it's a school!" The kibbutz is just the external form, "a dress," as members called it. School and kibbutz share some features, along with their differences, and many residents of Neot Smadar have mixed feelings about the kibbutz way of life.

So what is a school? Spiritual schools have cropped up throughout history, including Vedic schools and *ashramas,* Muslim madrasas, Buddhist and Christian monasteries, Jewish yeshivas, and many others. Most are steeped in and regulated by tradition: doctrines are learned and memorized, practices are drilled, a routine is honored. It matters little how "spiritual" or mystical the goals of a religious institution may be; the structure is invariably fortified by strict rules of conduct. The Buddhist *sangha* prohibits gossip and idleness, St. Benedict requires obedience and humility, Jewish academies devote effort to the study of ethics (*mussar*), and so forth.[1]

None of this applies to the school that is Neot Smadar. Early on Yossef had insisted that the community would run on the basis of "internal principles." He was referring to the natural workings of the liberated (or perfectly transparent) mind. Hence, the school is as elusive as true insight and as subtle as breath. I asked several residents of Neot Smadar, both veterans and younger residents, "What is a school?" and received different answers.

Some even denied that the question could be answered.[2] Perhaps that is as it should be, because, as everyone acknowledged, "school" means different things to different folks. After all, a school for Self-inquiry is largely a state of mind, not four walls surrounding learning equipment. On the other hand, the school at Neot Smadar is not just a state of mind; there is some institutional aspect, with a history and perhaps even rules, or at least guidelines.

One Saturday afternoon in 2014 I sat with Ilana—one of the two secretaries of Neot Smadar at that time—behind the art center. Ilana was one of the veterans of the community—an immigrant from Latvia who owned a nice library of mystical writings and was keen on Yossef's talks on the subject of numbers (Chapter 5). The afternoon air was close to one hundred degrees and dead still. The place was quiet, and even the goats in their pen behind Ilana did not stir. We talked for a long time, and early on I asked her about the school. Specifically, what is a school today?

> ILANA: That is a very big question. In the past, too, in Jerusalem, there were numerous discussions about this. Beyond the organization of the school— at its very heart—it is difficult to say. Personally, I don't deal with that question. [That is, it's a practical, not theoretical, matter.]
> ARIEL: But if you had to explain it to someone like me?
> ILANA: On those terms, a school is a place where everyone can learn intimately about him or her self and about the world. There is no doctrine— each does this in his, or her, own way. People easily misconstrue this. There is no Gurdjieff, no Rudolf Steiner, nor anyone else.
> ARIEL: So, what does it feel like to be in school?
> ILANA: It means taking a chance. Not to fall into views, hang on to opinions or dogma. The school means walking on an edge with a canyon on both sides. Today there are levels to this [commitment]: new people do not see it the same way as us older folks, and we have to meet them midway.

When Ilana finished her role as secretary, she submitted a report (dated April 1, 2015) in which she wrote about what Self-inquiry (in the school) requires, namely, daring: "Because [the student] dares without a teaching, without a forceful authority that most people are so eager for. There is no one to imitate or follow." Self-inquiry also requires courage: "It takes courage to look into oneself. It brings up conflicted feelings, emotional upheavals, a great deal of pain, and the knowledge and perception that it is [some-times] impossible to contain everything that comes out of the darkness."

I asked Ilana: "Do the younger folks believe you carry a secret?"

Ilana replied: "Yes, I think so. But they will need the strength to realize that this is not a teaching. The main thing, as far as I am concerned: under what conditions does your heart open. That is the essence. . . . You need to open up to life with your heart. This place, the school, creates the condi-tions. The secret is to respond to the conditions—but the conditions are not static and so this is not a teaching or a doctrine."

It became clear to me that the school at Neot Smadar is fluid, with both subjective attitude and some institutional dimension. It is both ever-changing and beyond time, and yet it does possess a history. I resolved to capture the sense of the school in its ephemeral sense by looking first at its history and its (original) institutional features. This may go against what Ilana was explaining on that day, but my readers—like me—may find this approach useful.

The History of the School

There are different ways of thinking about history. One refers to events in time, and a second may refer to the way the present is subjectively per-ceived in relation to the past. Most of the people who have committed themselves to study in Neot Smadar do not believe that the past is relevant to Self-inquiry in the present, even when examining how they arrived at Self-inquiry.[3] In fact, as we shall see, most do not regard knowledge—the accumulation of information—as relevant to Self-inquiry. So why look at the history of the school if it does not bear on Self-inquiry today? The an-swer is simple: I do it for myself and for readers who do not share the same discursive universe of Neot Smadar's school. It appears to me that the discourse of Self-inquiry, with its layers of paradox and self-referential denials, will become clearer if we understand Yossef, who founded the school, in a broader context and if we perhaps go a bit further into the past and begin with Gurdjieff. I do this, begging the indulgence of the mem-bers of the school, aware that they acknowledge the significance of Gurd-jieff (for Yossef) without clinging to his theories. Yossef would, at times,

Fig. 8. Landscaping in the 1990s

have students read passages from Gurdjieff, Ouspensky, Krishnamurti, and even Castaneda, although he regarded none of these as a model, let alone a teacher.

George Gurdjieff (d. 1949), the Greek-Armenian spiritual teacher, was profoundly eclectic in his spiritual roots and in his teachings.[4] Researchers attribute the core of his teachings to Sufi influences, but there were recognizable strands of thought from Buddhism, Hinduism, Chinese religions, and Christianity as well. One of his key early insights was the need for complete detachment from the ordinary pattern of automatic behavior in order to undertake a new path of total mental wakefulness. Gurdjieff set up a "study house" that combined inner work with physical labor, dancing, and music. This was not a monastic community and included families. The study at this place was ultimately individualistic, leading, in advanced stages, to a unique path for each follower of the master. However, early on the students focused on achieving "presence" and "quietude" while engaging in group activities and special projects (Fig. 8). "Presence" meant the merging of a bodily feeling with attentiveness and a feeling of deep peacefulness that descends and spreads throughout the body and saturates both thoughts and emotions.[5] Gurdjieff warned his students that the work never ends and that, while progress is necessary, there is a difference between "self-improvement" (which implies ambition and ego gratification) and the "improvement of being," which is a sort of longing of the heart, an inner prayer that reflects an elevated feeling from a genuine inner source (to which Ilana may have been referring).

Much of what we know about Gurdjieff and his teachings arrived via the work of his talented follower and author, P. D. Ouspensky. His influential book *In Search of the Miraculous* adds a great deal of theoretical and practical depth to Gurdjieff's literary work—much of it mythical in form—and includes the following central features, all of which are related to practice:[6]

1. At the core of practice stands the dictum "know yourself" as a rule to engage in the practice of self-study for the sake of understanding the "machine" that constitutes the human organism.
2. The method involved is not theoretical or scientific but phenomenological. That is, the method is Self-inquiry, which means seeing correlations between different functions of the machine. The observer must get to know "how and why on each separate occasion everything in him happens."[7]
3. At the earlier stages of practice, Self-inquiry is merely a "recording" in the mind of what is observed at the moment. This is not analysis, and it is certainly not any theoretical attribution of what one sees to some doctrine or scientific idea. Analysis, which can come only at far more advanced stages and is based on general laws, disrupts simple and focused observation.

The Gurdjieff program for self-study arrived in Israel in the 1950s and 1960s via Ouspensky's *In Search of the Miraculous*. In Israel it found fertile soil. Ilan Amit, who was one of the early students, writes in his biography of Gurdjieff about a moshav (farming community) that was founded in 1960 in the Lower Galilee—Yodfat.[8] The founders were students of a high school teacher (Dr. Yossef Schechter) who inspired them to lead a communal life while engaged in inner study. One of these students, Dr. Michel

Kung, organized the first Gurdjieff study group after reading Ouspensky and corresponding with Madam Jeanne De Salzman, who was at that time spreading the study method of Gurdjieff around the world.

Yossef Safra (1931–2003) began his own career elsewhere, as a theater director and playwright and a film actor of minor distinction. Like the residents of Yodfat, but elsewhere in the Galilee (at Rosh Pina), he engaged in self-study and in teaching in the 1960s. The school that ended up in the remote desert where Neot Smadar is now located came into being in Jerusalem, where Yossef moved in the early 1970s. The term "school" is far too reified for what actually took place. Yossef began by organizing a group that met on Wednesdays, then another one that met on Mondays, and so forth on other days of the week. The groups met initially at the neighborhood of Talpiot and then moved (with Yossef's home) to Beit Hakerem. The separate groups rarely met at the same time, although twice a year they all left the city on a retreat to an old Arab ruin (Hurbat A'lka) for a whole week. Like Gurdjieff's "study house," this was not monastic: families with children came along, and the study included music and dance in addition to Self-inquiry, reading of reports, conversations, and special projects that called for communal effort.

Like Ouspensky's Gurdjieff, Yossef was interested in methodical Self-inquiry in order to see through the mirage of the false self that our culture embeds in us. This activity, which Yossef called "limud"—and I have been translating as Self-inquiry—discerns the difference between the real and the imaginary, and that practice remains at the heart of the Neot Smadar school today.[9]

The early days of the Jerusalem groups, in the late 1970s, were deeply euphoric, accompanied by a feeling of infinite spiritual potential and joyful expectations. The meetings at the home of Yossef were (cigarette) smoke-filled, and the conversation often lasted into the early morning hours. A member of the second (Monday) group, Rony O., told me how he came to join:

> I was browsing among the books in the mysticism section of a Jerusalem bookstore ("Friedman"). I was into Krishnamurti in those days. The cashier noticed the books I was buying and asked me if I wanted to join a group that was discussing these topics. I said "sure" and gave her my number. A couple weeks later I received a call from a woman who identified herself as

Smadar, and she invited me to meet her in a café. We had a long talk, and I felt as though she was interviewing me, but she was pleasant and seemed to like me, because I was invited to meet her again and again. Finally she invited me to meet Yossef and the Wednesday group in a café. It was all very mysterious, sort of like the opening scene in Carlos Castaneda's *The Teachings of Don Juan*.[10]

The second group, to which Rony belonged, consisted of about fifteen people, a few of whom ended up in Neot Smadar. That group, like others, met once a week for a conversation on subjects of interest (attachment, the unknown, habits and patterns, the individual and the group, identification, and so forth), which could last for hours. In between the meetings, the members of the groups often had to experiment with a variety of living situations. Some were almost impossible to execute from a psychological point of view: one had to approach a stranger at a crosswalk and ask for help crossing the street. This had to be done without pretending to be blind or handicapped in any way. The key to this "experiment" was Self-inquiry.[11] One needed to examine the internal resistance, the impulse to justify the request, the flush of embarrassment. The more dramatic the situation, the stronger were the internal reactions and the material for Self-inquiry. Self-inquiry was also enhanced in other ways. For example, two hours a week were set aside for "nonintervention." During those two hours the experimenter did not intervene in the activities taking place around him in any way whatsoever. These could be conversing among friends, attending to one's children, or tending to chores or duties at work. The subject observed the inner dynamic that took place in that unusual situation and wrote a report describing this, which would be read out loud for the group.

A similar experiment set up a time when the subject did not offer up any "story from the past." This could be in a conversation with someone else or even while alone. For example, a spouse might ask you how your day was going or how the workday had gone, or perhaps why you were so serious or moody, and the response could not rely on a past narrative but had to consist of a precise accounting of the present moment. Not a word about the past could be uttered. This, too, was accompanied by a close observation of internal dynamics in response to an unusual situation.

Meanwhile, attentiveness was also sharpened by means of experiments that demanded a keen awareness. Every time one crossed a threshold, she had to turn and cross it again. Or, during urination, one had to pay attention to what exactly was going through one's mind. Absent-minded meanderings between one thought and another—our usual pattern—reflected a mechanical existence and could be cut through only by refining attention to the present moment.

It is not clear where Yossef acquired his practices. Some resemble the Gurdjieff agenda, but others may be among the resources used by theatrical directors to refine the performances of actors.[12] They can become powerful psychological tools when practiced repeatedly and with dedication, especially when they are reported in a group setting. But, as my informant indicated, none of this explained the attraction that these young people felt to Yossef and to the work they did in his groups. In order to get a sense of the pull, and to describe the magic of the groups, one needs to follow the talks that took place, to observe the mind of Yossef as it operated in real time. In other words, the school at its best was what Yossef said as people sat in a semicircle at his home, asking questions and responding to his own questions. The core of the school in those Jerusalem years was conversation with Yossef.

A Conversation in Jerusalem, February 1986

By his own reckoning, Yossef was not a guru or a master in any traditional sense, if at all.[13] Unlike a guru in a lecture, Yossef had to respond to unscripted comments made by students. That meant that he had to understand what they were saying (not always easy) and he needed to respond in the terms that they had just used. Furthermore, he could not stick to a single conceptual domain, using the same metaphors, but had to keep shifting in order to be truly responsive to different individuals. To borrow from boxing, Yossef was a counter-puncher, and he moved along with his interlocutors. The following conversation took place in Yossef's Jerusalem home in Beit Kerem, three years before moving to the Negev. The conversation opened, as usual, with Yossef asking what people wished to discuss that evening.

URI: Why do I identify with every thought that passes through me? Why do I identify with the form of my thinking? With the actions I perform? What is this?

DAVID: In every such conversation I find myself truly interested, and we always see that it touches the same root. And, in spite of the interest and the seriousness, I find myself today with exactly the same problems. I ask myself and the others here: What prevents me from understanding?

RUTH M.: I, too, am troubled by the same problem as David. I just want to add that we have always seen that the root of the problem is the "I" who acts as a center. What is missing is the ability to arrive at this point in practice.

YOSSEF: Aren't all the points raised by people here a function in one way or the other of a desire for achievement?

I find myself acting against something that I have already understood. I am unwilling to accept that fact. So I deny the understanding. I say, "I didn't understand, explain it better, perhaps I will understand." But did I really not understand what is being preoccupied with my own self? What is obsession with the past? What is inner conflict, and all the rest? Or what is it that makes me act against what I understood or despite what I understood?

RUTH M.: We need to understand if it is true that when there is a contradiction between the action and the understanding this is a sign that the understanding was false.

YOSSEF: How? Do we want to arrive at a "conclusive" understanding, a sort of intellectual headline? . . . All of this is related to a permanent urge for achievement, and there is the appearance of "understanding" something. Then the will enters the picture and imagines a future situation in which the effect of understanding has been attained. And when one finds himself acting against the "understanding," he draws new conclusions, and I say, let's stop there . . .

RUTH M.: It was possible that I did not understand, that I only concluded that I had understood. And then I am not acting against any understanding at all. I am acting against something I imagine.

Up to this point the conversation was crystal clear. Members of the group blamed their lack of understanding for a failure to apply the teaching in practice, while Yossef explained that the problem was thinking in terms of a goal and a path to that goal. The obstacle, in a word, was ambition. But suddenly the discussion shifted from cognitive misunderstanding to some emotional obstacle that accounts for the conflict between understanding the truth and acting on it. The shift is dramatic and relies on a new set of metaphors (negative emotions as demons) to which Yossef must respond (quickly) in their own language. This is a common pattern in these conversations, demonstrating Yossef's inventiveness and, perhaps, compassion.

MAYA: I think there was something there that had to be censored; a sort of Pandora's box, demons one does not wish to see.

Maya appeared to be implying that the obstacle to genuine practice is the repressed emotion that dominates our mental life. Releasing the emotion might somehow help (Pandora's box is not a very good metaphor for this). Yossef quickly disabused her of that assumption:

YOSSEF: The demons are a lot more dangerous outside the box than in, no?
But just a moment; am I willing to take a chance and let them surface into my awareness and look at them? Truly look at them? I know about them in a vague way: either when they are locked up, repressed with strong opinions about their danger . . . or when they are already active.
Why am I not prepared to give them freedom before they become active? Because when they are active they are not free. It is only an illusion that when I release something out into the world it becomes free.

In other words, releasing repressed emotions, such as jealously, fear, or anger, does not liberate anything and does not loosen the grip of these emotions on the subject. The emotion, with its strong cognitive component, remains an automatic response to some external or internal trigger. Freedom is much more than letting the demons out, although honest self-awareness is a good first step toward freedom.

YOSSEF (continuing): Its action in the world is a sort of reaction. The same reaction as being locked up. This is not freedom. Am I willing to take the chance of giving it [the emotion] true freedom in my consciousness, so it may be illuminated from every direction, because even outside it is moving and acting in the dark?
Am I able to be attentive [when the demon surfaces to conscious awareness]? . . . Do I recognize its passage?

The conversation, nudged sideways by Maya's psychological speculation, became increasingly abstract, as students wished to analyze the process by which the subconscious and conscious aspects of the mind interact to either obstruct or enhance progress in Self-inquiry.

YORAM: What is passage?
YOSSEF: Passage is a twilight condition. A twilight can be instantaneous [pre-conscious awareness], and in it I return to a complete "self-evident" certainty that this will take place [the unconscious will become subject to awareness]. . . . Every habit like that carries a basic demand or need for energy, no? In order for this to pass from potentiality to execution I need to bring myself to a certain fogginess in order that the self-evident will create the energetic push for achieving this. This is what thought does by creating a struggle for and against, and by means of identification it mixes up emotions which are used for this purpose.

In other words, our thinking creates binary oppositions and identifications with the "good" and the "bad" in order to generate the mental energy, the passion, that drives the process of becoming aware of a mental event.

YORAM: I saw something like that today. Around noon I started to notice that I really wanted to complain and that I was going to explode at someone, and this came up about ten times, and I kept blocking it with the sentence, "Be careful, this is about to happen, you are going to express this."
YOSSEF: You enhanced the battle, and so you strengthened the self-evident fact that it had to be done.
   This thing is just thought, and thought alone cannot bring about action. She [Maya] needs a cognitive friction that will produce energy by means of the emotions that identify with this thought and the emotions that identify with its opposite, and this friction with its emotional power brings about the result that the "self-evident fact that this must become real" will indeed receive an "external" realization. In every identification there is an enormous resistance to touch that which is self-evident about it. Identification sits upon something starkly obvious without doubt and which the identifying subject refuses to touch.

It is possible that Yossef was talking about nonconscious drives, desires, or beliefs and the process of externalizing them while identifying with their objects and believing them to be independent of us and truly external. Thought creates a dichotomy and recruits emotions in order to produce the energy that makes this possible. The identification is both a cognitive and an emotional lack of attention to the passage (between the nonconscious and conscious process) and the fact that what is self-evident is, in reality, not what it seems. The discussion touches on important material covered in Eastern and Western psychological epistemology as well as phenomenology, but here appears to be based on a refined practice of introspection. What is truly significant is that the school did not function as a place where sermons or lectures were disseminated but rather as one where students were shown, repeatedly, what sorts of insights about reality could be gained by Self-inquiry. No theories or doctrines were necessary.[14] In Yoga practice, physical discipline (posture, breath control) complements the theory. In Neot Smadar, physical discipline is not systematized but figures in a variety of ways.

The School at Neot Smadar

There was always some tension between "school" and Self-inquiry. School can be all too easily reified, while the activity of Self-inquiry permits no institutional structure. When the school left Jerusalem in 1989 and moved to the desert of Neot Smadar, this danger only increased because the place was exceptional: remote and extreme. The meaning of both school and Self-inquiry had to be constantly reexamined, with an open mind and with the capacity for accepting change. Moreover, two further dimensions were added to the life of the school: the farming economy and the community (Fig. 9). What had been limited to evening discussions with occasional retreats suddenly became a full life.

One of the first (and most interesting) decisions Yossef made was to appoint Ruth B. to be the head of the school. There were many alpha males in the group and also individuals with greater organizational, not to mention technical, experience. But Ruth was a veteran student and ideal for upholding the sensitive matter of linking Yossef with the members of the school. While several men rotated in and out of important functions (farm manager, treasurer, and so on), it was Ruth who communicated the instructions of Yossef over the next nine years. Hers was an immense and taxing job. According to Ruth, she had a natural proclivity for this sort of role, but she

Fig. 9. Desert retreat

was initially intimidated and often exhausted. She also reports that she lost many of her friends during those trying years.

At the same time, Yossef redefined his own role in the school as "sharat," as previously discussed. He held no office but had a say in everything—it was truly his school. The precise relationship between the school, the economy (meshek), and the community remained unclear and is currently undergoing renewed and vigorous examination (see the next chapter). The same is true for the relationship between Ruth B., who was the nominal head of the school, and Yossef, who had "stepped back." According to Ruth, Yossef was still very much in charge. An informant who was not part of the community but worked with the farm on a regular basis (as an expert adviser), told me that he could not reach any final decision with a member of the community unless Yossef was first consulted. At the same time, members such as Avi told me that they often bypassed or ignored Yossef if they felt that their work would progress more efficiently.[15] The respect for Yossef was not cultish, that is, blind. It was a dynamic trade, tit-for-tat, among strong individuals who constantly examined what it was that the sharat had to offer. And so Yossef retained his powerful status because the members of the community felt that he possessed extraordinary insight into states of consciousness rather than some global understanding of how an economy ought to run. Some individuals recall that the meetings with Yossef, especially the Wednesday-night meeting in the sukkah (tabernacle) were special, like a joyful holiday eve for which you wear your very best. The following summary of a conversation that took place in 1995 (six years after the move) illustrates some of the issues that came up during the early years of Neot Smadar.

"Self-inquiry in Neot Smadar"

Due to its subtlety, the subject of Self-inquiry never reached a definitive clarity, not even after years in Neot Smadar. The meeting on that night in 1995 began when Anat G. asked whether one had to be in Neot Smadar in order to practice Self-inquiry. Yossef responded sharply to the implied reification of a mode of awareness that defies space and time: "You can decide out of fatigue or despair that we must do something that defines us as a school, and then someone else will come and will decide on some other ritual or other, and so forth, and the whole thing will fall apart."

This was a brilliant answer fighting the impulse to institutionalize the practice of Self-inquiry. The Buddhist monk shaves his head, the Christian takes a vow; they both join some order and set themselves on a path to a goal. They acquire an identity. Yossef would say that they were moving backward, obstructing the real thing. Later that evening he said: "When there is contact with Self-inquiry . . . it is huge and awesome. Self-inquiry is a path of power. It is a state of mind that is in the moment and is free of movement in time." In other words, Self-inquiry can take place anywhere; it is a mode of perception that requires no special agenda or tradition: "Put the fork where the forks go, that is Self-inquiry. Clean the table perfectly, that is Self-inquiry. Self-inquiry is learning attentiveness, not an obligation."

Unfortunately, given our entrenched habits, Self-inquiry can be difficult. It demands courage, strength, and honesty if one is to overcome the constant "self-replication" of thinking and the crisis that this manufactures.

"Human consciousness is split," Yossef said, "we are all in the hands of merchants." In everything that takes place, someone sells and someone buys, someone profits and the other loses. However, he continued, "as I enter Self-inquiry, I no longer buy anything, including the opinions of experts in psychological matters." The man or woman who pursues Self-inquiry stands alone, with her back to the wall, with no one left to ask. Self-inquiry is power and freedom.

A student asked Yossef what his role as sharat entailed. Clearly there can be no teacher—there is no teaching at all. So Yossef replied: "My role is to prevent small groups from entering into struggles with other small groups, which is one of the main characteristics of human failure." This is seemingly a surprising—mundane—answer from someone who had been accused of being a cult leader. And yet, as usual, there was a deeper truth here. Among the more insidious consequences of mechanical thinking are socially destructive agendas: "I can't avoid negative feelings in my exist-ence," Yossef explained, "and at the same time I desire personal justice. . . . Where one cultivates the need for personal justice, relationships are not possible because it leads either to control of others or to a feeling of depri-vation." Seen in this light, the sharat is not a social coordinator or a sheriff; he is a mirror for those who truly wish to see themselves.

This conversation revealed a number of central themes in the work of Yossef: First, study (limud or Self-inquiry) is a process that transcends thought and time and that can take place anywhere. It is both concrete and elusive. Second, school is the context in which one avoids thought-driven repetition, which may refer to patterns. This work cannot be based on doctrines or on traditions. Third, society—even the group that makes up those who are studying with Yossef—is an abstraction. The only true social reality is the encounter between one person and another. Fourth, the attainment of freedom—the emptiness there—is a joyful and energized state of being. It involves action within inaction. Finally, the school requires a sharat whose job is to prevent the emergence of cliques—a key symptom of the splitting of human consciousness. This is due to the fact that we are deeply conditioned by others and influenced by the conflict that our (social) thinking generates.

Yossef's style in many of these conversations in Neot Smadar was more brusque and even aggressive than it had been in Jerusalem. In a sense, and as he put it, it was time to take off the gloves. Some of the conversations give the impression that Neot Smadar magnified the school's moments of crisis and that Yossef had to respond with what appeared to be anger, as when he said, in 1989: "You are not a kibbutz and are not capable of being a kibbutz and everyone wants to be a kibbutz . . . but it is a lie. It appears that a significant percentage of the people are in deep sleep and others have arrived here only for a temporary vacation."

This particular meeting led to a renewal of commitment to Self-inquiry by several of the participants in the conversation—a product of the sharat's efforts. In the words of Yossef: "A sharat is a person who has rolled up his sleeves and went to work with a small number of people and who is only able to point things out in a subtle manner for anyone who is interested." Clearly, there is nothing in the work of this person that resembles the sanctity or charisma of a spiritual guide. His authority comes from his ability to accurately describe what the members of the school community already sense from their own introspection. They have to validate this insight or it is meaningless. Of course Yossef had to be a great motivator and even manipulator in order to fuel the will of students to carry out the school's demanding agenda. But he was incapable of revealing unknown truths, and thus he was no teacher. The school for Self-inquiry at Neot Smadar, even when Yossef was alive, was teacherless in the strict sense of transmitting fixed knowledge or traditional facts; it even contradicted thinking. To be sure, Self-inquiry had to be learned, like walking, but it was something only an individual could carry out.

Just as the study required no teacher, the morality of the place required no explicit moral rules. Instead, right conduct follows from proper Self-inquiry. Yossef worked at clarifying this often, as he did on March 7, 1990:

YOSSEF: A school must be run strictly but by no means on the basis of co-ercion. The strictness needs to come out of the joy of this opportunity [to learn]. Without this joy any appeal made by someone who occupies a po-sition has the appearance of coercion. Then one becomes defensive. I am waiting for the chance to begin again with strictness but without coercion.
. . . A school is a strange place, you can't imitate it—that is impossible.
That is the root of the problem that I wished to discuss, the problem of

self-importance. Here truly there is a difference, and only those who wake up to this problem can prevent it. It is a screen, a screen to which structures of difference cling. When one only seeks to understand it with thought, it is forgotten after two minutes. And mindfulness is an act that you cannot perform with a screen in place. Because then mindfulness is split, and one becomes locked. When people want something, they become locked, hermetically sealed.

ARNON: Strictness without coercion can only come out of communal action. But people together are not strict with each other; they are only strict with themselves.

YOSSEF: On the contrary, people are not strict with themselves, so they see no reason to be strict with others. That's why we came—to learn private strictness.

YEHUDAH: It is as if I am unable to see the matter of self-importance, even though I know it is a great obstacle. I can only see aspects of its manifestation. I can't see it fully. . . . There is no basis for comparing self-importance with something else that I can see.

YOSSEF: In every single act is the entirety of self-importance—it is not a matter of aspects or manifestation. I can count them again:

A complaint is self-importance.

To correct another person is self-importance.

To defend oneself, to attack, to argue and resist, to emphasize my own [opinion] over and against yours for a momentary victory [is self-importance]. Notice that this pushes us, it fills the entire field and it undermines the school and it is a disgrace to each and every one of us and sabotages our relations.

Directing the actions of others by means of our imagination is self-importance.

We need to see these things actively before they assault us. It causes viciousness, pretensions, and a fear that is inescapable. I wish success to the man who tries to, who manages to escape this trap. He can't do this without strictness. And if he possesses this strictness, you will always discover it in time.

One can readily see how Self-inquiry, which reveals the power and pervasiveness of self-importance, would root out those factors that cause conflict among people. A school and a community that center on the school, where individuals understand the internal mechanisms that drive conflicts, would achieve an easy, spontaneous, harmony. No monastic rules of conduct would be necessary.

Clearly, the school for Self-inquiry is only an institution in some external sense. There is the sharat (Yossef), the sukkah where the important Wednesday meetings take place. There are the many activities, such as retreats, the reading of various reports, difficult projects, experiments (for beginners), and so forth. There are also the principles or conditions that one accepts as a member of the school community that undertakes Self-inquiry. But ultimately, these do not define Self-inquiry as a practice (which transcends time and place) and therefore do not constitute the "school" as a true reality. There is no teacher, no students, no lessons, no hierarchy.

Of the three points in the triangle that Alon has discussed in the previous chapter (the school, the economy, and the community), this one has always been the most elusive and perhaps ephemeral. However, this was bound to change with the departure of Yossef—and in many ways it has.

5

The School after the Death of Yossef

NEOT SMADAR WAS NEVER A CULT, and Yossef Safra was no guru, let alone a cult leader. The vast majority of the men and women who joined the school did so because they felt Yossef was onto something important and that his clarity of vision could help them deepen their view of reality. There was no ideology, no doctrine one had to sign onto, just a set of conditions that defined the school—to which members gave their assent. Those who could not do so were free to leave.

The passing of Yossef at the age of 72 in May of 2003 had a profound effect on the school in Neot Smadar. It is impossible to discuss the school today without paying heed to the way Yossef exited the world and to the discussions that took place afterward, in which a new way of organizing Self-inquiry and managing the school emerged. The school today, a dynamic reality, has been nurtured by those transformative events.

The Death of Yossef

This section paraphrases the weekly report that Anat G. wrote after Yossef died. Yossef choreographed his own death, turning it into a profoundly signifying ritual (rite of passage) that had a lasting effect on those who were close to him.[1] To show, with proper modesty, how he did this I yield entirely to Anat: the narrator's voice is hers, but she, too, relied on the testimony of others who were present for most of the events described, so this section is a composite of the narrative of friends who were happy to share.[2]

Friday Night

There's a full moon above Neot Smadar. After midnight a succession of quick gongs can be heard coming from the east. More and more rings fill the silence of the night. A clear fact passes through the darkness—Yossef is gone.

His house is lit up. It is clean, full of flowers, burning candles, and people warmly greeting the guests—that is, Iris, Ruth, and Yehudit. A hospitable home. The warm eyes of Iris and the inviting hand of Ruth settle the storm within me. I become quiet, quiet and alive.

Yossef rests in his bed, in a sparkling room with flowers and candles. He is dressed in white, his face at peace, beautiful, gentle, and young. His hands are long. People come and go intimately, without partitions or separation. They stand next to that man.

The Dying

Iris, Ruth, and Yehudit closely accompanied Yossef during his last days, and from their words the following picture emerges:

He died a happy man. He matured gradually but powerfully into the act of dying. It seems to me that in his last three days Yossef bid the world goodbye.

The surgeon in Wolfson Hospital had seen that his stomach was full of metastasized cancer cells and there was no point in operating. After a few months of consultations with various physicians, Yossef said, "Leave me at peace, I want to know the true situation, and I am returning to be master of my own body, and I am in charge from now on." He felt himself getting worse by the day.

On the final Monday he said, "Time is short" and began to weave the summary of his life and bid farewell to his own past. The medication brought up scenes from his past, as though real. He said goodbye to his own life.

Physically it was not obvious that it was about to happen. But he was so weak, and he realized there was no sense in waiting for something acute to take place. On Thursday the blood test results arrived and Dr. Eitan told Iris he should come soon and find out from Yossef, while he was still in sound mind, what he would like to do and how he, the doctor, could help him within the bounds of the law.

That night Yossef called Eitan C. and Savion and dictated a private will, touching on his children.

Sammy (Dr. Eitan) came on Friday at 3:00 p.m. It was clear to me that Yossef knew beyond a shadow of a doubt what he wanted and his decision was complete. He asked for a summary of his medical history. He felt his trouble began after his accident—that his leg had never returned to health. It was important for him that Sammy would become familiar with his medical situation.

The talk between Yossef and Sammy took place in the living room, in the presence of friends, and it lasted over two hours. Yossef had his usual energy, sitting on the couch, erect and full of vitality—he connected immediately with Sammy. He was sharp and clear. The two made a strong connection. The talk was equally important to and for Sammy and Yossef. Yossef tried to communicate the full impact of his decision, and Sammy kept asking questions in different ways in order to ascertain that Yossef wanted this wholeheartedly.

Sammy knew that Yossef was dying, and Yossef knew it was a matter of hours.

Yossef spoke about the village doctor, who visited homes and saw his patients as people and not as clinical cases. Sammy said that people do not wish to open up to their doctor. It was unusual to find a village doctor because it was unusual to find people who wish to see a doctor in their homes. He explained that when he wears a doctor's hat he can function only under the constraints that bind physicians, but if he removes that hat, he agrees completely with Yossef. In this situation the physician and the man became unified. The meeting of the wills of Yossef and Sammy the man and the doctor made them one. Yossef wanted to be recognized as a man, and Sammy told Yossef about his own life, about his decision to convert from anesthesiology to family practice, a decision with no turning back.

They spoke in the most personal manner and kept returning to this point: "I understand that this body needs to go, and I do not wish to suffer. You and I are sitting in clarity and talking as one. The body has finished—it has done its duty, and I want to help it." Sammy tried again and again to ascertain Yossef's will, and Yossef explained, over and over, that this was his decision. He told Sammy about Kafka, the tuberculosis patient who said to his doctor: "Kill me, if not, you are a murderer!"

Sammy said he would do everything he could within bounds. They understood one another, and Sammy fulfilled Yossef's wish. They both understood that they will make it possible for Yossef to go to sleep and the body will do its own thing. At the end of the conversation Sammy said: "I'm giving you strong morphium that will put you to sleep. But what if you wake up in four hours and desire a cup of tea?" Yossef said, "That is out of the question." Then he asked for his children, Geffen, Tzofnat, Noam, and Yael, spoke with them, laughed with them, and said goodbye.

When they left, he lay down quietly, awake and clear, and we all bid him farewell. He looked at me with his long, penetrating gaze. I thanked him for everything. Yossef said: "I am feeling good with the knowledge that I am going to sleep. I love you all. Thank you to Dr. Sammy."

Then he said: "One leaves, one comes, comes and leaves together." He closed his eyes and sank into a deep sleep. We did not cry near him; we wanted to let him go in peace and not burden him. We sat in his room and followed his breaths. At 11:00 p.m. something caught my attention and I sat next to him. His last three breaths followed, and he was gone.

Sammy's act, the rare way he did it, moving as one with Yossef, allowed Yossef to go in his sleep, a peaceful death. There was so much love in all of this. The house was flooded with a feeling of compassion and grace, and there was even the lightheartedness of eating and laughing in the living room. It was not heavy.

I felt, when he died, that something huge, beyond my own boundaries, had opened up and took me with him, and I could only feel his own joy.

I was privileged. He had so much to show us about life, and now he showed us about death. A man with his entire existence and vitality goes somewhere else, and there is no gap between talking about it and actually doing it; this is impossible to grasp.

Yossef asked the same thing, that we wash and prepare him. I felt that he returned to being as innocent as an infant. It is a great privilege to respect the wish of the dying, and we did it lovingly. He asked us, "After you wash me, straighten out the room and the house, and when it is all done ring the gong so people may come here." He asked for a secular funeral, without a Rabbi or a Shiv'a.

After the Dying

Yossef was an actor, a director. He founded Neot Smadar, a place where we can create, be joyful and playful. His death, too, he staged—he did whatever he could. He remained without desires, hopes, or unfinished affairs, and his body wanted to leave. He said that his illness was nothing compared to this immensity. Life itself does not die because it is life. The body falls apart; you need to know when to let it go. As you live now, that's how you will be in the future, and you will die the way you live now. And whatever you fail to achieve in this singular opportunity you were given—that's how your death will look.

The Yossef who ran this place had died days earlier. He did not wish to continue the suffering, not only his own, but that of those around who were taking care of him. When asked, "Do you have anything to tell us in Neot Smadar," he answered: "I think it would be a crime to do so. I have spoken to you for twenty years. There is no need for a final word."

When we talked about the cancer and I told him, "The cancer threatens to destroy your body, it is like a parasite, threatening to take your food," he said: "So you want to prevent larceny by larceny. If you look at it, you understand that you can't deal with violence through violence. Cancer is in all of us. It is the product of human consciousness, and just like when a jealous person dies the jealously does not die with him, cancer does not die when the individual dies who has cancer.

"Cancer is not an enemy, but that doesn't mean there is nothing to do. Cancer is an integral part of the body. The activity of the cancer is exactly the same as the activity of human consciousness. It uses the energy of life, but it separates itself and takes only for itself, without consideration of the environment. If you look at it thus, then you see that humans are the cancer of this planet."

As far as I can tell, the fact that Yossef did not see cancer as an enemy that had to be vanquished—this was a turnaround in his understanding. Win or lose, it was not a war.

In the matter of memorializing the dead, he tried to explain that when the particular individual died, this is not significant. "Who remembers Caesar Nero despite his fame, who remembers my grandfather—what was he? The individual as such disappears in the passage of life. Life continues in other bodies, in other figures. Life is a single flow."

I feel that in the way he died he gave us another perspective on realism, that you can walk toward death in a manner that is pure, complete, and joyful—there is no threat. I asked him if he was at peace, and he said: "I am very much at peace because I know that the moment is approaching and I am glad to return home, whatever that means." His face, from the moment he fell asleep, registered no conflict. He gave himself over.

Many people came to Yossef's funeral, family and friends. We stood there, all of us, in the wind and the dust, facing the wildness of the desert, the green vineyard, and the setting sun. It was a tight circle of beautiful people in an ancient ritual of farewell. I never felt more clearly that the body that dies is not the man who lived. A strong wind blew there, and passed equally among all. I felt peaceful in the space, the color, and the infinite light of the sky. All was right.

"Yossef," said a representative of the Kibbutz Movement, "was a listening man, a man of dialogue. Many people should ask your forgiveness for the suspicion, the persecution, the contempt toward the one who had the audacity in the face of the known and who was not afraid to shock the familiar and absorb massive resistance."

Ruth, Hannah, Israela, Alon, Yael, Tzofnat, and Iris spoke—and their words took off in the great wind of the moment—about gratitude, about the invitation, about the meeting that changed our life, about the thirsting for a connection, about the loneliness of man and his efforts to understand, about compassion and grace that produced cooperation, about humor and power, about a fresh man, who was attentive and determined and who gathered us as one gathers abandoned eggs. He showed in his life, in his beauty, wisdom, and love, that there was another possibility.

Final Observations

I see the soft light of life in the faces of the people. A light that is absent from the faces of the dead. What turns a living person into a dead one—the instant of passage where he who was like me up to now is no longer like me. It is a wonder that cannot be fathomed.

I feel that there is no panic; there is stability, wisdom, and sensitivity. There is interest. Yossef the man was one of us for over twenty years, and now he has left his space. Each one of us now has an enormous space, and each has a task. Yossef has said a number of times recently, "You have this wisdom, let it take hold in reality." His presence had something confusing, contradictory in that it tempted us to rely on him and hold on to him—and now that is gone. He left completely in an act with no return.

Yossef woke and strengthened in us the learning movement, and he pointed to the possibility of an intelligent human existence—he never said a word about what will be—the answer was in the situation itself, and we have to discover it and develop it by means of cooperation. In our years in Neot Smadar Yossef undermined the walls of our practical skepticism and showed us that it is possible to realize that which is beyond routine thought. He used to say: "This is the time and the conditions are not right," a phrase whose depth became clear as the years went by. Yossef was a sharat. This means an uncompromising being, who points to facts, and a presence that is giving for its own sake. He touched me in a direct way and in hints in sharpness and in humor, in silliness and seriousness, in hardness and softness.

The first condition I accepted years ago in Jerusalem was to support him. Over the years I tried to understand this condition, even while carrying it out. In his existence Yossef echoed a sound within me and was a real presence in my life. I loved him. I could not imagine this, but somewhere I feel relief, an expansion. Being with him filled me, and now that he has left, he has liberated me of focusing on him personally. Now the condition is the condition of my own reality, supporting the learning movement, a movement that crosses boundaries and belongs to no one.

I am being cautious—perhaps it's a reaction, and there will be a letdown—and when we touch on daily issues we shall encounter personal walls, but this is the opportunity of our life, for each and every one of us to mature and be born into a reality where we are friends and where we can live our daily life in a wise, questioning, and attentive mode.

An important chapter in our life has ended, and now we have a lot of work. And that brings joy.

Anat's report on the passing of Yossef and her reflections on his work represent a definitive rejoinder to those who considered him the leader of a "cult" and his "followers" brainwashed. The rationality, self-awareness, and compassion exhibited in this document can only be the product of an autonomous, indeed empowered, mind.

Yossef on Mourning

On the Wednesday after Yossef died, the meeting in the sukkah included the reading of a conversation with Yossef after Gil had died over a decade earlier. Gil was a young man when he died, and he left behind his wife, Hannah, and two young boys. Gil had been one of the most beloved men in Neot Smadar, a brilliant individual who was also warm and extremely funny. Yossef spoke to the group about mourning Gil's passing:

When a person is aware that every thought about pain and sorrow is about oneself, he must release the departed. Every crisis like that brings growth and change. My personal pain is between me and myself; there's no need to spread it around. The deceased has been freed from this life, and now he is in some other reality, we don't know what. We are here to free ourselves from tradition, from our proclivity for leaning on things we learned early.

When the body ceases to exist, something opens up, dissolves itself into the pervasive human consciousness, and blends with all things. It is important to depart from this world in a state of acceptance, for then the contribution to the negative aspect of human consciousness is minimal. Whatever is not under the control of consciousness passes into the totality of life. A person who is here and binds himself to someone who is not here, that is not good or healthy. And the person who is gone would like us to live without all of that.

In Self-inquiry, such an event, if you treat it correctly, becomes a true change in your existence. The change is the letting go of obsession. And if there is true relief, that is validation by the departed that you are doing fine.

The Self-inquirer says, "Why must one suffer? There is no room in my life for suffering." Sorrow is different from suffering. I felt sorrow when I saw Gil suffering, but I cannot feel sorrow toward him now because I do not know where he is now. Confusing sorrow and suffering is self-pity and self-importance.

. . . Death happens every one thousandth of a second. It is part of life and is with us, and that is a good thing. Without it you could not live, like there can be no numbers without zero. You speak about death as something negative, frightening. We hang on to life. The contact with death is the knowing that it is part of me, not outside of me. In every seed of my life death is present.[3]

How Do We Decide?

Is there any connection between the existence of a spiritual school and the running of a community such as a kibbutz or a collective economy (meshek)? Does the "inquiry" extend to life in general, and does it influence routine decision making? When Yossef lived and functioned as the sharat, he dictated many of the decisions, and it was a learning (inquiry) matter for students to just accept his decisions—even to disregard their own judgment on some matter or another. But now that he is gone, and no individual has this role, who makes the decisions, and how are the decisions reached? Here, as we consider the question of how a school deals with the death of its founder, we see the distinction between Neot Smadar and religious groups such as cults, devotional sects, monastic orders, and others. For example, in the case of the Indian Radhasoami group, Mark Juergensmeyer has made the following observation: "Whatever one decides about that issue [the Swami's succession], it seems clear that the actual succession of guruship at the time of a master's death is never as certain and smooth as the theory of spiritual reincarnation implies it should be."[4] In contrast, Yossef was not a master, properly speaking; there is no theory that might rationalize succession; and there was no true question of anyone's inheriting his position. But there was the matter of preserving the school and the community.

The one lengthy discussion dealing with this question, on August 13, 2003, shed some light on the question of authority but was far from clarifying it. If members of the group had extended the principles that guided them before (when Yossef lived) to their new situation, they might have said something like this: "I may have certain opinions on the matter before us, but my opinions represent my brain at work, a mechanical and conditioned thought process that it is my task to separate from my true identity and from the objective matter at hand. That true identity is pure energy, a place of supreme quietude; it has no opinions and holds no preconceptions. As a result, I enter the discussion with no personal agenda; I am free like the wind, and it is unpredictable where this freedom will guide me as matters are brought up for decision making. It is a mystery that can only reveal itself in real time, but it goes without saying that I shall try to abandon all personal agendas."

The task of the school was to focus on the individual student—Self-inquiry was not a collective process. But the true identity at the core of the individual person is a universal Being, perhaps something like atman (though Yossef avoided such terms, and some today reject any such metaphysical affirmations).[5] If so, the person's progress in Self-inquiry might lead him or her to that which is universal in all people, and if many succeeded at that extraordinary task they might perhaps share a common vision, or at least a mode of seeing. This seems true in theory at least. A skeptic will wonder if such a theoretical goal means anything for students who have not made a great deal of progress, or whether the theoretical conception carries any practical implications for those who are still on the path of learning.

The conversation in the sukkah—about three months after the death of Yossef—demonstrated the fragility of Self-inquiry as a practical tool of governance. The specific matter under discussion was the invasion of damaging porcupines and whether some of them should be killed in order to thin out their population.

At the time of this discussion, several months after the passing away of Yossef, Dalit was the head (secretary) of the school. One of Yossef's first students, a woman with a mild and compassionate disposition, Dalit was perfect for the role at that time. She encouraged her colleagues to open up but not give in to negative feelings: "The question has come up, how do we make decisions, that is the topic for discussion this evening."

The matter of the porcupines, important as it was, may have been merely an opportunity for ironing out decision making, "because we do not wish to decide in a democratic manner," that is, by majority vote. Dalit stated that now that the sukkah has replaced Yossef, decisions needed to be collective, but added, "What happens when many people have a different perspective?" Is it possible to leave the sukkah at the end of the evening when the final decision is acceptable to everyone, even if some individuals had wished for a different outcome? Can a true consensus be reached, based not on unanimity and not on a majority vote but on something else?

This sounds confusing. Either one practical solution to a problem emerges that is shared by all or everyone agrees to follow the majority. What else can there be? Omri, a contemplative man, suggested one possibility: "We need shared clarity in this forum. This is a sensitive and dynamic subject on the border of art and begins with a direct observation of my own self in order to see, clearly, where my own interests are." From subsequent conversations with Omri I surmise that by "interests" Omri did not mean practical outcomes that benefit the individual but rather how the self acts as it gauges internal deliberations. A practical issue that demands resolution is a keen opportunity for Self-inquiry.

Following Omri's suggestion, the conversation moved to procedural matters: Why shouldn't a specialized committee deal with practical issues that are not central to the life of the community? When might such a technical matter reach the sukkah even after a committee had considered it? Dalit reminded the gathering that no rules, even procedural ones, would be legislated and the intent was to look at any situation together and develop "a shared view" (mabat meshutaf). But Hagar, who was very active in that night's deliberation, raised an objection: "How proper is it to decide that a 'shared view' is something that is essential, that we reach it, and that we do not move unless it is reached?" In the past, Hagar continued, that had not been the case; one simply accepted decisions made by others (mostly Yossef). Hagar appeared intent to solve the problem of using Self-inquiry as a practical tool of managing life by reminding her listeners that Self-inquiry also implied simple acceptance. The relevant phrase was "crashing against a decision" that was not one's own—simply agreeing to accept what the school gives. However, Yossef was now gone, and, as Avi stated a bit later in the conversation, "Unity is the foundation of this school."

But how could unity be achieved when individuals differ on a matter of principle? Someone described the conflict: some people categorically refuse to kill animals, while others consider the damage these animals inflict on the water pipes and the cost to a poor economy. Both perspectives are valid as far as they go. So can a global picture emerge, "a shared view" whereby both of the conflicting perspectives are accepted? As the conversation continued, three approaches began to crystallize:

1. *The shared view:* If all participants approach the exchange with a truly open mind and all opinions are freely aired and everyone's point of view is respected as equal, a unified view could emerge. This applies even to a question such as one on the killing of animals or working on Shabbat.

2. *Delegation:* Such a unified view is unlikely to emerge and may not be necessary in every situation. Self-inquiry as a practical tool may entail one's willingness to let go of influencing every event and, in Hagar's words, "letting those who need to decide, decide."

3. *Process:* The process of coming together to discuss any matter is just as important–perhaps more important–than the issue at hand. Deliberations should be an opportunity for Self-inquiry, as Omri had described it. Neither unanimity nor delegation will ultimately matter if the process fails as an opportunity for Self-inquiry.

The question of a shared view was discussed for the next hour, deep into the night. Because Self-inquiry is an individual undertaking, the school in Neot Smadar had not taken up the question of a shared view and it remained vague. Several interpretations emerged in the discussion, but Ruth

B. seemed to have formulated her own understanding in the most explicit way:

> In the final analysis the common thing we all share is the intention to look at the human condition in which I find myself, with all its consequences. And all our undertakings are designed to have this perspective illuminate every situation in our life. When this illumination takes place every specific topic is dwarfed and it does not matter how a decision is arrived at and who makes it.
>
> So, if I am discussing "shared view," I have the same vision that each and every one of us here has even if our opinions and our emotions are conflicted. And if I look at this state of consciousness I will see that we are part of the same web, the same movement.

When Dalit finally called an end to the meeting, the question of the porcupines and the more interesting matter of a shared view both remained open, with a standing invitation to continue the conversation. The porcupine population was eventually thinned out, but the relationship between Self-inquiry and practical decisions remains a dynamic and open-ended affair.

Analysis

The discussion may seem disorganized and disjointed to the casual reader, but that is far from the case. In fact, it exhibits a remarkably focused attention to a small number of critical issues:

1. The need to avoid legislating rules of conduct while deciding how to act in specific situations.
2. Determining whether a shared view is necessary in making a decision—in order to avoid coercing those who disagree.
3. Recognizing that conflicting personal interests are at work but, just as important, there are conflicting principles about such matters as life and death.
4. Recognizing that both interests and principles can generate the stubborn loyalty of individual opinion.

5. Arriving at an understanding of whether Self-inquiry leads to a unity of view or whether unity must come from the rational analysis of objective conditions (damage to crops and farming equipment, costs versus benefits, and so on).

It seems to me that during this lengthy meeting everyone said something important and made perceptive comments. But due to the fact that there were over thirty people there and someone was always prepared with a quick response—sometimes to a comment made a few turns earlier—the thread was not always kept intact, and a great effort must be made to sort out the key points. The issues that dominated, excluding the matter of the porcupines, were as follows:

- Is there a unified way of seeing?
- Are practical decisions based on this perspective? Should they be?
- What are the obstacles to having this unified way of seeing?
- What is the difference between "seeing" and having an opinion?

Underlying issues that did not dominate but emerged toward the end of the meeting without being worked out were these: What is the task of a school? Does the school inculcate a way of seeing that can be related to "shared view?" Can that spiritual agenda have any bearing on the conduct of life on a daily basis?

This issue of the porcupines was merely the trigger for airing views on how major and minor issues are to be approached in the absence of the figure of Yossef. Previously Yossef "was" the school and unfailingly exhibited the sort of vision to which members aspired. He was not charismatic in the sense that a special aura clung to him; in fact, he had to constantly earn the assent of the others and only did so because of his ability to impress with the clarity and focus of his vision. Thus, although he had been merely a "sharat," his decisions represented the perspective that cut through the trifles of individual agendas. He was the wall against which they chose to crash. He embodied the conditions of Self-inquiry.

Now that Yossef was gone, the group itself—the sukkah—was to replace him. What that entailed, however, was not the desired singularity of perception but a troubling multiplicity. Some compensation had to be found, represented in this discussion by the repeated references to "view" (*mabat*). But because no single individual could identify this view in any other person, it was sought in the narrow space between consensus and some transformative point of view—hardly a reliable substitute for the sharat. The gift and the challenge that Yossef left to students of Self-inquiry was the valuing of true freedom to pursue Self-inquiry as an individual pursuit while living and working in a community. Could this challenge be met in the absence of the sharat? Could the school generate institutions that serve the community's need for a shared view while allowing individuals to pursue Self-inquiry?

The School Today

Today, over ten years after the death of Yossef, the school still occupies that "edge" that Ilana was talking about, that is, the narrow space between institutional existence and the individual path. The sharat (Yossef) is gone, and the men and women who perpetuate the work of the school have drafted a number of working papers that do three things: they describe the function of the school, prescribe proper conduct within the school, and emphasize the tenuous nature of the school as a reified entity. Some of this material cannot be published yet. The following, in a paraphrased translation, are available for sharing:

Neot Smadar was established in order to realize the intention to create a school for human Self-inquiry. The school exists due to a real and urgent objective necessity to change the condition of humans in their relationships with themselves, with others, and with the environment. Self-inquiry is possible when a person realizes three things:

- That in one's own person and in the world at large there is constant struggle, dissatisfaction, alienation, and suffering
- That the individual person, due to ignorance of his or her self-ignorance, takes an active part in this destructive reality
- That a change in one's situation—and that of the world—must begin with one's own self, thanks to an awakening and insight and

without a dependence on any external authority, be it a person, a
book, a method, or any path whatsoever

Self-inquiry is personal. It is an observing state of mind, an interest and
intention that a person maintains individually while engaged in relationships that embrace the fullness of existence. In its nature the school is a
dense fabric of conditions, principles, and arrangements that are designed
to emphasize the human condition in its various expressions. These conditions and principles are not rules of conduct but gateways to awareness
that enable the student to transform her daily life into an existence that is
marked with questioning, observation, and the intention to come into contact with a real perspective on the student's situation as it truly is.

In his journey the Self-inquirer discovers that the activity of thought—
mechanical and reactive—does not allow a true approach to seeing his own
situation. Instead, it pushes and obscures such a vision. A true vision demands a foundational movement toward Self-inquiry in order to observe
the full range of disruptions, along with their roots. Such inquiry can exist
only when the conditions, the principles, and the arrangements of the
school are not designed by the students but are provided by an understanding that originates from a different level of order. This understanding takes
into account, with caring and a broad perspective, the fact that a student in
the school will do whatever she can in order to resist her routine perspective
on life. Every student who says "Yes" to the school becomes a partner to the
understanding of this basic fact—that "*I do not determine the conditions,* and
when I treat the conditions with my full attention, I support the existence
of the school for Self-inquiry."

The school invites each person to join as an individual. The community
of students develops as a function of the joining of individuals. Self-inquiry
is a personal journey among the group of students, who take into account
a special system of conditions and principles. When the entire community
of students participates in this matter, each person according to his or her
ability, a unique field of inquiry develops that permits a true consideration
of relationships and cooperation, with respect and trust.

The new student who joins the school gradually becomes aware of the
guidelines to Self-inquiry, to school principles and meta-principles, to school

norms, and so forth. There are several of these, and the process of exposure to them is intertwined with deepening Self-inquiry. I have accepted the suggestion that publishing them in this book creates a reification—something akin to legislation—that runs counter to the spirit of the school itself.

The Journey of Self-Inquiry in the School

The volunteers and young individuals who arrive in Neot Smadar (including for the seminars and other programs) cannot see the school. What they—young men and women in their twenties, often from places like Spain, Portugal, Germany, or the United States— do see is a working community where people of all ages work together and often stop to have oddly meaningful conversations. In the summers, when everyone (including children) joins the consuming projects, there are also Wednesday-night meetings in front of the dining hall, and these, too, appear to the newcomer as unusual. But the school itself has no walls and no staff. The volunteers may have been drawn to Neot Smadar by their interest in ecology, organic farming, or communal work or because they need "something different." Most volunteers leave after their few months, returning to college, going into the army, or packing off to trek in Nepal. A few may be asking bigger questions about the direction and meaning of their lives, or perhaps these questions come up as a result of their attentiveness while in Neot Smadar. They may decide to stay longer, and they may be invited to join a seminar (on construction or agriculture) or to join a preparatory group. Those who respond and undertake a preliminary investigation into Self-inquiry may be invited to join a preliminary study group, which will be led by one of the veterans. During the summer of 2015, the initial groups were, in order, the "new arrival group," the "open group," and the "closed group." Each was led by two or three veterans (e.g., Shlomit, Rakefet, Tessa, Orit, or Eitan), and each successive group implies an increasing involvement in the community and a deepening sense of responsibility for the work and Self-inquiry.

As the study intensifies and deepens, the individual may come to recognize that a more focused approach may be necessary that will be more deeply personal and will also embrace others who wish to study as he does.

This person now accepts the principles that guide the school, beginning with the fact that he is not the one who determines the conditions. With this acceptance the student will have opened up an inquiry into the hidden nature of presence. The school will support this inquiry, but not by helping him accumulate information and knowledge. The study is more about generating insight by shaking up the seemingly solid foundation of customary habits of mind.

This study proceeds along individual paths—there is no single and uniform outcome. However, intensive and honest Self-inquiry can, in a general sense, lead to a clarified view accompanied by a sharply reduced self-preoccupation. Individuals who reach these advanced stages of Self-inquiry will have moved beyond the conditions that previously served self-study, and they require another level. Members of Neot Smadar today discuss these levels as "circles" and describe a movement from the outer (first) to the inner (third). This is an extraordinary level, a calling. It includes a sense of being prepared to engage in the study of the freedom to adhere to some purpose, without external support. This calling demands a genuine sense of responsibility for the human condition, accompanied by a refined sense of compassion and charity; it has nothing to do with status or honor, nothing even about self-actualization. Individuals operating at this rarefied level support and lead the school. They facilitate the work that takes place in the "outer circle" of the school, aware of their own reality and the immense difficulty of passing on the spirit of the place. In reality, several members of the school who could belong in the third circle, men and women like Shmuel, Amnon, Ilana, Yoram, Rony, and others, have opted to define themselves as members of the second circle, along with the younger generation (e.g., Gadi, Dagan, Guy, Eleanor, Vered, Adva). The distinction describes not one's rank in the community or on the farm (Dagan, for example, is the CEO or farm manager, merakez meshek) but rather a form of self-understanding that is subject to constant reexamination.

The flesh and bones of the school, the level at which it accomplishes the bulk of its work, is the second circle. This is the space where Self-inquiry becomes refined, where the student learns to truly open herself up to presence and self-observe clearly and honestly. This is achieved individually but carried out most effectively in group settings. Self-inquiry is the subject of

Chapter 7, but the exceptional quality of Neot Smadar, its magnetism for young people who identify it as special, radiates outward from those exceptional individuals who lead the place from the third level. Their secret is compassion and the way they have acquired it.

Thinking about Thought and Numbers

The passing of Yossef does not mean that the school in Neot Smadar has stopped dealing with the most subtle questions regarding the human condition, specifically about thought and consciousness. No single person sets the tone, of course, but the observations continue to be subtle and to exhibit both a refined phenomenology and an implied philosophical acumen. One example of this is the report submitted by Alon after the Passover retreat of 2014, in which he set out twelve questions about thought. The questions addressed the nature of thought as a conscious function, its temporal operation, its psychological relationship to the awareness of subjectivity, and so forth.

There are several academic fields that deal with such questions, including cognitive psychology, cognitive neuropsychology, neurophilosophy, and even computer sciences and robotics. One of Yossef's early students (Amos Arieli) is a neuroscientist, and Yossef had invited other scientists for dialogues on the brain and on thought. But here the reader must become sharply aware of the theoretical gap between causal (reductive) accounts of thought and the subjective feeling of what it is like to think—the two are not the same! A neuroscientist may observe the fMRI (functional MRI) brain images of a Buddhist monk in deep meditation, but the subjective meditative state is not the same thing as the activation of certain brain regions.[6] Alon and his colleagues are folk phenomenologists, interested in the field of consciousness as an experienced domain in which thinking takes its place alongside perception, feeling, and so on. From that perspective one wishes to know (for example) whether thinking includes, as a felt matter, the activity of the self-aware subject or perhaps the semiaware subject, and thus whether thinking promotes egotistical agendas. Self-inquiry can help with such subtle agendas and promote not academic information but rather existential insight leading to a better life. One of the more in-

Fig. 10. Circles before Shabbat

triguing means by which Self-inquiry comes to perceive the work of the mind in thinking is through numbers.

Numbers have figured prominently in religious and mystical literature throughout history. Some of the greatest mathematicians and physicists (Pythagoras, Newton) have been attracted to numbers as mystical entities, and in the 20th century Gurdjieff assigned numbers a prominent place in his teachings.[7] Yossef also used numbers extensively, but he rejected metaphysics, magic, and anything that could be considered remotely mystical (saturated with mystery). According to Ilana and other informants, Yossef's attitude toward numbers was an outcome of his insights as to the depth of, as he called it, "the movement of numbers," and it bore no relationship to mystical numerology. Instead, numbers were simply meant to exhibit the way the human mind (thought, perception) operated. As a physical embodiment of the play of numbers, the community of Neot Smadar created a complex dance, called "circles" (*ma'agalim*), that is done on Fridays before the festive Shabbat meal (Fig. 10).

On July 11, 2014, a meeting was held at Ilana's house in order to explore some elements of this vast and complicated topic. In addition to the hostess, there were also Omri, Noam S., David, Shlomit, Iris L., and I. The purpose of the meeting was to provide me with a basic insight into the subject. The subject was close to Yossef's heart, and he had exhibited astonishing inventiveness with numbers while trying to make an important point about human thought. The meeting at Ilana's lasted several hours and was lively and focused. It began with general observations about the nature of numbers and thinking about numbers and quickly moved to technical details that will be omitted in the following account. Lost in the woods, it was evident that I would need help in seeing the forest, and Ilana volunteered to show me the way. She put together a document that greatly oversimplifies the subject and omits virtually all the numerical razzle-dazzle. The following represents her account:

The world of numbers is a rich, complicated, and somewhat magical place. It is open to an objective and clear viewing by those who seize the opportunity to uncover its secrets, but this is not easy to do.

In the field of numbers every numerical event and relationship between the numbers is simultaneous. However, thought can only describe these events in a linear, temporal manner. Thought is only capable of opening a narrow channel—an angle—within the field of numbers and describing it sequentially. Once we understand this, we are able to observe and understand the movement of thought itself. This is a critical skill for one who wishes to understand the self, his very own nature.

In order to achieve this self-understanding one may observe the movement of numbers, separated from the relationship of numbers to the material world, which it supposedly represents. "I have discovered that when I observe the world of numbers, the numerical movement, I do so with thought." Such thinking is separate from and independent of the emotional self. Put another way, numerical thinking is different from the internal identification with "what is mine" and "what is not mine." However much pleasure one gets from numbers, one cannot say that 5 is mine and 7 is not or that one loves 4 and hates 6. Emotional thinking and attachments carry no objectivity and lack clarity. For example, emotional thinking usually forces us to compare. One of the most interesting characteristics of thought is that it operates by picking out contradictions and contrasts. When one says: "I don't like this," this implicitly and unconsciously contains the thought

"I like this other thing." But understanding numbers allows us to see that emotional comparison requires two entities, that is, that there is a numerical base to this kind of thought process. Once you are aware of this twofold activity within yourself, a third observes the dissonance between the first and the second, some balance is restored.

But this is just a start. In fact, the situation is far more complex. Every number, however large, can be reduced to a number between 1 and 9. These numbers cannot be further reduced. They are the sources of the infinite range of numbers. For example, the number 9 pushes every number all the way to infinity. For example: 17 is 8 plus 9. And then 26 is 17 plus 9; they are all the reduction of 8. And this can go on forever. Likewise, we can cautiously see that when thinking proceeds by means of a chain of association and ends up constructing some mental narrative, the subject usually loses contact with the original thought that started the chain of association. It becomes difficult to return to that original thought and examine its own source.

Thinking about numbers provides us with important insights into the nature of thought and helps us understand our own thinking process. Here is another example. One learns in childhood about squaring: $4 \times 4 = 16$. This is simple and obvious. But one day, I stopped and asked: "Is it possible that there are two 4s in the world of numbers? If not, what is the second 4 in the square of 4?" Here are a number of descriptions that provide an answer to what the square of 4 might also be

$1 + 3 + 5 + 7 = 4 \times 4 = 16$ (the sum of N consecutive odd numbers is the square of N)
$(1 + 2 + 3) + (1 + 2 + 3 + 4) = 4 \times 4 = 16$ (the filling of the number 3, that is, $1 + 2 + 3$, and the filling of the number 4 always results in the square of 4)
$3 \times 3 + 7 = 4 \times 4 = 16$ ($3^2 + 7 = 16$)

These are simple descriptions of the same thing; there are far more complex ones. None is more correct than the other. What all of this shows about our inner world of thought is important. People often enter into a conflict over some subject or other thinking that they hold opposing viewpoints. On examination it is possible to show that these are distinct descriptions or perceptions of the same idea. The impression of disagreement is actually false.

Ilana's discussion of numbers in her correspondence was greatly simplified for me and for the reader of the book. She emphasized that at times fifty or more individuals would dive into far greater depths and complexity in the movement of numbers. At such times they share a unified attention to the numbers and to the movement of numbers. And then the activity of thought, which is usually based on contrasts and conflicts, comes to a rest, which allows the participants to transcend the limitations of human thinking. There is a shared interest, often rapt, a shared meditation really, that produces harmony and a sense of deep peace.

The subject of numbers does not come up as often as it used to when Yossef lived. Some members of the community, such as Ilana and Noam S., occasionally discuss numbers with young volunteers or seminar participants, who enjoy these discussions. But I had to return to the words of Yossef himself to discover why he had valued numbers so much as an activity in the school: "Numbers are relationship. If I look at my relationship with you, we can never reach a common way of thinking because each of us responds according to his own system of conditioning and there is no end to it. In the world of numbers this does not exist; they require a shared way of thinking—they are universal."[8] I saw this shared mode of thinking in Ilana's house, and I saw it budding when Yoram explained numbers to the young seminar participants, who were thrilled by the subject.

6

The Art of Listening

NEOT SMADAR IS NOTHING IF IT IS not one long, extended conversation. Its dominant shape is the circle, which comes in many different sizes. The inner circle, the "core," is the sukkah—the tabernacle. It was one of the first construction projects of the new school or community. Built of stone and timber, it looks like a Kwakiutl communal lodge and serves as the meeting place for members of Neot Smadar's inner circle every Wednesday night. The sitting area is circular, with a heating stove in the center—where a fire would have warmed the council of Native American elders. Wednesday is the same night that the earliest meetings had been held in Jerusalem when Yossef began meeting with the people who would later found Neot Smadar.

There are conversation circles everywhere. Every branch of Neot Smadar's economy has set aside a circular space for talking in a group. Some are built-in, such as the patio shared by the fruit-processing plant, the winery, and the dairy. Others are improvised, including my favorite. This is the stone and pebble fixture up on the northern hill, by the vineyard with the Merlot grapes, where the sun can be seen peeking over the Moav Mountains of Jordan at 6:00 a.m. and where I spent Saturdays meditating. Most circles are thatch-covered, like the "smoking hut" by the dining hall, but others, like the one shared by the garage and the metal workshop, use an existing porch roof. Most of the meeting circles are strewn with pillows— the one at the goat pen is, and so is the one in the date grove, where the "pillows" are rolled-up webbed sacks, the same ones used to cover the dates

Fig. 11. Conversation around a fire

when they turn brown in order to keep the birds off. But often people just sit on the lawn under a shady tree (Fig. 11). In homes, guests or friends remove their shoes and sink onto a couch or easy chairs arranged around the ubiquitous coffee table. They can count on food and drink, at the very least coffee or tea; the host will just bring this out without asking. The Hebrew term is *kibbud,* which derives from the word for honoring a guest. This goes all the way back to biblical times, but although many Israeli households today have dropped the custom, here it still runs on, stronger than ever. There are no television sets and no fancy stereo equipment, and most residents don't even have a computer. The only alcohol I ever saw was wine at Shabbat meals.

During the summer, when everyone dines outside—buffet style— conversation circles (from pairs to six or seven) form spontaneously on the lawn and steps outside the dining hall. And, in that same space, the biggest circle of all assembles when a communal project is under way. During those weeks the Wednesday meetings of the tabernacle give way to community gatherings that include everyone except for children and those parents whose turn it is to watch them. These gatherings include even the volunteers, at least the ones willing to sit and listen from 9:30 to 11:00 p.m. before rising the next day at 5:00 a.m. So over a hundred people gather around, all sitting in circles on chairs, steps, the ground, and the grass. Everyone can eyeball everyone else, and they do.

Conversation is the lifeblood of Neot Smadar's communal life, but it is not gabbiness, let alone gossip. In the form of a monologue it plays out in the voice of one man or woman who has been chosen to read the weekly "diary of the place." Far more common is the dialogue between two colleagues or friends, the eight-way exchange among co-workers during break, or the stunning "multilogue" among the thirty or forty veterans sitting at the tabernacle and working out some issue.

Nothing can get done without such verbal exchanges. Running an economy obviously depends on communication, but, more important, so does the governance of the community: the way authority is negotiated and transmitted, especially when rules are seldom written down. Most important of all, conversation is the way that the public aspect of Self-inquiry takes place in the school and the way its insights and wisdom pass from the inner circle to the periphery. In Neot Smadar, as in few other places, spiritual matters are more important than material substance, but nowhere else have I seen so much attention paid to the way communication plays out between one person and another. The place excels in the art of conversation.

The Religious Dialogue

Jonathan Z. Smith has likened religious experience to a sort of map—a culturally constructed discourse that builds worlds. These maps may be paradoxical and self-cancelling, but they overshadow the territory nonetheless. Many scholars today subscribe to this discursive understanding of religion, and in the following chapter I apply this mode of analysis to the unique form of mysticism practiced in Neot Smadar.

However, our focus at present is not the use of words to construct worlds—it is not about ideology—but something more specific and incisive: the dialogue. Religious literature overflows with examples of dialogue and with supreme valuation of the direct verbal exchange between one man and another, between God and man, or in any other combination. Think of the Hebrew Bible, beginning with Genesis (think of God and Adam, God and Abraham, God and Noah, and so on); the Talmud's profoundly dialectical method; the Hasidic Tsaddik and his followers; the religious psychology of Martin Buber.[1] And this applies equally to Christianity (Jesus and his disciples), Islam, and the great Asian religions, Hinduism and Buddhism. The Hindu scriptures, beginning with the Vedic Brahmanas, the Upanishads (Yajnavalkya's intense debate with contemporary scholars, Uddalaka Aruni's instruction to his son Shvetaketu), the dialogue of the *Bhagavad Gita,* the dialectics of Hindu philosophy, and others.[2] Buddhism features the dialogues of Buddha and his followers, the enigmatic exchanges between the Zen master and his disciple, the Buddhist-Hindu debates, and many others.[3]

The religious dialogue favors discovery over the sermon, the lecture, or even scripture because it is spontaneous and challenging for both sides equally. The teacher who engages in dialogue while avoiding the lecture is taking a chance and demonstrating something vital about truth itself: it cannot be set down or fixed but must flow from one moment to the next and is accessible in a contingent form as far as humans are concerned. If it is not perceived in the exchange itself; it is not the truth. The dialogue also reveals a profound psychological truth: listening is a supreme exercise in attentiveness, in presence, and in empathy. Without these qualities the spiritual life is an empty gesture or mere tradition. Dialogue is the simplest expression of the deepest levels of conscious experience involving the other.

Yossef used to say something similar. He would often begin group meetings by saying: "Let's be perfectly naïve about this"—that is, don't quote books you have read or cite theories of learned experts. Tell me what you see in the simplest way right here and now. In one early Jerusalem exchange a student brought up her desire when she first awoke in the morning. Yossef asked her what she wanted, and she hesitated, then said she wished to have a good day. So he repeated the question, and other students joined in with things they desired, such as "success," "recognition," "satisfaction," or, more concretely, "good coffee," and so forth. But Yossef kept repeating the question. When the students finally gave up trying to come up with a satisfactory answer, Yossef explained that desire is its own entity. We want because we want. Desire is an autonomous force that creates different objects; it is not the objects that create desire. We think that "success" breeds desire in us; it's actually the other way around. Desire targets something we call success because desire sought it out. The desire was there long before it had an object in view.

This was a valuable lesson presented in an impressive display of dialectical insistence. It matters little whether we call this religious or psychological insight. Either way one sees a dynamic use of words to communicate the idea that our attention creates the world that we perceive and our attention is bred by desires over which we have little control. Later on in the training we may learn to live with this truth by actually seeing both how we saturate the world with value and how we are controlled by unconscious mental patterns.[4] For example, we divide our colleagues into those who annoy us and those who please us without necessarily realizing that what we find annoying or pleasing is our own contribution to the situation. And this seeing can liberate us—this, after all, was the goal of spiritual practice in ancient India, where many of Yossef's insights originated.

The words could be obstacles, too; after listening to Yossef, his students felt a temporary sense of clarity but quickly resorted to old patterns of behavior. Then they lost confidence in whether they had even understood the sharat properly, and they would return and raise their renewed doubts in the next meeting. Yossef, like many other teachers, would then talk about their ambition to improve—their goal-oriented desire—and explain this in the context of that very same desire he had originally discussed.[5] In early 1999 this subject came up again, and Yossef refined his teachings about desire and the energy behind our drives and urges. He stated: "At our core is pure energy that feeds on nothing (except perhaps the sun). Our behavior in the world limits this energy and channels it according to the demands of the "I" (self) and the way the self is conditioned to interact with other persons. We become confused between the energy of motivation—the "I's" energy, which is nothing, and pure energy at the very core of our being." I cannot tell whether Yossef got this insight from personal experience or from reading sacred literature, but it sounds like the teaching of an ancient Buddhist or Hindu philosopher. However, the Israeli teacher added a phrase that explains why he thought conversations would be useful in Neot Smadar: "However, the contacts of the self [with other persons] can actually shatter the 'I' (releasing the inner energy) and thereby explain why one feels so alive in a place like this [Neot Smadar]."

Dialogue in Practice

In November 2015 (as in the years before), a retreat into the desert took fourteen groups into an isolated location for several days and nights of camping. Each group, consisting of about fifteen members, set up a primitive camp for a simple and contemplative experience—as a group. The desert stay was unscripted, but a central feature was direct and even intense verbal interactions—conversations—such as "Tell me who you are?" In this exercise, the group split into pairs who sat facing one another and took turns answering this deceptively simple question: "Who am I?" Each individual took five minutes to answer while her partner listened without responding, and then they switched. This turn-taking lasted for a whole hour. According to Avigdor, who reported this, once the usual clichés are disposed of, the exchange becomes extremely difficult but also remarkably liberating.[6]

I think Yossef repeatedly indicated that an honest exchange of words between two individuals who are engaged in Self-inquiry challenges the conditioned self, shattering patterns that throttle our internal energy. An honest conversation can be liberating, or it can open up the door to more advanced work. So did I see any such conversations in any of the conversation circles?

There are radically different levels of verbal exchange, just as an initial meeting with a psychotherapist bears little resemblance to a meeting three years later. At the highest levels one can only read, with fascination, the records of Yossef's talks with his advanced students. Some of these have been included in chapters of this book. Equally interesting, in another sense, is how skills are transmitted to beginners in Self-inquiry. I believe I witnessed such useful verbal exchanges on a number of occasions. Two of these were led by Anat and Eli and involved the Construction Seminar. About fifteen men and women signed up for the seminar—which lasted for about three months. The participants spent most of the day engaging in desert-oriented, ecologically sophisticated construction projects on a hill

Fig. 12. Duration walk in the desert

adjacent to the community. But they also shared in the life of the community and participated in guided activities that represented incipient Self-inquiry techniques. One such activity was a "duration walk" followed by a conversation circle. Anat invited me to join two of these walks. The fifteen seminar members participated, men and women between twenty-five and thirty-five years old, none of whom had much experience in group work or in spiritual practices. Eshel was chosen to lead the group. It was a stunning morning—6:00 a.m. in early July—and as we took off, the soft golden light of the rising sun radiated off the austere table-top mountains to the west, where we headed. He walked easily, meandering through the edges of the community, then climbed a hill and led us through the fringes of the desert to the northwest of Neot Smadar. We walked silently behind him, a line of walkers, each focusing exclusively on the person immediately ahead (Fig. 12). The direction we took, the pace of the walk, stopping to sit down, getting up again—all of these were up to the leader.

We finally arrived at our destination, a circle of fruit crates around a fire near a grove of pear and apple trees. Hot tea was poured, and after a few moments of silence Anat asked Eshel: "What would you like to share?" Eshel was slightly older than the other seminar participants, perhaps in his mid-thirties. He stared into the fire and thought for a while. As I watched him hesitate, I speculated on what might be going through his mind: "What could he share, his thoughts right now or what he thought during the walk? Should he talk about his body, about the morning? There was too much to say but all of it vague." He said: "At times I just wanted to keep going, into the desert."

> Anat: Why didn't you?
> Eshel: I felt a responsibility to the group.
> Anat: What did you feel about the group?
> Eshel: I thought about what it could do or not do. I felt that Ruti could not keep up.

Ruti, a short, fragile-looking young woman with short black hair, looked at him with a slightly surprised expression. Anat pressed on: "What did it feel like to have this thought?"

This question was followed by a long silence. Eshel came from an Israeli culture where thoughts always found a voice but feelings were often mute. What does it feel like to have a thought? He was clearly considering what might constitute a proper answer for such a question. He seemed to feel—most of the people in the group may have been feeling—that there is one correct way of answering questions, of talking about thoughts and feelings, in Neot Smadar. Avi had been in the community longer than the others, and he interjected: "It feels like responsibility. It feels like what you want has to take into account what the others in your group want."

Eli, who was co-leading the seminar along with Anat, asked: "How do you know what they want?"[7]

> Avi: You sense it. Somehow you just know.
> Anat: What do you sense?
> Avi: You feel the line behind you and take it into account.

Neither Anat nor Eli pressed the point (about projecting one's inner views on the external world), and the conversation moved to other themes.

A couple of weeks later, Anat chose Tamar to lead the group, but Tamar demurred. This was shortly after morning meditation, and the world was still sleepy and semidark. But Tamar's resistance was fully awake. She giggled nervously and refused to look up; she kept kicking the grass with her boot and changed the topic. Anat did not let her off the hook, but it took fifteen minutes of persuasion before the walk began, with her leading the group.

During the conversation around the fire that followed, Anat explored the young woman's reluctance to lead and her feelings about walking at the front of the line. Tamar was tall and skinny and painfully self-conscious. Asked how it felt to lead, she said it was difficult. "Why?" Anat asked. Tamar took several moments to answer that question. She did not seem to be thinking about her answer so much as working up courage to just speak. Finally she said: "I was worried about being judged."

ANAT: Judged on what?
TAMAR: Am I taking a good path? Am I going too fast or too slow? Is everyone getting bored? Things like that.
ANAT: Are you having any such thoughts right now?

Tamar blushed and giggled. She kept her eyes on the fire and remained quiet as Anat and Eli looked at her gently, waiting.

Both Eshel and Tamar were hesitant to speak and appeared very concerned with how their responses would be received. They may have experienced themselves in relation to the group and actually felt the group as an inner force with a competing will. There were complicated social and psychological reasons, no doubt, but Anat and Eli were not interested in theories. They tried to coax, some expression, in words, of what it felt like to be in this position; as facilitators they did not get very far in showing how deeply conditioned and socially constructed the ego-self was. But the seminar had only just begun, and there was no rush. Using words, in the form of simple questions, they began to teach the young students to turn their gaze inward and to develop a vocabulary for describing what they see.

There was nothing mystical (in the customary sense of that term) about this sort of work, but it struck me as both valuable and gentle. If anything, these exchanges reminded me of psychodynamic therapy, informally practiced.[8]

It is important to remember here that there is something technical about listening as an aspect of Self-inquiry. This can be termed "nonresponse"; it is an exercise in attentive and sympathetic hearing without responding. The listener makes no effort to answer, to solve a problem, to defend a position, or to pursue any other agenda. Instead she cultivates a deep attention to the desire to respond or to whatever else is taking place at the actual moment that the words are spoken. This critically important skill came up in many of my discussions with informants, who explained: "In looking to respond we move our attention to our own agenda, our own ego, and lose track of what is going on at the present moment, out in the world."

In other places, away from Neot Smadar, I have been seeing the same disturbing pattern. Conversations—or, more precisely, listening—is a dying art. Talking is not the issue; it's the listening that seems to be falling apart. I can't help thinking of Milan Kundera's hilarious depiction of this situation in *The Book of Laughter and Forgetting*:

> You know what happens when two people talk. One of them speaks and the other breaks in: "It's absolutely the same with me, I . . ." and starts talking about himself until the first one manages to slip back in with his own "It's absolutely the same with me, I . . ."
>
> The phrase "It's absolutely the same with me, I . . ." seems to be an approving echo, a way of continuing the other's thought, but that is an illusion: in reality it is a brute revolt against a brutal violence, an effort to free our own ear from bondage and to occupy the enemy's ear by force. Because all of man's life among his kind is nothing other than a battle to seize the ear of others. The whole secret of Tamina's [the heroine's] popularity is that she has no desire to talk about herself. She submits to the forces occupying her ear, never saying: "It's absolutely the same with me, I . . ."[9]

True, empathetic listening requires a presence or mindfulness and a self-silencing (based on discipline) that I have come to associate only with meditative states because it seems so difficult for people to achieve.[10]

I recently came across a new book written by Andrew Newberg and Mark Robert Waldman. The book is titled *Words Can Change Your Brain,* and it offers twelve conversation strategies to build trust, resolve conflict, and increase intimacy.[11] The book is based on extensive neuropsychological research but also shows the fruit of insight derived from Buddhist meditative practices. The debt to Buddhism becomes clear when you look at the twelve strategies of "compassionate communication":

1. Relax
2. Stay present
3. Cultivate inner silence
4. Increase positivity
5. Reflect on your deepest values
6. Access a pleasant memory
7. Observe nonverbal cues
8. Express appreciation
9. Speak warmly
10. Speak slowly
11. Speak briefly
12. Listen deeply

These strategies cover both speaking and listening, and in both the ego's many agendas can play a disruptive role. On the other hand, the good listener comes across as a Dalai Lama figure, calm and compassionate. And according to the authors, the listener enjoys the same outcome the Dalai Lama repeatedly praises, namely, happiness. Has there ever been a community where all twelve of these conditions have been observed? That is highly doubtful. Certainly there was often little warmth in Yossef's speaking style, and he often failed to respond in a positive manner or even to truly perceive his listener. I believe he favored truth, cold truth, over empathy. But he made a difference in the way his students understood the dynamic patterns of the self—he often called this "mechanical thought"—and in the way this can thwart true communication and therefore Self-inquiry. A community where the true self—not the highly conditioned busybody who runs our life—is sought in meditative states of inner-silence conversation can become elevated. When that happens, some sort of fraternity can sometimes emerge—not because togetherness is a supreme value (as in a community) but because relaxation, presence, and inner silence lead to attentiveness, which somehow leads to empathy. I saw this repeatedly during my time in Neot Smadar.[12]

I found myself in such conversations with many people. There was Anat, of course, and also Shlomit and Alon—all three of whom I had already known. Then I found myself in delightful talks with Avigdor and Isaac, with Iris L. and Ilana and Iris T., and with so many other men and women in the community, or in sad conversations with Hanna and even with Dudu and Savion, who were no longer living there. It was not always easy to explain how a true exchange, a compassionate giving way to the act of listening, could happen. But I saw elements of conversations everywhere in the community and came to realize that the listening and sharing were the beneficial fruits of cultivating a good understanding of the self. That's what all those circles were about. And that is how, ten years after Yossef had died, his former students looked to advance the study of the self and, indirectly, community.

One Shabbat Dinner

At the first Shabbat dinner of June 2013, I sat with Isaac and his family, and Shlomit and then Iris L. joined the table. After the meal there was fruit on the table and some red wine, and what had just been chitchat developed into a full conversation. All around were other such tables, all covered in white linen and surrounded by family members and friends. The area buzzed with voices and the shouts of children chasing each other among the tables. Shlomit told me to ask Isaac's wife, Galit, the same question I had asked Shlomit the day before. I could not remember the question, and Shlomit reminded me of the talk she, Isaac, and I had had the previous Thursday in the Pundak (restaurant, literally "Inn"). Later that night I looked at the notes I had taken of that conversation:

Thursday morning I went to the Pundak for a cup of coffee and to write my notes for Wednesday. Isaac and Shlomit were both working there that day, and as I began to write, Isaac came over. I was sitting at one of the tables next to the fish pond in the back courtyard, under a shady tree. A light breeze ruffled the pages of my notebook, and the coffee was superb. I had already been there several times, always at the same table and always with my notebook.

ISAAC: Why are you writing?

ARIEL: I have to or I forget what I saw and heard yesterday.

ISAAC: You misunderstood me. I meant, why do you write . . . in general?

This was a question I was not used to hearing, and I didn't know how to answer it exactly. I had always written. Usually I wrote because that is what professors do (to promote their careers or to disseminate knowledge). I no longer felt motivated by either of these, but I felt compelled to write anyway. So I said: "I write because I write. The way the tree moves in the wind. I write because it's who I am."

Just then Shlomit came over to the table and, as always, she was carrying some cakes. On a plate were six slices of a rolled-up date cake that went splendidly with espresso. Both she and Isaac had a glass of herbal tea. We sipped and chewed silently for a while. Then I asked her: "If you had to make a choice, which single item would you regard as most meaningful in Neot Smadar? Which one of Yossef's lessons have you found most significant?"

Shlomit smiled and said: "That's a really good question." Then she became silent for a few moments and spoke again: "I'll need a few moments to think about it."

ISAAC: Do you mind if I say something while you think? I think there was something missing in Yossef's method.

ARIEL: What do you mean?

ISAAC: Yossef focused on understanding thought as the key factor in human consciousness.

ARIEL: Do you think it was too psychological and not religious enough?

ISAAC: I don't know. Maybe. If you feel some presence all around you (he waved his hand at the beautiful oasis in which we were sitting) and you know that it is greater than you—let's call it divine—then understanding thought and its mechanism in minute detail becomes unnecessary. I think that modesty and empathy are superior to tinkering with the way thought operates.

ARIEL: Let's assume you are right. How does the feeling you describe translate into everyday behavior and relationships?

ISAAC: It just does. It changes you. Too much mechanical tinkering hardens the personality. It only reinforces weaknesses—it does not help you transcend it to a better place.

ARIEL So you feel there is not enough "God" in this place?

Isaac: I'm just talking for myself, but that's the way I feel. We hardly deal with this directly.

Shlomit: I don't agree; I see it differently. It may be that there was not enough God in Yossef's method, but there was heart. For example, for a whole year, many of us were selected to become a "prince," each for a whole month. That was a great opportunity for learning to care for someone else and to give unconditionally.

Isaac: But that was so rare . . .

Shlomit: Isaac, you are wrong. Yossef placed relationships at the center of Self-inquiry (limud). Just as in the example of the princes, over the years he made suggestions and observations that were all about working with the heart.

Ariel: Does either of you believe that Yossef's work has produced an ideal society in Neot Smadar?

Both vigorously shook their heads. Shlomit reminded Isaac that he had not been in the community during the early years and then said: "This place is far from perfect, but if you need a single test for the quality of a place, look at how the children are raised. We have done a fantastic job raising our children. They read the best books and learn to be accepting, creative and nonviolent in school and at home."

Isaac nodded in agreement, and we finished the cakes.

So I now asked Galit: "If you had to choose, what is the one single most meaningful thing about Neot Smadar as far as you are concerned?"

Galit looked at me and began to think about her answer. Other people had joined the table, but no one said a word. We all waited for her to answer. Finally, she said: "This place gives me the context or the conditions to feel that I am like everyone else."

Iris asked: "What do you mean 'like everyone else?'"

Galit replied: "I'm not at the center of the universe, as my ego would normally wish to be. It's OK to just stay in the shadows; I don't feel threatened by that."

I asked: "Why do you think that is the case? Is it because this place is a communal environment?"

Several people answered at the same time: "No!"

Then Shlomit's voice emerged from all the voices: "For years we practiced "Staying in the Shadow" and "Non-intervention." It's not a community thing; it's a school thing, some of the better aspects of Yossef's teaching."

Galit said: "I think one of the most important rituals or actions that we have here is the reading of the weekly report. Personally, I really enjoy doing it myself. It's amazing how attentive everyone becomes during the readings and the freedom to say what is on your mind without being censored or interrupted."

I asked: "What else do you appreciate about Yossef?"

Galit responded: "He had an amazing ability to raise the energy level in the place when things began to falter, when we had doubts or were just exhausted."

Several voices rose in agreement when Galit said this, and Ruth C. added: "He had a way of seeing how we dissipate our energies. Remember when he forbade entertainment like radio and idle chatter?"

IRIS: He didn't forbid it. He just challenged us to give up these things for a month.

RUTH: That's true. It was hard at first, but then I did feel more energized.

GALIT: Just the effort of living up to a challenge . . .

ISAAC: A vow.

GALIT: . . . or a vow, was energizing. He knew when to toss those things at us.

ARIEL: Galit, earlier you mentioned that you had a lot of freedom in reading the weekly report. Was there anything you were not allowed to say?

GALIT: No gossip. You were not to mention people by name, especially if you were reading something critical.

ARIEL: Why not? Isn't the idea of the report, or of the school in general, that things emerge into daylight—even if they are unpleasant?

GALIT: Not like that. This could lead to account settling and vindictive behavior.

ARIEL: But I thought the people who are already in the sukkah (where the report is read) are advanced and beyond that sort of thing, that you are mature enough to be trusted with each other. As you just said, this is a school, not a community.

IRIS: Yes, that is true. But the school has to function in the real world. And in the real world feelings get hurt and you need to create a space of trust where you know that your feelings would be protected.

Attentive listening at Neot Smadar did not imply a soft acceptance of whatever was said. It often looked like sharp criticism, but it emerged from careful listening. One day when I worked in the kitchen, the following exchange took place during break, when we were all sitting around a table in the "smoking hut":

NISSAN: Today washing the pots I could not help thinking, "Why me? Why am I stuck with the job of washing pots?" The thought kept coming up . . .

MICHAEL: You should have told me—I would have traded places with you.
ALON: You mean to say that if you had that thought that you did not like or
enjoy what you were doing you would immediately want to change it?
MICHAEL: It's good to offer someone the opportunity to switch places, to get
relief or give it to someone else.
ALON: No, I am talking about your own thoughts coming and going, up and
down (*Alon gestured with his hand*). I am talking about the need to become
attentive to them.
MICHAEL: If I feel that I need a change, then yes, I would want to act on that.
ALON: Why?
MICHAEL: In order to feel better.

At this point, before his comments changed from reflective to judgmental,
Alon became quiet. He didn't even seem tempted to say: "Perhaps you need
to learn self-restraint. You know, patience or forbearance." Instead he simply rested in what had to be an act of quiet self-restraint. Perhaps he had
already said too much.

I saw many exchanges like that in Neot Smadar, usually between an elder
and a young volunteer. These struck me as teaching moments, but the
teaching was always implicit, and I could not tell when the lesson attained
its goal. There was a long tradition of using conversational exchanges as
teaching opportunities. After all, Yossef's approach was deeply dialectical.

Following is part of a conversation that took place in the sukkah in the
mid-1990s. Yossef, acting as the sharat, explained how dialogue functions
in the context of Self-inquiry. The lesson seeks to remove the biggest obstacle to a true conversation, our inner resistance. Yossef spoke as follows:

When there is an opposing view there is always tension. It is a kind of holding oneself in a nonrelaxed way, and relaxation is more important than anything else. The initial reaction then rests, and I am free to see what is going
on. Learning how to listen is not holding on with all your might to the initial
reaction. Let it be mobile. I do not truly lose it [the value of what is said]
because if it is correct it will show itself in the deeper perception. There is
something in us that perceives the entire situation. If our reaction was accurate, and that is rare, and I am not afraid of losing it, it will become manifest
at a deeper level.

This is difficult to grasp . . . if a boy comes to you with an excessive request, the initial response is "What are you talking about?" But the connection needs to be toward the boy; what made him approach you? The connection [to the boy] is from the heart. I can connect to him with an empty mind; it doesn't come from thought. And then I feel the boy, what stands behind his request. It is a moment of contact of one with the other.

I did not know Yossef, but if he practiced what he taught—listening from the heart—this was a softer side of a hard man. It means that in addition to the "jolt" that he prized so much (truth in the face of self-deception), there was compassion, which I saw in many of the older residents of Neot Smadar. The connection between attentive listening and compassion is thus at the core of Neot Smadar conversations. However, this is a technical matter, and far from self-evident. Omri explained the connection between listening (without responding) and compassion in a number of conversations. His analysis is available in Chapter 10.

7

Everyday Mysticism

SCHOLARSHIP ON THE SUBJECT OF mysticism today largely tends toward the view that it is no more and no less than a verbal performance, an act of communication, perhaps an exegesis. This flies in the face of popular conceptions, which still see in the mystical event something truly transcendent. Here is how the *Oxford English Dictionary* (*OED*) puts it: "Belief that union with or absorption into the Deity or the absolute, or the spiritual apprehension of knowledge inaccessible to the intellect, may be attained through contemplation and self-surrender." In contrast, academic definitions of mysticism begin by reminding readers how difficult this phenomenon is not only to define but even to identify. For example, is mysticism a matter of experience (as the *OED* implies), or does it also, perhaps solely, include interpretation? Can experience, separated from that which is "inaccessible to the intellect," even be had?[1] Because a definition of mysticism demands that one take a position on such issues and because this chapter discusses precisely these matters, my understanding of mysticism emerges gradually as the chapter progresses.

The mystic in the popular imagination is a hero, a spiritual genius, and the states of reality he or she can access are truly extraordinary in the knowledge they convey and the intensity of their experience. Here is an example from Swami Ramdas's *In Quest of God:* "Ramdas, you are free, nothing binds you. You are free like air. Soar high and high in the heavens until you spread everywhere and pervade the whole universe. Become one with Ram

[God]. All Ram! All Ram! What a grand spectacle to see the dazzling light of Ram everywhere!"[2]

Surely one need not be a Hindu to attain such intimacy with God, to break free from the confines of the limited personal self, to see light and experience supreme joy. Jews have reported similar experiences, as have Muslims and, not least, Christians: "Ascending the tabernacle, the soul comes to the house of God. While it admires the members of the tabernacle it thus is led to the house of God by following a certain sweetness, an indescribable interior pleasure. It is as if a musical instrument sweetly sounded from the house of God, and while walking in the tabernacle he heard the interior sound and, led by its sweetness, he followed what had sounded, separating himself from every clamor of flesh and blood until he arrived at the house of God."[3] The language is different and the metaphors vary, but something seems essential: the proximity to God and the exuberance (which the OED neglects to mention).

Following the common understanding of mysticism, one would be hard pressed to understand Neot Smadar as a mystical community or its now deceased founder (Yossef) as a mystical teacher. There is no talk there of God or any other divine being, indeed no explicit metaphysics of any kind. One rarely encounters the same techniques that engender the sort of experiences described above, and no one has reported ecstatic flights of the imagination—or soul—to supreme and blissful spheres. And yet Neot Smadar is indeed a mystical community, and it practices something I call "everyday mysticism," which is extraordinary without any of the theological fireworks one sees elsewhere.[4] To fully understand what all of this means, we must review the way that scholars today understand the subject of mysticism—how they reject the essentialist (common) view and what remains of it—and what this implies for secular postmodern mystics working on a communal farm in the desert.

Mapping and Unmapping Mystical Paths

Like the debate on religious experience in Chapter 1, the question of mystical experience and religious traditions has taken a strong constructivist turn since the publication in the 1970s and 1980s of several edited works dealing with the topic.[5] Today only a minority of academic researchers, like Robert C. Forman, argue that a unitary and pure state of consciousness underlies the diverse forms of expression used by mystics as they record their mystical theology.[6] The Buddhist practitioner of shunyata (emptiness) and the Hindu yogi ultimately reach this unified state despite the different maps that got them to that goal. The constructivist maintains, in contrast, that the map stays with the mystic till the very end.

Consider the following three examples, taken from the Mahayana text *The Heart Sutra* (*Prajñāpāramitāhṛdaya Sūtra*), from the roughly contemporary Hindu text Patanjali's *Yoga Sūtras,* and from the Christian text of Hendrik Herp, *A Mirror of Perfection.* All three can be regarded as road maps—theological, philosophical, and psychological at once. They point the way to Truth, which seems to lie both in the words acting as signs and somehow beyond them, too. There are good reasons to believe that Forman has a point, namely, that something essential takes place beneath the level of mystical discourse. But there are better reasons to follow Steven T. Katz and the entire generation of scholars (including Bernard McGinn, Robert Gimello, H. P. Owen, and others) who reject this position. Finally, there are strong and intriguing reasons to believe that there may be a third position that does not seek to resolve this dispute but changes the conversation altogether.

Heart Sutra *(portion)*

Listen Sariputra, this Body itself is Emptiness and Emptiness itself is this Body. This Body is not other than Emptiness, and Emptiness is not other than this Body. The same is true of Feelings, Perceptions, Mental Formations, and Consciousness.

Listen Sariputra, all phenomena bear the mark of Emptiness; their true nature is the nature of no Birth no Death, no Being no Non-being, no Defilement no Purity, no Increasing no Decreasing.

That is why in Emptiness, Body, Feelings, Perceptions, Mental Formations and Consciousness are not separate self entities. The Eighteen Realms of Phenomena which are the six Sense Organs, the six Sense Objects, and the six Consciousnesses are also not separate self entities. The Twelve Links of Interdependent Arising and their Extinction are also not separate self entities. Ill-being, the Causes of Ill-being, the End of Ill-being, the Path, insight and attainment, are also not separate self entities.

Whoever can see this no longer needs anything to attain. Bodhisattvas who practice the Insight that Brings Us to the Other Shore see no more obstacles in their mind, and because there are no more obstacles in their mind, they can overcome all fear, destroy all wrong perceptions and realize Perfect Nirvana.[7]

For anyone seeking an escape from the suffering that characterizes this existence—for the Buddhist "mystic" (to create an odd hybrid)[8]—this is a strange map indeed. It tells the Mahayana monk that the map itself is quite "useless" (rather, lacking in inherent nature, empty) in what Richard H. Robinson and Willard L. Johnson call paradoxical witticisms "that played the conventional level of truth against the ultimate, erasing dualities between subject and object, conditioned and unconditioned, pure and impure, conventional and ultimate, even same and different."[9] Indeed, the shunyata theory negated accepted Buddhist metaphysics (the Abhidharma), which had described and explained the circumstances that made one committed to Buddha's teachings (over and against, say, Vedic teachings) and to the idea of escaping samsara (rebirth). Now the map points out that there is no inherent difference between samsara and nirvana, and there is no self or being that must escape samsara.

What would "experience" consist of for one who trains with this paradox in mind and who finally attains nirvana (or another state based on the concept of emptiness)? Clearly it would be logically absurd to expect a description that is based on the work of language with its function as marking difference.[10] "Ztt! I entered. I lost the boundary of my physical body. I had my skin, of course, but I felt I was standing in the center of the cosmos. I saw people coming toward me, but all were the same man. All were myself. I had never known this world before. I had believed that I was created, but now I must change my opinion: I was never created; I was the cosmos. No individual existed."[11]

The clever and often hilarious performances one sees in Zen literature result from recognizing that every distinction, bred by the illusion that things possess intrinsic nature, is false. Of course that is the end of the map itself. And so the map constitutes what I consider a conceptual aurobor (tautology) of the highest order. The only way to follow the map is to get rid of it: to un-map the map!

Patanjali's Yoga Sutras

This is the teaching of yoga
Yoga is the cessation of the turnings of thought.
When thought ceases, the spirit stands in its true identity as observer to
the world.
Otherwise, the observer identifies with the turnings of thought. (1.1–4)[12]

The cessation of the turnings of thought comes through practice and
dispassion.
Practice is the effort to maintain the cessation of thought.
This practice is firmly grounded when it is performed for a long time with-
out interruption and with zeal.
Dispassion is the sign of mastery over the craving for sensuous objects.
Higher dispassion is a total absence of craving for anything material, which
comes by discriminating between spirit and material nature. (1.12–16)

The *Yoga Sutras,* roughly contemporary with the *Heart Sutra,* demonstrate a familiarity with Buddhist thought and terminology. For example, as
in Buddhist soteriology, Yoga also shows the way out of suffering, which is
due—to a great extent—to grasping or seeing permanence in what is im-
permanent. But the Yoga school, like Sankhya metaphysics, was radically
different from Mahayana Buddhism in its teachings. To begin with, it was
dualistic; it recognized consciousness or pure awareness (*purusha*) as real
and eternal. But there was also material nature (*prakriti*), which—unlike
pure consciousness—was the mind's reality: the way sensory reality was
processed by and shaped the working of the mind ("turnings of thought"—
citta-vrtti). In this philosophy, or perhaps psychology, mind was regarded
as an aspect of material nature and was distinct from consciousness. But
mind misattributed its perceived reality to consciousness in an error that
caused suffering.

And so, as far as the yogi is concerned, the map is real. It informs us in a
rather precise way about the psychosomatic nature of reality and sets out a
clear and practical path for attaining the goal of practice. This goal is known
as Samadhi, which is pure contemplation: the elimination of the mind's er-
rors, allowing the objectless radiance of purusha to shine through. But like
all "mystical" soteriologies, this one too sets up predictable cognitive paradoxes: Edwin Bryant makes this point, quoting the preeminent Sankhya

text on this: "No one is actually either bound or liberated, nor does any-one transmigrate; it is only prakriti in her various manifestations who is bound, transmigrates and [sic] released."[13] Nonetheless, prakriti is not empty in the same way that Buddhist psychology regards reality; rather, it is distor-tive and error-causing and can be controlled by discipline (Yoga).[14]

So, what would the yogi who relies on this map experience in samadhi? The *Yoga Sutras* tell us: "Pure contemplation is meditation that illumines the object alone, as if the subject were devoid of intrinsic form" (Miller, 3.3). This is undifferentiated consciousness: "In this state, the mind is no longer aware of itself as meditating on something external to itself; all distinctions—between the yogi as the subjective meditator, the act of meditation, and the object of meditation—have disappeared."[15] No mental construction (such as names and concepts) remains, and thus the experience is apophatic—just as the Buddhist shunyata was, but it is more likely to be described by meta-phors. Ramana Maharshi describes it in this way: "Absorption in the Self con-tinued unbroken from that time on. Other thoughts might come and go like the various notes of music, but the 'I' continued like the fundamental *sruti* note that underlies and blends with all the other notes."[16] Despite the meta-phor, we understand that the reality of the experience here is purusha, which is real and permanent, and the yogi knows that what cannot be described is not the same thing as that which lacks all characteristics of existence.

Hendrik Herp, A Mirror of Perfection, *Part 4*

> We now turn to the third and most perfect life, which is called the super-essential contemplative life. It is symbolized by Mary Magdalene, who had chosen the better part; for just as we have been created to dwell with angels in glory, as scripture teaches, so too we will be raised higher in the choirs of the angels when we grow in divine knowledge. The superessential con-templative life has the highest grade of divine illumination. Therefore, we should ascend all the rungs of virtue, and pursue especially true renuncia-tion, as much as we can, and thus we will make ourselves ready blissfully and profitably to receive from God the supreme influx of the superessential contemplative life.[17]

Hendrik Herp (d. 1477) was a Dutch Franciscan monk whose best-known work was *A Mirror of Perfection*. The work consists of four parts:

the first deals with mortifications that act as preparation for the mystical path. This is followed by active life, the contemplative life, and finally the "superessential" contemplative life—from whose description the preceding text comes. Like other Christian mystics, Herp was deeply steeped in a particular mystical tradition (early modern European Lowland) that formed a distinct version of broader Christian mystical theology. As the editors of the volume put it: "Given his sources (especially the Lowland mystics Ruusbroec and Jordaens), the ascent into the superessential life has a Trinitarian dimension: the Holy Spirit operates on the will or the loving faculty; the Word operates on the intellect; and the Father acts on the memory."[18] In other words, A Mirror is largely an exegetical work. For example, the final stages, in which the spirit possesses "all the deliciousness, the riches, the knowledge and all that it can possibly desire," is first and foremost a commentary on the great Flemish mystic Ruusbroec (1298–1381) and other Christian sources. While it lays out the mystical journey and prescribes training methods, it does so by quoting the Psalms ("With the holy, you will be holy," Ps. 17:26) and Exodus (19, 27) even when it says that "the Spirit of God flows into him as a superabundant living, supremely sweet spring, in which the loving spirit is being baptized and immersed" (159).

Like the Buddhist and Hindu maps, Herp's is both rather brief and complete. It provides a recognized cosmology, psychology, and soteriology. And its roots, like those of the other maps, grow directly out of a traditional and textual worldview. Finally, although the experience itself is described in Trinitarian terms, it is ultimately (like the Buddhist and Hindu experiences) apophatic: "For all the words and everything that one can learn and understand in a creaturely fashion is alien to, and far beneath, the truth that I have in mind. But he who is united with God and enlightened in this truth can understand the truth by (the truth) itself."[19]

The three examples hardly represent the full range of mystical worldviews and practices. There are also apocalyptic forms of mysticism, feminist, political, prophetic, visionary, affective, erotic, and so forth, many of them kataphatic or highly expressive.[20] The three I have chosen illuminate the case of Neot Smadar's everyday Self-inquiry, if not "mysticism" as an academic category. All three maps suggest that the peak experience (to borrow from Maslow) transcends the map itself, but this gives no one license to claim that such an experience is singular and universal. The contextual-ist (constructivist) researchers who deny the essentialist claim will engage in comparative work only to the extent that they are looking at map making and map reading (literature and practice, respectively).[21] Such work might show, to give one example, that where scripture is hallowed (in Christianity, Juda-ism, Islam), map reading may point to a transcendent experience but scripture (the substance and medium of the map) is retained as a symbol or sign of the experience itself. In contrast, traditions where scripture is regarded in more contingent ways show the map being left behind as a useful means at best.

A strong psychological assumption underlies the contextualist agenda. Every human experience, even those that ostensibly transcend verbalization, is either shaped or filtered by cultural factors. The empty (Buddhist), pure (Yoga), and divine (Christian) experiences are distinct to the very end. Mys-ticism is not just a cultural-exegetical activity but is also a demonstration of the ways that culture constitutes our deepest states of consciousness.[22] Hence, mysticism is no single phenomenon unless we apply the term to the making of maps of reality (including the self, society, and the cosmos), which are then read in a way that questions that same reality to such an extent that a new vision of being emerges. Such an understanding is broad enough to encompass academic definitions (for example, Bernard McGinn's) but may be so broad that it both glosses over distinct types of mystical systems and includes secular modes (the labor mysticism of A. D. Gordon, the stories of Kafka, postmodern poetry, and so on). Still, it is a valuable working defi-nition as long as in "reading" (of the map) in this context one also includes training and practice, which are often ascetic and are usually embodied as meditation, sleepless nights, harsh diets, pain, movement and work, strict sensory discipline, and others.

Finally, it is important to add that mystical practice has always served various social agendas, even when the mystic appears to be a solitary indi-vidual operating against social norms. If the mystical map is constituted by sociocultural work and the mystical reading is an act of un-mapping—that is, questioning the map's own contours—the social implications can be striking. This is particularly true in the case of prophetic mysticism but also applies in the less obviously social examples cited earlier. A strong example is the Aghori mystic in India, whose practice leads to the evisceration of social taboos (for example, purity) and the promotion of universal social welfare. This area of mystical research has begun to interest researchers in the past few decades.[23] Understanding the social role of map construction and reading may appear to undermine mystical theology as a "pure" religious activity, but it illuminates mysticism as a contemporary phenomenon, particularly in a secular, globalized context in which social and moral engagement dominate. It is one of the keys for understanding everyday mysticism and the mystical community in places such as Neot Smadar.

Mysticism in Neot Smadar

Like the mystical texts of early Buddhism and Hinduism, the mysticism of Neot Smadar is apophatic in the sense of drafting a psychological map that needs to be erased. It must be erased not because it is false but because mapping is the wrong activity; it is a sort of skillful means (upaya)—a raft that must be discarded at that other side of the body of water. The map is drafted in long conversations—the drafters refuse to attribute this activity to anything but direct observation—and the reading, the unmaking of the map, is achieved by means of providing the conditions for attaining the right sort of insight, including conditions that have, or appear to have, ascetic characteristics: hard work in difficult conditions (physical demands, fatigue, heat); shock (truth telling, mirroring, "experiments," controlled deception); collectivism (conversations, shared property, workplace rotation); and others described in the next chapter.

The school at Neot Smadar is part of a living process, and its members have assiduously avoided any temptation to enshrine a doctrine or teaching that would act as a guide for the traveler. There is no sutra and no Torah to draw on here; the map that does exist must be pieced together by looking at conversations in which observation and introspection play dominant roles. There have been dozens, or hundreds, such conversations over the years. A small sample should illuminate some of the more salient features of the mapping.

What Is Real, and What Is the Self?

Imagine a conversation between several ninth-century monks in a Shankaracharya monastery in India. They are all advanced meditators, all sophisticated students of Shankara's monistic philosophical system, which holds that there is only one true reality, namely Brahman. The rest is maya, which is the phenomenal world of sensory and cognitive error. The monks might ask, What is Brahman like? Can we know it? Does our phenomenal experience reflect Brahman in any way at all? If Brahman is all there is, where does error (ignorance) come from, and how can it be removed?

In Jerusalem in December of 1985, essentially the same conversation took place among individuals who were not monks, meditators, or students of Advaita Vedanta (or any other philosophy). They were ordinary men and women who had been training in simply sharpening their introspective skills. The conversation began when Iris asked whether God exists and can be known, but Yossef, who was uninterested in theology, turned the focus to the question of the Unknown and the Unknowable, that is, the ultimately Real. What followed was a conversation in the mode of mystical ontology and epistemology.

Yossef began by asking, for the sake of clarification, "Do I desire to turn the unknown into the known? Is that what I mean by "coming into contact?" Is the "I," or the mechanical thinking associated with it, able to bring to it [the phenomenal self] the unknown? Is this your question in general? . . . Is the unknown not part of the known?"

Iris, who had raised the initial question, responded, "As I see it, no."

Yossef replied: "Hold on. The known to me is not everything I know. That is, there is something that is not known to me but in the realm of the known. It is knowable.[24] Is there something that is not subject to knowing? The known and the unknown that is knowable are both in the realm of knowledge."

Amos, who was one of Yossef's first students and is a professor of neuroscience, spoke: "I feel that we are constantly coming in contact with the unknowable but we translate it into other things and lose contact with it."

Yossef said, again by way of clarification: "Yes, I ask, this contact, it is the contact of the known with these (unknowable) things?"

Amos replied: "Yes."

But this seemed to violate common sense, and Kobi immediately pointed it out: "That's impossible. If I can't know it, then I can't discuss it, including talking about contact or no contact with it."

But Kobi, like most of us, seemed to assume that the "unknowable" was

somehow entirely transcendent, whereas Amos thought of it in more concrete psychological terms. He explained: "When I step outside and see a
panoramic view, what I see cannot be described; it is beyond my grasp. But
I encounter this all the time."

Yoram, another of Yossef's veteran students, refused to accept that a totality is the unknowable: "Every view is knowable. If need be you can send
someone to bring every single stone."

But this was not what Amos meant: "No, that's the detail—the view before your eyes is different."

At this point the conversation turned to phenomena and noumena, all of
it based on the introspection of men and women who were not trained in
philosophy. Yossef explained: "I think Amos means to say that every experience we have is grasped only in the capacity to grasp it. That is, it is grasped
in the realm of what is known, and the part that is unknown is dominated
by the other, which gives the experience its [cognitive] significance. In other
words, every encounter with a phenomenon includes the mysterious just
beyond what we know." Amos continued on the theme of that mysterious
element: "Everything you take apart, you may be able to understand and
communicate, perhaps use it, too, but you lose from the living essence."
Yossef added to this: "There has to be something more basic that precedes
the parts that cannot be taken apart. I don't know how to say it, but it is
something instantaneous."

Iris then stated that she did not understand. And, indeed, the subject had
now turned to epistemology, because Yossef had introduced the subject of
time in the act of seeing. He explained: "Amos is basing this, as I understand him, on the argument that taking the totality apart, setting boundaries so it is known, follows the act of seeing." In contrast, the mysterious
unknown requires the instantaneous present; it cannot be assembled, as it
were, in time.

At that point Shaul remarked: "The difference between the mysterious
and what we know is how the brain processes it. If it makes an impression
on the brain, if it becomes an impression, then it is known." In contrast,
he added: "If someone somehow comes into contact with that unknown,
there is no way he would be able to communicate it because there is no instrument to create an impression." We can translate these comments into

religious terms to make them a bit more concrete: if God or Brahman or some other Noumenous becomes a subject of experience, there is no way for our human brains to process this information and therefore no way to communicate it.

This observation made Yossef shift the focus from the Unknown Other to the human, that is, to the knowing self: "If I come into contact, it is hard to be precise with these words. If there is contact with the boundary between the known and the unknown, what is it that bounds the known?" In other words, how does our world of knowledge change by virtue of having come into contact with something special?

Amos gave one answer: "It's possible that even when there is something that is unknown, there is a feeling of something missing in the known, a feeling of absence."

Yossef turned to make the matter more explicit: "Let's stop here. The known can be defined. It can be symbolized and communicated. The unknown does not receive a symbol or a sign; there is no conceptual scheme that captures it. It lacks content, because these are aspects of the known. When you encounter a phenomenon or event, is there anything in it that cannot be captured by such content-bearing instruments?" The question invited a metaphysical answer: what is the noumenal that humans throughout history have regarded as God and other such entities?

The group in Jerusalem was not religious in any strict sense and, as mystics now forced to put into words something that transcended communication, the people sitting around Yossef offered a number of options. Miriam said: "I think we can call that "life." We can explain and describe the detail, say of a plant, but not life itself."

This was discussed for a while, and then Uri offered, "Vitality."

Yossef then returned to the original question (about God), pointing out to Iris that her question was both metaphysical and epistemological: "Your question had two parts. The first part, How is it possible that humans invented such a thing (as God)? And is there such a Being that oversees us, that cares for us, punishes, rewards, etc.? The other part of your question was about the mysterious. And when I say mysterious I am no longer talking about some Being or non-Being: can I as a limited being have any contact with whatever that mystery is? What do you say, Amos?"

Amos answered by pointing out the obstacle to true contact with the un-known: "Roughly speaking you can say that knowledge about contact with life can only come when there is no contact with life—only with a thought. Our thinking also allows us to be aware that we are not conscious of the liv-ing experience. If I understand Yossef, when you are perfectly quiet, when you are inactive, you can come in full contact with the experience. When you are active and thinking, you lose that contact." In other words, acting and thinking are obstacles to realizing the truth. Self-inquiry is the process of achieving this realization, and it requires a sort of dynamic inactivity.

This is what Yossef then explained: "And inactivity is a sort of movement. It is not static in the sense of being inert . . . we can't take it apart, but it's a fascinating question. This is because this movement has no beginning; it does not come into being as a result of some causal factor, and it is not bounded by anything else. So how can one react to it?"

Amos added: "I would like to call this 'riding a wave.' When you're on the wave and feel it, you are not separate. You do nothing—you don't fall or jump off. You can't separate your awareness of the wave from the wave."

What then followed was a lengthy and detailed examination of how Self-inquiry acts psychologically as the tool with which human conscious-ness encounters the absolute truth of the present instant, which thought later interprets as the Other.

Later that evening, Yossef asked: "What happens when I meet something that I can't fit into any content? Something more powerful and sharper than my sense of time? Every activity comes to an end. When this stoppage of all activity takes place, we react to that. What is the stoppage?"

Savion replied: "The entire system of response is absent."

Yossef said: "And immediately it (thought) becomes active in response to that. This is very tricky. On the one hand, we see that the source cannot elicit a response. On the other hand, when a limited being that is used to manu-facturing contents and formulas encounters something that is sharp, strong, extremely fast, and not of his own kind, that being stops. It is a shock for him. The stopping leads to some response in his system of responses. . . . Think of it like a shooting star. It is instantaneous, a blink of the eye that cannot pro-duce a response in terms of contents. We stop and then react. But we react to the stopping (of the system of responses), not the shooting star."

The conversation had moved now into tricky monistic epistemology and psychology: where do our impressions come from if they can't be the result of a response to something like Brahman? How does a monist account for the origin of error if the true event (Brahman) cannot be the cause of it? Yossef and others explained that these erroneous impressions emerge from the stopping (of responses) in the instant of encountering the primordial event. But some members of the group, like Yoram, asked how that could be. The stopping itself is unreal; it is not a thing. It, too, is an error.

Yossef then provided a psychological answer: "Yoram is asking how I produce impressions of things past, such as the shooting star? And I say, if this is true, what gets arrested as an impression? I am very scared that there will be no activity. That makes an impression. An impression of what? Of something that is about to be arrested, almost, and that was very special. This is what makes the impression.

"The question is, how does this impression acquire some content? But I want to take this slowly and carefully. Something here became impressed with what happened to me. It almost lost the capacity to react. It stopped, and there was great excitement. This imprinted something: that it stopped because of this event. But the event is already gone. So is the picture that I have, is it of the event itself?"

Although the question of mental contents is both important and interesting, what is of primary importance is how one can encounter the true event in its immediacy. That, after all, is the goal of Self-inquiry. Yossef answered thus: "If there are no contents or preconceptions that I carry with me to meet the event, then there is just the event. There is no event that I am undergoing, just an event. There is no prearranging self, only event."

Savion asked: "Can there be a meeting with the event without that preconceived impression, without any separation at all?"

Yossef replied: "We say the preconception exists of necessity, but if the self is inactive, then there is just the event. Not a meeting with an event.

"This brings us back to Iris's question: the meeting with the Unknown is the dream of humanity as a preconceived notion. As long as man dreams about such a thing, he dreams about something impossible, that needs to be clear. The preconception cannot meet an event in its totality because it has split it up, created a division in it."

It is not clear to me (as a scholar of Hinduism) that anyone in that room had a taste of "vidya" or "jnana," that is, direct knowledge of Brahman (the instantaneous kind, without characteristics).[25] What is clear is that sharp introspection can raise, on an existential level, the question of ultimate reality and its relation to personal and social experience. The map that is thus drawn is different from the three discussed earlier in the chapter: those of Buddhism, Yoga, and early modern Christianity. It is not a map that depicts emptiness, dualism, or theology. Instead it is an informal variation on monistic Vedanta: the truly real transcends thought (and time) and leaves no impressions on our mundane experience. There is an attempt to explain "ignorance" or *avidya* (including giving an answer to Kobi's question at the end), but, like Shankara, this is bootstrapping and thus a failure. This monistic map carries distinct psychological implications (about the self, perception, thinking, and so forth), but little of that is explored here. The subject of consciousness (for example, the yogi's pure contemplation) is also missing from this conversation—but not from the map that guides Self-inquiry at Neot Smadar.

The mapmaking here, the conversation, contains its own crystal-clear reasons for ditching the map after the fact. When Amos tells Yoram that he is unable to hear the sound of his voice because all he hears are the words ("content"), what he is explaining is the total control of conventional practice over the mind. In other words, the answer to Yoram's question is that our mind's habits are, in fact, a sort of fiction. If this view is followed to its extreme, we can say that the entire evening in the Jerusalem apartment with its exquisite introspective observations also produced a sort of fiction.

The following conversation is more psychological and examines a number of linked questions: if the map is correct and Reality itself is in some sense perfect, and if knowing Reality (the removal of error) is so valuable, why do we fail, and why do we suffer as a result?

"Why Do We Suffer?"

The next conversation took place eleven years later, in mid-November of 1996. The participants had now been living and laboring in Neot Smadar for seven and a half years, advancing their Self-inquiry while struggling to turn the desert into a sustainable economy. Everyday life was extremely demanding, especially in the way it challenged any attempt to integrate work with Self-inquiry. The conversation touched on a basic theme in both Buddhist and Hindu thought but turned solely on self-observation.

YOSSEF: Who has a question for this meeting in the sukkah, which we have not held for a long time?

ANAT G.: I have a topic, not a question. In the way that our life here proceeds, in a rhythm and in economic necessity, and in the context of intensive relationships, and in the thousands of details of this place—it sometimes seems to me that our life here takes place as a collection of minute details and the everyday becomes small, like collection of details. The details are important: the financial difficulties, the work that needs doing . . . but there is a feeling of limitation. Sometimes it seems like there is a contradiction between one and another detail, and then you see antagonism.

Is it possible to open up a narrow opening to something that breathes, that is broader, in this picture? What causes us to get lost in the minutiae?

YOSSEF: That was an opening to a question. Now focus all of that into a question, and I will invite people to respond.

ANAT: It is not a new question . . . is it possible, in the midst of life's detail, to find some space? In this life precisely . . . there is no other. Is it possible to do so while working, constructing, raising the children . . . can we find a space?

ARNON: You [Anat] are talking about the distress that results from the gap between my restlessness and the peace I seek. If the conditions here were more peaceful, that would obscure that which makes our life restless.

YOSSEF: What is that restlessness? What causes a person to lack inner peace? People here are no different from people anywhere else. What causes one to be so?

A Buddhist would possibly answer this by saying "grasping," and a Hindu might say "desire" or "attachment." In Neot Smadar there were no doctrinal answers. One looked inside honestly for an answer:

AVI: It's a fear of being truly available.

YOSSEF: What makes him unavailable?

AVI: Fear about myself. Fear of losing.

YUVAL: A constant movement toward something.

YOSSEF: And how do I perpetuate it?
YUVAL: In thought.

But then Yossef elaborated all those answers, which he accepted: "Because I live in continuity! Just look at that."

YOSSEF: A continuing motion, *time*. That is our problem. As long as I have not liberated myself from that, I am not independent and autonomous, and as long as that continues, I am not free. Time is linked to my self-perception as continuous, and that is the problem, and we have not cracked it yet here.
HANNAH: Why does continuity produce dissatisfaction?
YOSSEF: The continuity lays before me desired situations in the future, as opposed to the past, and the capacity to compare produces dissatisfaction.
EITAN: It can always be better.
YOSSEF: Before me is dissatisfaction. When I treat life as a continuous motion, there is comparison and conflict. The conflict leads to dissatisfaction.
HANNAH: What is the conflict?
DALIT: Permanent desire.
YOSSEF: The past brought me to the now. The past holds nothing complete, only fragmented reality. I am at a place where one is engaged in struggles and fear and there is a desire for something else. Can I die to that situation? I am always looking to improve the situation and blame it while looking for better conditions, but there are no such conditions as long as one lives in time.

Yossef's explanation was consistent with Buddhist critique of Hindu theories of time and was easy to understand.[26] But it left another issue unresolved:

YUVAL: But how does this coexist with what Anat had described as actions in time?
YOSSEF: Work and action is a movement in time. But why must *I* be in time?
YUVAL: I need my attention in the actions I perform. I come here in the evening to talk about being outside of time, but all day long I do things in time.
YOSSEF: No! We are trained to do things in time. All the things I do (like raising a child)—why does it make me exist in time? Let's try to understand why we are creatures who are trapped in time and if it is necessarily so.

What followed was a lengthy discussion about human conception of time and the recognition that humans, as material beings, must function in time. But Yossef pointed out that the problem is not time but our relationship to time:

> YOSSEF: It's true that this is the way you look at the world: a description that jumps from one instant to the other; from the smaller to the bigger. But this entire matter, when we are observed by an observer who measures, what happens to the observer himself? Time requires a point of departure according to which you measure the process. There is the measurer—without him, what is there?
>
> YUVAL: The conclusion is that if there is no measurer, there is no time.
>
> YOSSEF: If there is no *measuring*, there is no time.
>
> YUVAL: But matter operates in time.
>
> YOSSEF: That is because of our language as we try to describe something that is not in time; that is outside and beyond the measurer.
>
> YUVAL: Let's say a person who has left time and lives without the movement of cause and effect goes to a stream. He sees a boulder fall—will he not observe a cause and effect there? Will he not know how to be careful?
>
> YOSSEF: Continuity is an extension of points of reference that become possible due to the images that make reality concrete. Is that clear? Even to express a certain cognitive conception, you need continuity. By means of this continuity we try to understand something that is not thus. We manufacture this continuity, spend energy with it, and live in conflict.
>
> MEIR: This undermines our happiness.

The subject of this conversation is the perceived gap between the difficulties presented by everyday struggles and the ideal state of affairs that ought to emerge from success in Self-inquiry. I have excluded a great deal of material but kept the essential elements of the answer. It is that our empirical cognitive self exists in time, while true Reality is extratemporal (as seen in the previous conversation). Indeed, to a great extent subjectivity is measurement, which produces a temporal progression of yesterday-today-tomorrow. This, in turn, causes comparison (to past and future events), and comparison is the root of dissatisfaction. Yossef suggests that although the work of the self takes place in time, it is not ultimately necessary that the subject exist in time. The conversation offers no way out of time, no soteriology, but does offer a clear explanation of suffering. Readers of the *Bhaga-*

vad Gita will recognize the situation described in this conversation and correlate it with the teachings of jnana-yoga (knowledge of the true self) and with karma-yoga, on the practical means of continuing to work in the world while maintaining the self outside of the bonds of time. The solution offered by karma yoga is to learn to perform actions without regard for the fruit of the actions, that is, without making work an extension of the ego's desires and fears. The best example in Neot Smadar of such actions is the pursuit of collective projects, as seen in the next chapter.

One solution to suffering has already emerged in a conversation that was summarized in Chapter 1, "Group and Self," from 1986. That conversation does not fully address Anat's issue—how to combine work in time with the peace that depends on another mode of being. However, it offers thought-inspiring possibilities of how to overcome human suffering. Among other things, Yossef said the following:

> Self-inquiry begins with the study of obstructions; it is the study of my situation as it is, and as I imagine it to be. . . . It is a necessary process for man, an intimate familiarity with himself and a knowledge of his existence so that there will be no events taking place in darkness. . . . These act as motivation, thoughts, and conflicts. It is a dysfunctional situation of disorder. The brighter the light, the greater the order.
>
> This takes more than the need to be active. It requires an enormous discipline of caring, that my life become less wasteful. The spreading of our interest in such a wide range of interests, opinions and opposite opinions, and taking a side in everything that takes place around me—all of this activity is a great disorder. And it blocks the light. Preventing this requires discipline. And it will not happen without a very strong concern, which is accompanied by an extraordinary discipline, a special kind of caring discipline, of sensitivity, not a forced discipline that moves according to some idea.
>
> All of this depends on recognizing our own role. Am I aware of the fact that I cause suffering to myself? This is very important, and I don't want to cause any further pain to myself. . . . I do not want to be a partner in that. How, if I am not a partner, can you possibly cause me pain? It is this awareness that brings about the caring, the responsibility.

In the previous conversation Yossef might have followed his diagnosis (suffering is due to the temporal nature of the self) with a prescription, but he did not. But one solution was indeed available to those who participated in the conversation of April 1986. A good way to undermine ordinary subjectivity—which manifests itself as self-preoccupation—is to end the isolation of the self by means of relationships with others. Yossef remarked that the realization of this truth, that our existence depends on *eliminating isolation,* solves the problem of suffering.

It is important to note that the conversation is promoting not codependence but rather a deep realization that the individual self is ultimately false.[27] Similarly, the individual other (the image we have of other people in our own minds) is equally false and one errs in blaming others for one's own experiences and actions. What is required, rather, is discipline in recognizing the subtle ontological truth here, along with care in following through on a daily basis. This conversation, and others like it, lays down the first markers on the road to autonomy. But, paradoxically, that same road leads to community, one that is based on individuals who seek to achieve self-transcendence and thereby develop compassion for the other and responsibility for one's own destiny.

8

Constructing the Art Center:
Communal Project as Ascetic Practice

THE VISUAL EMBLEM OF NEOT SMADAR is not a goat or a date tree—the true lifeblood of its fragile economy—but an immense and exotic tower that rises above the art center at the heart of the community. The pinkish-blue-beige building draws visitors like a magnet, and up in the tower is a museum that quickly explains what at first appeared like a drug-induced apparition. The photographs in the tower are from the early 1990s, when the construction took place—and the images fix the event in time. The people shown—members of Neot Smadar—are the same ones who live here now but permanently locked into their youthful selves, with long hair and the erect bearing of young people. In the background is the stark desert—the oasis of Neot Smadar was still years away. One is reminded of those old photographs of early Zionist pioneers—people like my grandparents—who "conquered the wilderness" (as the myth has it) and dried up the malaria swamps in the early years of the twentieth century, when photography in Palestine was a novelty.

There were other projects in Neot Smadar over the years—some impressive in their own way: the lake, for example, or the entire neighborhoods that were built to resonate with the desert ecology. But the art center project was immense and, in a sense, primordial. According to Yoram, plans for it existed in Yossef's mind, and even on paper, during his early years of Self-inquiry in the Galilee. Other projects undertaken during the Jerusalem years came and went, but this grand one remained as an idée fixe. The other projects called for cooperation and joint effort; this one would exceed all the others and call for something greater than effort: self-giving, indeed asceticism of the highest order. The word "asceticism" itself never came up, but the conception, including its ultimate goal, was there. On February 28, 1990, Yossef declared: "I have seen no movement here from obligation to connectedness. Where there is no connectedness, people invent the obligation. The latter implies a split within the self, and our school offers people the opportunity to switch from the state of mere obligation to connectedness. This is a unique state of mind, holistic and all-encompassing. While obligation depends on reward and punishment, in connectedness barriers come down and you care for the other without concern for your ego, that place where calculations of cost and benefit play a major role." In other words, Yossef was pointing to the possibility that a healthy society is based on a deep change in human consciousness, which ceases to function with the individual self as its center. Social relations depend on inner work, not vice versa. Neot Smadar was to be a new society, a new culture that required a new approach to the self. This was no easy thing to achieve. In fact, it was far more difficult than even the erection of an immense building erected by amateurs in the hot desert. The building was but training for that other project, and it was asceticism in its purest sense.

The word "asceticism" evokes negative images of irrational self-deprivation, austerities, and even self-hurting. According to the *Oxford English Dictionary* it is "severe" self-discipline and is usually oriented toward religious goals. The history of religion offers thousands of examples, particularly in Christianity and Islam, but they are certainly not lacking in Hinduism, Buddhism, and Judaism as well. In fact, one of the most familiar ascetic narratives involves Marpa's torments of Milarepa by means of the repeated construction and destruction of his home in the mountains.[1] Naturally asceticism is a central focus of academic study, figuring in the landmark works of Friedrich Nietzsche, William James, Emile Durkheim, Max Weber, and a vast number of less-known nineteenth- to twenty-first-century scholars. Alas, as Vincent Wimbush has recently noted, there is little consensus on the meaning and function of the universal human practices that fall under the heading of asceticism.[2] In the words of Yossef quoted earlier, we see an intention that is geared toward a deep understanding of the self and the connection made possible by that understanding to a society that is based on mutual sensitivity rather than the pursuit of individual agendas. The uplifting of humanity to a different level of existence is made possible by that new understanding. The conditions, which I have described earlier as ascetic in nature, can serve as the ground for this new understanding.

This understanding of "training" (my translation of "asceticism") resonates with recent social-psychological theories of asceticism. For example, Richard Valantasis has argued in multiple publications that asceticism at its core is personally and socially transformative: "At the center of ascetical activity is a self who, through behavioral changes, seeks to become a different person, a new self; to become a different person in new relationships; and to become a different person in a new society that forms a new culture."[3]

In this sense asceticism is not limited to "religious" goals, narrowly conceived. Training for a marathon is ascesis in some sense, and so is the training some receive to form special military units. In fact, as a psychological and social mode of being, asceticism may not even be teleological or goal-oriented. If Geoffrey Harpham is correct, it is the basic mode of enculturation or cultural assimilation as a whole.[4] At any rate, there was nothing theological (or teleological) about the art center project, but it does need to be understood in the context of a cultural agenda that I have already discussed as a form of everyday mysticism: that is, the erasure of the maps that constitute a worldview in order to achieve new visions of the self and of sociality. And of course, this takes a very long time.

The monumental project of constructing the art center would stretch well over a decade. To give just one example of the time it took, the doors alone (one hundred of them) took over four years to fabricate, each with seventy layers of polish. Today, anyone (like myself) who wishes to understand how Neot Smadar is a school-based community and not a kibbutz—in fact, anyone who wishes to understand Neot Smadar by means of a single gesture—need only visit the art center itself and read the story of its construction.

With the help of Anat G., who guided me through the building, I was able to piece together the complexity of the physical undertaking. The construction naturally began with the measurements and the digging of

Fig. 13. Foundation work on the art center

the foundation, moved to the cement basement floor, and to the rising cement and brick walls for which no external scaffolding was required (Fig. 13). Although the work took place after regular work hours, almost everyone in the community pitched in. Some spent a great deal of time and effort, others less. A few people stayed away. More skillful members of Neot Smadar did specialized work such as drafting plans, designing and fabricating venting pipes, or fashioning the molds for precast figures into which a mixture of cement and glass would later be poured. These precast figures (such as penguins, owls, and dolphins) formed a major part of the building's façade. Less skillful workers mixed cement or helped with the carpentry tasks. The work proceeded day and night, and people came and went as their schedules and stamina allowed.

The tower presented nearly insurmountable technical difficulties for builders with no experience in that sort of thing. Avi, Yuval, and Gil ran that operation and were fortunate to find a man, Hertzel, who was a retired builder—the man who had constructed the control tower at the Ben Gurion airport as well as others around the country. Hertzel supplied them with the material and with the knowledge to do the job: the key was a hydraulically driven cement mold that rose (on twelve pistons) as the cement dried and the work on the tower progressed. The mold for this specific tower had to be fashioned in the wood shop, and the pistons had to be assembled. Yuval described the very precise execution of the project, including the construction of a bridge for the workers as the tower arose. He also described the grave personal difficulties that arose due to issues of authority and personality—a theme that repeats in the accounts of many workers. Still, the tower was a success and now stands visible for miles around.

The floor also presented a major challenge that drew a crowd of volunteers. The planners wanted colorful patterns that would be durable and made with nonsynthetic materials. They decided to use colorful cement poured into floral patterns bounded by brass and aluminum strips. In order to produce the desired material, they used white cement mixed with quartz sand, multicolored gravel (indigenous to the desert in these parts), natural pigment, water and polymer. The work became increasingly sophisticated as four Chinese workers led the way, but the cement was not always cooperative, and the polishing of the cement had to be done continuously as it was drying.

The work seriously tested the limits of individuals, demanding an intensive cooperative effort by a group of people who had only recently moved from the city and their own professional worlds. The fatigue of physical labor was an issue, but it was dwarfed by the ordeal of working together (without a professional structure of authority) while letting go of individual concerns. It was Iris L. who made it possible for me to understand just how psychologically and spiritually difficult such a project truly was, when seen through the eyes of the participants. If the art center is a metonym for the school that Neot Smadar claims to be, this is due to internal struggles that accompanied the mere pouring of cement and laying of bricks.

The Work

According to Yoram, one of the oldest men in Neot Smadar, the idea for the art center existed in the mind of Yossef before he even moved to Jerusalem and set up his urban commune there. In the life of Neot Smadar, this is prehistory. Kobi, who passed away a few years ago, wrote that the actual planning began in Jerusalem with a few artist friends who wanted to set up a cooperative workshop. Yossef shot down the idea of a joint commercial venture, telling these young artists that they were not sufficiently spiritually mature to handle money together. So instead of building an art center the group rented a workshop in a Jerusalem neighborhood and gradually developed social and psychological skills for working on common projects.

Once Yossef moved with the younger members of the school to the desert, the idea of an art center progressed to a planning phase. Yossef appointed Yoram, Kobi, and Shlomo to draw up the plans. Shlomo was a fine architect and a terrific drafter, a logical choice for the planning group. Some time later, Anat S., who was much younger than these men, arrived at the community, which was not accepting newcomers at that time. But she managed to receive an audience with Yossef. According to her recollection, Yossef was sitting in his underwear and playing the organ when she entered his house. Hearing that she had just finished studying art, he told her about the art center. He described a building covered with precast figures: "When finished the whole thing will look more like a statue than a building." He asked Anat if she could design and execute the precast work and complete it in six months. The young woman responded enthusiastically, and, in what she later regarded as youthful stupidity, she boasted that she could finish the work on time.

She became part of the planning group, a regular occupant of "Room 113" where the planning took place. This work had three main phases: dreaming up ideas, translating these into architectural plans, and presenting the plans to the appropriate governmental agencies for permits and financing.

The point of greatest difficulty was the transition from the dreaming to the planning. Yossef, working with the creative members of the planning group, knew nothing about design and drafting. He would wake up late in the morning and arrive at Room 113 hours after the others had begun the day's work. Then, arms flailing and gesturing wildly, Yossef would describe his new and ever-changing ideas. Sometimes he would grab a pencil and attempt to draw these on paper, but he was hopelessly incompetent at drawing, and it often took days to translate his vague gestures into coherent two-dimensional designs. Meanwhile Yossef would also toss out numbers for height measurements, for angles and for area sizes—none of which worked out with the design that he himself had suggested. The planners were infuriated by these exchanges, which could take entire working days, but this hardly failed to dampen Yossef's enthusiasm. On the contrary, Yossef was the only person in Room 113 who never showed impatience or fatigue with the overall process—as though they had all the time in the world.

Kobi reported that he, along with Shlomo and Yoram, would slave over a plan for days and weeks, bringing it to a state of near-perfection before showing it to Yossef and promising to work out the final kinks. Yossef would look at the plan, listen to the explanations and then toss the plan away, demanding that the men start again from scratch. "Start a new page," he would say.

This happened again and again. The designers would work out a sophisticated plan with minor, workable flaws, only to dispose of it and start all over. Shlomo, the architect, had the most thorough experience with planning, though Kobi had studied architecture and Yoram also was an experienced planner. Shlomo's own difficulties with Yossef were not resolved, and he decided to leave the community, working elsewhere as an architect.

The planning showed that the construction would consist of several major phases: ground preparation (including measurements), laying of foundations and construction of air ducts, cement and block work (for the tower and the five buildings), the making of the precast figures, and the installation of floors, electricity and plumbing, doors, and metal work (windows and handrails). The overall structure would be over twenty thousand square feet, and the tower would rise to sixty feet. Yossef insisted that not a single inch of this grand construction would be the work of professional builders. But the project required a complex organization, and Yossef not only dreamed up the building and drove his planners crazy; he also set up the organization and appointed the individuals who occupied the various positions.

Avi was the work manager, the man who oversaw the practical implementation of the plans and organized the workforce. Kobi was appointed the general manager, and Yoram was the adviser and engineer. The workers were divided into crews, each with a separate leader, assistant leader, and regular crew members. As the construction progressed, the personnel changed; the leaders rotated, and regular workers shifted onto and off of different crews. Everyone involved had other duties in the economy of the kibbutz—their participation in the art center construction was only part-time. For example, the ground preparation began with Yoram, Alon, and Dalit, but all of them moved to other roles in time. Dalit, for instance, became the secretary of the planning room (113). A few individuals, most notably Gil Zohar, were accomplished in so many ways, and made themselves entirely available; they floated among the crews and helped wherever their skills were needed.

In some ways the organization was sensible—after all, Yossef despised experts and expertise—but in other ways it was perfectly set up to induce conflict and stasis. When one thinks of a large construction project—say one for building a hospital—the overall enterprise is designed to maximize efficiency (high speed, low cost) and quality. After all, someone is paying a great deal of money because the need for the hospital is urgent. The end determines the means. Moreover, the authority embedded in a project derives from its financing and from the expertise of those in charge. Information flows from those who have authority to those who do the work, under supervision. These workers are hired based on their ability to expertly carry out specific tasks with speed and accuracy. The whole thing is an information system with a single clear goal: timely completion of the task to a high standard and under budget.[5]

In Neot Smadar, the plan kept shifting because of Yossef's dynamic approach to planning and because of the way he handled his planners' work. The system of authority had three competing centers (not including Yossef himself): Avi, Kobi, and Yoram. Avi had had previous experience as a small contractor in Jerusalem, but he was the youngest of the three and had been with Yossef for a shorter duration. Kobi and Yoram had been with Yossef for years and were both extremely strong-willed and imposing. Avi reports being intimidated by the other two men; he believed that Yossef had appointed him for this job because of his energy and willingness to push people, sometimes harshly. "Dealing with my feelings of inadequacy was my Self-inquiry," he told me, "my crisis to recognize and outgrow." The other two found him somewhat disorganized and saw him as a man who did not mind taking shortcuts; both of the others were fastidious and cautious. In contrast, Avi found that being overly cautious slowed down the work, and he believes that Yossef appointed him manager because his approach got things done. The three men found it difficult to cooperate, and Kobi finally left the project for other work in Neot Smadar.

According to everyone who recollected the project, conflict was endemic and was constantly used as material for Self-inquiry. Yoram claimed that the conflicts with Avi lasted for years. He found himself angry at what he called Avi's "messiness" and "improvisation" and at Avi's inclination to take shortcuts to save time and money. Neither man would yield. Avi reports that at some point he decided to continue working past 10:00 p.m., the nominal stopping time, which caused a sort of proprietary rancor among the others. So he gave as well as he got. Dalit, who spent time working in Room 113 (the planning room), reports that the men there kept "firing away at one another, and at Yossef."

The fighting often included Yossef. When Yossef kept interrupting a planning session with suggestions that displayed his ignorance as an architect, Yoram describes yelling at his sharat, as Yossef called himself: "Yossef, you're getting in the way!" According to Yoram the older man remained quiet when the younger man yelled at him. Others report that Yoram once became so enraged by Yossef's suggestions that he grabbed a computer monitor and threw it on the floor before storming out. Yossef remained unfazed by such tantrums. After all, he was often the cause: "Drop everything you have been working on. Let's go with my idea all the way, and then either we abandon it but learn something important or we adopt the idea." Indeed, it is important to recall that the entire project was not just about construction but mainly about engaging in Self-inquiry, seeing and understanding one's limitations, obstructions, and so forth. But other things made Yossef mad. If he felt that people failed to show up, worked indifferently, or refused to listen, his anger would flair.[6] However, it was difficult to say when such anger was genuine. Avi told me of a horrible fight he had heard in Room 113; when he looked in, Yossef and Anat were screaming back and forth at the top of their voices. But then Yossef spotted Avi at the door and gave him a hidden wink before returning to the drama. I later recalled reading about such a scene in Ouspensky's description of life and work on Gurdjieff's estate.

But conflict was not limited to the men who led the project. In fact, it appears that it was in the nature of working together under extremely difficult conditions that tension, disagreement, or open conflict would emerge.

Avigdor describes his feelings about Alon, with whom he found himself working for a short time: "I was in a situation of knowing nothing—truly I knew nothing about construction. I lacked confidence and wanted to learn, obeying other people's instruction. It was like being a permanent underdog. There was a time I worked with Alon. He is someone who takes responsibility for everything, signs out for every nail. I felt constantly supervised. I lacked the space to make mistakes and things got very extreme—I felt I could no longer work there. But it wasn't really a conflict . . . I brought it up some time later, and Alon was surprised." Avigdor's insight—in his subsequent report on the work—offers a glimpse on the value of conflict for the process of Self-inquiry. His observations are not a criticism of Alon but actually a report on his own state of mind, a sort of revelation that leads to ever-deepening self-awareness.

Some workers, encountering the same difficulties of inexperience, failure to solve technical problems, and having to take orders, seemed to have a somewhat easier time. Iris reports: "I was not accustomed to being in this situation or knowing nothing, only taking orders and instructions. It was difficult and fascinating. . . . The area of the construction was completely exposed to the sun, without a trace of shade, and it all radiated extreme heat. Preparing myself to go was more important than what I did there. I learned to drive tractors, transport cement in every conceivable container, and I felt great." The fights in Room 113 repelled Iris, and she found the actual work on the building far more rewarding.

But there were plenty of conflicts at the construction site itself. Anat S. reports that when Gil came to work on the tower the relationships among the construction crews were not good. Each group leader was locked onto his or her own agenda, and they all barely spoke to each other. Only Avi spoke to everyone—it was his job—and Gil himself showed interest in all the work that took place. He was unique in this. And he was one of the few, Anat reports, who supported Avi.

Effort

As Iris has noted, the work was physically demanding, and the desert conditions were unforgiving. Alon, who was as physically tough as any of

Fig. 14. Pouring cement at the entrance to the art center

the others in Neot Smadar, recalls: "So we started pouring cement and it was getting to be evening—there were numerous complications, and the hose was giving us problems, too. It went really badly. At some point I was so exhausted I literally fell apart. I left the cement area, sat next to one of the buildings, and could not move. My whole body collapsed. This cement work, which ended late, was an astonishing, crazy effort. This hyperexertion was one of the themes of our life during those years. So, too, was the theme of not keeping score of profit, fatigue, time, or how much or how little sleep to get. It wasn't even about testing your own limits."

Dalit reports that even after a cement-pouring machine was available, Yossef often insisted on using hand-held buckets, which passed from one worker to the other. He also insisted on mixing the cement manually (Fig. 14). Many workers objected to this inefficiency, and, given the enormity of the task, their point was valid by any objective measure. But Yossef was looking at something else.

It appears that for some the main source of hardship—and the call to sacrifice—came not from physical limits but from the conflict between responsibility to the building project and domestic obligations. Many builders had small children who had to be watched, fed, and put to sleep. There were times of crisis with a frustrated spouse and even greater problems for the single parent. On this conflict between domestic and community obligations, Yossef said to Alon: "We're setting up a particular order, and each one tries to maintain it as best he can. These are the conditions, and you organize yourself accordingly. That's the material you need to confront."

For others the source of difficulty was neither physical fatigue nor domestic obligations but a strong distaste for construction work. Ronen, for example, loved the farming work and his work with the water system—and felt revulsion toward everything having to do with the main project. Sent to work on the mud bricks, he simply left the worksite and went home. It was clear to him, he reports, that he was packing his belongings and leaving Neot Smadar. Ronen had never liked the work he found himself doing with Avi and Gil, not even during those earlier years in Jerusalem. The building project seemed like a marathon, and he regarded himself as a sprinter: "You start pouring the foundations for a house and in the middle of your work they add another story to the building? What does that have to do with me?" After a long period of hesitation and a cup of coffee, Ronen put on his shoes and went back to join the other workers at the brick-making site. He committed himself to the work.

It became clear to me as I read these testimonies that if a community did emerge out of the individual workers who constructed the art center, there was nothing organic or spontaneous about it. And a community was not the "goal" of the project; Self-inquiry was. The two of these, combined, were the product of many separate decisions, each made under difficult circumstances, painfully arrived at when the goal that Yossef had established was met with a personal assent. When asked what kept him at the construction work, Ronen said: "My signature. Yossef made us sign a declaration that we take it on ourselves to finish the construction of the art center. That's what kept me there." The signature, he later explained, was merely the external form of a deeper commitment to the project or, to be more precise, Self-inquiry under difficult conditions.

But maybe, just maybe, there was more to it than that. Some aspects of the work did become community magnets, like a holiday. For example, the cement work that nearly wiped out Alon called for a major recruitment of hands. Everyone showed up, large crews manned the equipment, buckets passed from hand to hand, sandwiches and drink were passed around—it was a carnival. Alon recalls: "What I remember is the surreal lack of efficiency—it embarrassed me. But I loved the cement work and always got involved." Galit reports that despite all the conflicts she had witnessed among the leaders, "what remains from the entire period of working on the art center is a flavor of cooperation. It is a very strong taste of working together." This was particularly true in the afternoon, when everyone left their specialized tasks around the meshek (farm) and joined the common effort.

At that time Galit was the head of a crew and worked on the building full time. She may not have been aware of the struggles that other workers had to undergo in order to join, or perhaps she has forgotten this. Dalit reports more realistically that people arrived despite being overcome with fatigue after a long day doing other work with which they identified more closely—in the field, the goat pen, the Pundak, and so forth. Whatever else motivated them, how could they desire to continue with this interminable obligation when their own short-term projects had not yet been completed?

The question that remains open is whether art center work succeeded in serving as a nexus that drew individuals out of their personal worlds to engage with something that was greater than that—a common "project." Although I have emphasized the ascetic element, the working to the edge of tolerance as a tool of Self-inquiry, the project also had a sort of "moral" vision. One committed to something greater than one's own personal agenda, something even greater than life. Was this a success? It was mostly the planners, the work leaders, and a minority of the workers who felt connected. These men and women developed a strong identification with their own work on the building—it became the center of their working life. All the others had to struggle, to undergo a test, before they could commit themselves to the art center construction. But even if that "goal" was not met, another one became clear: even failure at completing a task can awaken self-perception and enhance the process of learning inner truths. Meanwhile, Yossef, the teacher, had set up a diametrically opposed learning agenda for the two camps. Those who became overly attached to their personal work on the art center had to be undermined, while those who did not care about the construction had to be turned away from their individual worlds. It seems to me that Yossef's quirky and often infuriating behavior around the project can be understood along these lines, and it is also clear that not everyone realized this at the time. However, now they do; it goes without saying that I would not see any of this today if the reporting witnesses did not realize the wisdom of Yossef's painful agenda in retrospect.

Alon reports that he saw Yossef pressing each and every worker to the limit of his or her capacity, always finding the vulnerable spot or the limiting character traits that showed most sharply at work. With Shlomo it was his pride and rigidity due to his high accomplishments. Yoram, too, he incited or motivated on that point of professionalism, and he was so successful that Yoram simply had to shatter that computer monitor in his moment of rage. Finally Yossef confronted Kobi every which way. When people once asked Yossef why he was yelling at the men in Room 113, he answered: "I'm mirroring those men. Yelling seems to be their way of communicating, I'm merely using their language."

But it was more than that, of course. Yoram, the ostensible "victim" of Yossef's diatribes, described them in his own words: "During all my years of working together with Yossef in Jerusalem, we never fought. Then one day he said something like this: "When someday we shall find ourselves in a conflict you need to remember that the one who's confronting you is on your side. We're examining something together." So what was Yossef examining, what was his intention? There were two or three major tasks that he had set for the workers on the project: supreme effort—what religion scholars would call "ascesis" (training through effort)—and the ability to disengage from the ego's desire to constantly identify with its work. Avigdor described the first of these: the project provided "terrific conditions for self-study. I see it in that you are always in a situation where you can't get everything done. Your work is never finished. There will always be a time when you need that extra effort, the 'plus one.' When you remain calm, you develop the ability to recruit that 'plus one.' This place is designed for such learning."

Omri described the second task, which was far more difficult than going beyond your limits. He wrote about Yossef's treatment of his planners, the tearing up of the plans: "This is something that we have since forgotten, the possibility that your plan will be tossed aside and the flexibility to let it go. Today no one stands between the designer and his identification with his product." This identification is far subtler than merely becoming attached to work one has invested with great time and effort or than the achievements one takes pride in. It's a way of thinking; it is thought itself. It reflects a pervasive attitude about action and time. Alon may have been alluding to this when he commented on the endless discussions about various aspects of the project. He recalls that Yossef suggested that they set aside the urge to decide right away. "Not every discussion has to lead to a decision—whether you like the idea that comes up or not." The act of thinking about a plan, or any act at all, does not have to rush toward a result—it can stand on its own.

Acting without attachment to the product and thinking without hurrying toward conclusions—this sounded a lot like the *Bhagavad Gita* and Krishna's advice to Arjuna. It also resonates with Gurdjieff and Krishnamurti. This was an extremely common theme in the work that Yossef did with members of the school, both in Jerusalem and later in Neot Smadar. The ostensible topic of a particular discussion might be something like "identification," or "mechanical thinking," or "what is school." But the underlying subject was the pattern of self-deception, attachments and negative emotions associated with the desire to achieve.

He would say something like this: "The fear of losing heightens the feeling of loss. It becomes a permanent element in the brain, a strong and permanent mold that constantly seizes on new contents. If this is of interest to me I must become familiar with the mold itself. The "what do I lose" is always changing . . . but I am interested in the deep-rooted pattern that is an aspect of the human mind as a whole. Due to the fear I create attachments and thereby increase the fear of loss."

This is how he may have accounted for the behavior of his project leaders. That is, they became attached to their diagrams and identified with their ideas and their craftsmanship, and all of this was rooted in the fear of loss. To be free of loss one had to recognize the pattern, that which Yossef called a "mold," and break it. You do this by abandoning your designs and do so without a fuss. For Alon this might have been reliance on rules, for Dalit the struggle against her lack of assertiveness, for Avigdor dealing with authority, for the leading men having to deal with competing personalities, for Anat S. the letting go of plans, and so forth.

Conclusion

In the context of the ascetic disciplines studied by scholars of religion, the work on the art center was unique. What was unique was not the effort, the heat, or the psychological stress. Instead it was the communal nature of the test. In order to break the mold of personal predilections and to sharpen Self-inquiry, one person needs another. In their clash, they are allies. Dalit talked about the "viciousness" of Self-inquiry, by which she meant the unmasked nature of the conflict that triggers it. But she also called it "the most amazing gift there is." A polite and tactful encounter could hardly induce Self-inquiry because it builds molds rather than shattering them. In the process of discussing the material that went into this chapter a few members of Neot Smadar became concerned that it paints a negative picture of the community and the school. Others—the majority, in fact—did not think that was important because the picture was truthful. One member, Omri, said, echoing Dalit, "Self-inquiry is blood."

This material fits well with Richard Valantasis's theory of asceticism as a way of remaking the self in the context of a new culture.[7] After all, the psychological ordeals do have a significant influence on Neot Smadar's sociality and personal outlook. But there is a major difference. Most theories of asceticism regard it as intrinsically teleological: it fortifies worldviews and is geared toward explicit goals. The school at Neot Smadar rejects ideology and regards both thought and goal-oriented action as slaves to time and therefore obstacles to clarity and freedom. They also "drain one's energy," as Yossef put it. I believe Yossef would reject any teleological theory (ascetical or other) as an explanation for the project of the art center. In a sense he would be correct, because any purpose that might have been accomplished by the work is no longer part of reality. The workers were not fundamentally altered as human beings; they are not "better" in any sense at all. However, if the project succeeded, it is because the process of the construction—not its product—allowed the workers to see that process and the lesson of the moment is all there is.

9

At Work in Neot Smadar:
Making Wine, Milking Goats, Learning
the Lesson of the Bolt

Making Wine

For a volunteer who arrives in Neot Smadar—as I did—the place is first and foremost a place of work. The eight-hour workday, beginning before dawn and often extending beyond sundown during special projects, presents a challenge, much of it physical. Clearly one does not transform the desert into a source of livelihood without hard work, and few people today go to the desert for a month or more just to hang out. Even the most casual volunteer understands that work, often physically taxing, is the core of life here.

The word itself connotes this. *Avodah* is drudgery and effort, much like labor in English and *travail* in French. Work is what we do because we must if we are to obtain things we need or value, like food and shelter or, in more fortunate settings, luxury and prestige. But Neot Smadar is a school—it is not a kibbutz or a collective farm. So are there two communities folded into one? Does the place suffer from some sort of multiple-personality syndrome? Or does the contemplative activity that describes Self-inquiry—rarely categorized as "work" ("limud" means "study")—extend to the field and the factory so successfully that workers do not even realize they are both working and inquiring into the nature of the self?

These questions may seem like academic hair-splitting, but they are not. In fact, the community has been struggling to answer them both in theory and in practice. Some members have even proposed a nominal split so that those residents of Neot Smadar who do not wish to engage in Self-inquiry will remain at the outer circles of the school and focus on working in the meshek. I am fascinated by this question because Neot Smadar as a contemplative community may offer ways of thinking about work as something more than instrumental activity—as a set of conditions in which Self-inquiry can take place successfully.[1] In order to pursue this line of investigation I have turned to Miroslav Volf, who has written extensively on work and its role in the religious (Christian) life.

Volf defines work in the following manner: "Work is honest, purposeful, and methodologically specified social activity whose primary goal is the creation of products or states of affairs that can satisfy the needs of working individuals or their co-creatures, or (if primarily an end in itself) activity that is necessary in order for acting individuals to satisfy their needs apart from the need for the activity itself."[2] Work often, though not necessarily, contains elements of coercion and subordination. These may apply to social and professional entities (boss, supervisor, employer), time and space constraints, market forces, and other factors outside of the worker's own wishes or needs. But for Volf, the most important feature of work is its instrumentality: the needs that work fulfills are by definition external to the work itself (in contrast with hobbies or play). Finally, as a theologian Volf adds a normative dimension to his understanding of work. The needs met by work apply not only to the individuals but to their "co-creatures." Work, in this view, ought to be a "new creation," that is, a sort of cooperation with God.[3] This approach is consistent with Saint Basil's (ca. 330–379) own understanding of the value of work in the context of monastic life: "So it is clear from this [Eph 4:28] that one must work, and work diligently. For we must not reckon the goal of piety an excuse for idleness or a means of avoiding toil, but as a prospect of training, of even greater toils and of patience in tribulations. . . . For this way of life is good for us not only because of the rigorous treatment of the body, but also because of love for our neighbor, so that through us God may provide sufficiently for the weak among the brothers."[4]

Given all we know about Neot Smadar, it would be absurd to expect a theology of work or even the implicit romanticism of a Jewish work mystic like Aharon David Gordon (who influenced the early kibbutz movement).[5] But perhaps, if we expand (yet again) our concept of theology or religious thought to encompass what is generally termed the contemplative life (for example, mindfulness at work), this would be a meaningful exercise. Precedents for such an approach to work—that is, its instrumental value in promoting contemplation—are potentially familiar to some in Neot Smadar via the literature on Gurdjieff's ideas about Zen.[6] It is safe to say that among the needs met by work in Neot Smadar (food and shelter) one finds contemplative needs of the individual, social or community needs, and the expansive needs of a universal human ecology. Do we see any of that in the work that takes place in the garage, the goat pen, the winery, the food-processing plant, the orchard, the fruit-packing building? The evidence, alas, is ambiguous and comes from my own experiences and observations. The next three sections (wine, goats, garage) deal with contemplation, intrinsic and extrinsic interest, humanitarian husbandry, leadership, and other matters that allow us to examine the meaning of work in Neot Smadar. In the process we shall see that even Volf's theology of work requires a fine-tuning if we are to understand how work may be regarded as a true aid to contemplation and Self-inquiry.

Making Wine with Shmuel

The boutique winery of Neot Smadar is sandwiched between the food-processing plant and the dairy, surrounded by a lush garden with a gazebo at its center. For several years now Shmuel has been running the place. I spent more time working in the winery (*yekev*) than any other place, and so it was Shmuel who showed me—with little fanfare—what contemplative work and equanimity of character mean.

I knew nothing about wines and winemaking when I started, and, in truth, the work was usually either mechanical (bottling) or physical (washing barrels) and only rarely "stimulating" (wine tasting and mixing). The winery is an octagonal structure with each side measuring approximately twenty-five feet. One enters from the north side into a square entryway, a wood-paneled tasting room with an octagonal chilling column at the center. Wine is on display here—all of it organic—and for purchase. There is Mus-

Fig. 15. The vintners with pomance

cat (sweet), Harei Edom (Neot Smadar's special dry red, the winery's best), Shiraz Merlot, Merlot, Sauvignon Blanc, and several liquors (plum, peach, apricot, pear). The wines and liquors stand on a handsome bar, and there are shelves displaying other products such as olive oil and vinegar. The windows are shaded with potted plants. The mood is delicate, without the pretentiousness of some boutique wineries: the framed photographs show people at work—picking grapes and tipping crates of grapes into the crusher (Fig. 15).

The main room is dominated by its octagonal shape, which is framed by steps on the northern side that lead to offices and a mezzanine walkway that wraps around the entire structure. Along the wall are numerous large demijohns inside baskets and several large potted plants. There are more large photographs of workers in various stages of winemaking. At the center of the room is an octagonal marble working space and a sink. The floor is a star pattern that grades subtly toward the center onto two drains. There are two large walk-in refrigerators—one holding about thirty wine barrels and two large nirosta vats, the other with finished products (bottled wine). A cheap work desk stands against the wall beneath the steps to the mezzanine with a bookshelf (holding *Wine Bible, Vintner's Art*, binders and files, and so on) and a white writing board on which Shmuel writes notes and reminders to himself. The whole place stays cool during the day thanks to the chilling column with its underground vent that leads to the space underneath the marble octagon at the center of the main room.

Work begins at 6:00 a.m., but not before I make coffee (as Shmuel checks upstairs on his eggs in the heated plastic hatchery), and we drink it outside, by the garden, with a few dates that Shmuel keeps stored in a plastic container in the refrigerator. Shmuel goes over the day's tasks in a soft and calm voice, unrushed. Reflecting on my work in that winery, it occurred to me that there are ways of thinking about labor as noninstrumental activity without resorting to Volf's theology of work or any other existing theory—not even that of Zen work as a symbolic gesture regarding metaphysical emptiness. A way of conceptualizing what Shmuel does at the winery may be that of Mihály Csíkszentmihályi's "flow"—that is, finding intrinsic satisfaction in the act itself—but even that is not quite satisfactory.[7] A surprising parallel to what I found with Shmuel is the work of Trappist monks—whether making wine or beer or mowing the lawn. According to August Turak, that work is driven by the ideas of service, selflessness, and authenticity. The latter is the value that monks appreciate above all others—the capacity to know and be who they are in truth at every given moment.[8] And that is where they resemble the workers in Neot Smadar.

As an American I think of work as a goal-oriented activity: I work to earn. Shmuel, too, harvests grapes to make wine to earn money for the community to pay the bills. We work now in order to benefit later. The reaping depends on the sowing as the effect follows the cause in time. The more we all work, the more likely we are to subscribe to temporal thinking as a mental force and to experience the present moment as something that leads to a future eventuality. We don't necessarily live in the future (though many do), but we evaluate the quality of our situation in the present by means of its relationship to the desired or feared future.

Shmuel fully and effortlessly works in the present. Of course, he has to plan his actions, set goals, and examine likely consequences, but even then he is fully present now. He is not invested in the future—that is, he does not gauge his present circumstances based on future outcomes. At work he shows no anxiety or worry, no yearning, no trace of anticipation. He works with the mantra "*Na'avod benachat,*" which means "We shall work calmly," that is, we shall focus on what we are doing right now. I might also add that he demonstrates no attachment to the past and, like a dog, holds no grudges. Shmuel's relationship to time exhibits a high degree of what the *Bhagavad Gita* calls "*samatvam*" or sameness—that is, equanimity. He strikes a precise balance between being attracted to something good (as desire) and feeling aversion from something bad. I discussed this quality with others rather than Shmuel himself. Avigdor, who spends his days working in the wood shop, related this trait to Self-inquiry: "Our conversations with Yossef illuminated the point that thinking is essentially temporal and causal. It was a task of Self-inquiry to see this and to learn to deal with the consequences of such a pattern. It's about freedom, actually."[9]

In 2015 my work at the winery came as preparation for the harvest. It was intensive and often strenuous. However, it all began with the annual wine tasting, a late-June ritual in the Neot Smadar winery. In the past a man, Arkadi, would come (charging 10,000 shekels or about $2,500) to taste the whites, the reds, and the sweet wines, and he described them in that specialized jargon of professional wine tasters: astringent, round, soft, smoky, fruity or oaky, rich, aggressive, full-bodied, and so on. Arkadi sat in front of a table with about twenty wines (of different vintages), with a spitting bucket filled with paper towels, and with various snacks such as crackers and goat cheese. He is a Russian immigrant who speaks Hebrew with a thick accent and always begins the tasting with several jokes. He decides how to price each type of wine (and vintage) and even how to package it. He also explains which wines, not yet ready for bottling, should be mixed with which others—specifically for the blend called Harei Edom. We all tasted right along with him—I tried to match the qualities he identified in a wine with what my mouth registered. Like music appreciation or learning to talk about your feelings with your spouse, this is an acquired skill.

In June 2015 Shmuel stated that Neot Smadar had decided to avoid the high cost of inviting Arkadi and that he would run the wine tasting. He invited Arturo and two young men who had some experience with wine to join the two of us in the tasting and then asked each one in turn what he thought about every wine. We tasted in order to decide the fate of each barrel; to finalize the new Harei Edom blend, the new red wine for domestic use, the new topping wine; and to decide what was to go back into which barrel, which combination of the best and the not-so-good. There were four barrels of Cabernet 2013, Shiraz 2014 in four barrels (two good, two not as good), and Shiraz 2013 that could all go in the same barrels; Cabernet 2014 could be mixed in its own barrels (the barrels were mostly 200 liters or about 50 gallons). There was also Merlot that was rejected, and Shmuel would spend the next few weeks extracting the ethanol from this wine in a beautiful old-fashioned distiller upstairs—the same room where he kept his hatchery.

Barrels had to be emptied, washed, refilled, and labeled. A smallish pump ran on and off for hours, and hoses kept changing positions as the wine flowed this way and that. Extra barrels were washed, dried, smoked out with sulfur tablets, and put away. The barrels had been stored in the refrigerator and had to be squeezed out of tight spaces using a hand lift. The whole lot of them then had to be returned to that same refrigerator. The number of actions performed (by Shmuel and myself—and for two afternoons with Arturo) was staggering. One day Shmuel made the following list on his white writing board:

1. Bottling of Sigal (semi-dry red). Transfer to the 1000-liter vat, emptying of the 700-liter vat.
2. Filtering and bottling of Edom (emptying of the 1000-liter vat).
3. Bottling of Rosé in 400 bottles.
4. Separating 70 liters of Edom for domestic use.
5. Separating Chardonnay into a barrel and three demijohns.
6. Making more vinegar.
7. Bottling several liquors.

We got through only 1 and half of 2, which Shmuel noted with no sign of frustration. All of this (and the constant cleaning, the spraying with sulfur dioxide, the topping of barrels, the distribution of wine to the Pundak [restaurant] and the kitchen, and much more) precedes the next harvest and the initial stages of winemaking. This will begin sometime in July with the storage of grapes in the refrigerator, the dumping of grapes into the crusher, the separation of skin and pulp—the noisy work that calls for more hands and muscle. In the summer of 2014 this work was done by Shmuel's son Or and Avivit's daughter Shaked in addition to Shmuel and myself. In 2015 the work was far quieter but equally demanding in its own way. The tasks followed one another relentlessly, each with its many subsidiary actions. Most of the jobs I had to do were new and required instruction. Shmuel is soft-spoken, and the winery is an echo chamber (especially with the pump running), and my hearing is not so sharp under the best conditions. I often asked him to repeat his instructions, but Shmuel never lost his patience.

He explained what he was doing even when I did not ask for an explanation, and he delved into the science—the chemistry of winemaking—because he felt it would interest me (it did). He assigned to me responsible tasks and gently checked to make sure I did not make mistakes, which I did often. His voice never rose, he never became short, and he was both courteous and, during breaks, warm and funny. If there was any hierarchy in the winery as we worked together, it was the superiority of knowledge and experience over its opposites but not of the one who embodied knowledge above the novice. Finally, there were no fantasies about remote or proximate future goals that made all that work "worth it." Nothing was said about earning, about becoming accomplished or renowned, nothing even about a wonderful vacation just after the yearned-for harvest. Each day was like the one that came before and like the one that followed—perfect or painful in its own way.

Still, none of this was boring. There was a deep sense of joy and intrinsic interest—and a perfect example of that was the experiment of combining wine with herbs. It was begun in the summer of 2015 and concluded by the end of that November. Shmuel took a sweet red wine (an organic Cabernet and Shiraz mix) as a base and began to experiment with herbs that Tessa provided for him. Every day for a week we tasted different combinations of herbs, and then I forgot about the matter. In December 2015 I returned to Neot Smadar and tasted the final product, which was then available for sale. The (dessert) wine was intriguing and delightful. The mix, as it turns out, includes sage, thyme, hyssop, sheba, geranium, fragrant oxeye laurel, jasmine, lavender, and fruit of "Tsur Hagilad," which is considered to be the biblical plant used in the production of persimmon perfume.[10]

There is no guarantee that everyone in Neot Smadar works with such profound equanimity. Furthermore, I cannot be certain whether this state of mind is acquired via Self-inquiry or the community selects residents with such a disposition. But the work ethic and leadership in work environments aims to induce the sort of self-reflection that could potentially lead to such presence. I saw this on the date farm, in fruit-picking work, and nearly everywhere else.

Milking Goats

Equanimity, I can assure the reader, is far harder to find while working with goats. Toward the end of May 2013 I asked Daliah—the work coordinator— to assign me for work in the goat pen. I wanted to work with Adva, the woman who ran the goat farm (whose name means "water ripples"). The night before she had objected to the idea of a book about Neot Smadar, and I wished, naïvely, to continue that conversation.

I arrived at the milking shed at 5:45 a.m., and the place was already mayhem, with goat hooves clanking on wood, women yelling, machines whining, and steel clanging. Adva was not in the shed; Maya and Rachel were running the place with a frantic but calm control, while Michael was running in and out on different errands. Maya was a tall and chiseled Israeli woman, and Rachel, equally tall, was a suntanned French volunteer; both were fierce-looking and shy. Neither woman carried an ounce of extra body weight. Like all the other community work locations, the goat pen had a loose hierarchy. Adva ran the place—she had been there longest— and Maya "supported" her and was being groomed to take over later on when Adva rotated to something else. Then came a long-term and usually younger worker (Nurit), after whom came the long-term volunteer (Rachel), the youth worker (Amir), the volunteer who had signed up for the construction seminar (Michael), and the short-term volunteer (on that day this was I). Adva was in another shed, clipping goat hooves, with Nurit helping.

The entire operation was a paradise for milking goats. It was a very large complex of yards, divided by gated fences—about two acres in all. Large boulders protruded here and there, and thick tree branches were arranged among them for those goats that felt the need to climb up and view the others from above. Neot Smadar's goat products—milk, yogurt, and a variety of cheeses—were highly valued among Israel's health food and humanitarian consumers. The yard-soil was frequently replaced: the strong odor associated with goat products is largely due to bacteria in goat manure, and the repeated cleaning made the flavor of the milk products far more subtle. The goat operation was ethical: goats left their confines several times each day in order to range outside, and the mothers were allowed to nurse their offspring for over two months—a rare practice among commercial goat dairies. Moreover, the goats did not have their horns cut off, as was done on so many other goat farms. Furthermore, those goats that were sold for meat (most males and older females) were sold to local Bedouins for personal use and not to commercial slaughterhouses. The result of all this was far lower productivity, at just over 3 liters a day per goat, but the product was highly sought after in Israel's better markets.

Maya asked Rachel to teach me how to milk the goats. The shed had two long, elevated platforms along the walls, one for eighteen milking goats, the other for twelve. Outside were ladder ramps—for incoming goats on one side and outgoing on the other; a gate separated the two. When I arrived, both platforms were fully occupied, and the milking—all by machine—was progressing at a furious pace. This is what I learned from Rachel in the blur of activity: Fill the troughs with pellets of goat food kept in ready buckets for quick turnaround. As the goats lower their heads to feed, the locking arm engages above their necks. Push the blue actuator on the left, then touch the electronic sensor on the left suction handle (there were two) to a tag on the left rear ankle of each goat to activate the suction. Attach the suction cup to the udder nipple, and the machine will do the rest. The milking machine stops automatically, and the cups drop off when the milk stops flowing. The exact amount obtained from each milking goat registers electronically.

The udders are large and full to begin with, and the skin is tight and sensitive. The goats become persnickety if you fail to attach the suction cup quickly, and they will kick you—though not hard—in an exasperated downward motion that nails your wrists. When the milking is done, the udders appear to have quickly aged—the skin is loose and wrinkled in a rather pathetic show of lost fecundity. The nipples are then sprayed with a disinfectant, producing a cold sensation that the goats do not enjoy. A handle on the wall releases the neck holders, and the goats are shepherded out via one ramp while a new group comes up the other ramp for another round of milking and the process starts over again.

Before long I got the hang of it, and then Maya sent me outside to shepherd a new group of goats into the shed. This was harder than milking. The goats stood around in the milking pen, about fifty of them. They respond to human voices and gestures, but reluctantly and (it seemed to me) only when they detect honesty or at least conviction. Goats will not abide irony, half-heartedness, or timidity. But they also resist force; they push back against it. In this respect, Maya was impressive—a woman of clear intentions and commanding earnestness. The accepted verbal cue appears to have been "*Boyi, boyi*," which means "Come, come" (spoken to females), and the accompanying bodily gesture was the waving of both arms in a wide, symmetrical motion, which seemed to suggest "Go, go." The goats did not mind the contradiction and obeyed Maya, albeit grudgingly, with a certain loss of self-respect. Me they found annoying and preferred to disperse rather than move in any one direction. My "Boyi, boyi" was weak and self-conscious, not to mention somewhat self-deprecating. I waved like a beseecher, which also failed to move them.

The Shepherd's Philosophy

Two years later I discussed this episode with Isaac, who had been the head of the goat farm for years before handing it over to Adva. Isaac had not arrived at Neot Smadar with the original group but had joined somewhat later. He is an athletic man in his fifties who had played on a prominent soccer team in his youth. He understood the way that Self-inquiry operates in goat farming, that is, what it is about working with goats that illuminates the working of the human mind.

> ISAAC: Goats are just like humans in some basic way. If you nudge them in any particular way, they will resist and push in the other direction.
> ARIEL: Yes, I saw that—but is that like humans?

ISAAC: It's exactly the same. Even the biology is the same, although for humans the pushing is not necessarily physical or in space.

ARIEL: Can you explain?

ISAAC: Tell someone anything and your listener, if he is honest, will note some inner resistance. Ask him to do something, and his initial reaction is "Why should I do this?" Yossef used to talk about this, and I agree with what he said: human interaction is about encountering resistance and opposition. Sometimes we overcome it (when we act), but it is always there, inside. It's how our brain biology conditions us. We are animals.

I saw the merit in this observation, and it was undoubtedly true as a cultural aspect of Israeli life. Tell me how great your son is at school, and I will immediately think (or say), "You should see what my kid can do!" Americans are less demonstrative than Israelis about their resistance, but they are also far less likely to ask you to do anything for them. A decisively nonscientific sampling of my experiences tended to confirm Isaac's observation, even if I did not share his belief that the basis for this was biological.

ARIEL: OK, so goats are like us in that sense. What do you do with that insight?

ISAAC: When I interact with humans, I neither push nor pull. If something needs to be done, I make sure they know what needs to be done, and the rest is up to them.

ARIEL: Yes. And goats?

ISAAC: It's the same with goats. They know what needs to be done, and I just let them do it.

ARIEL: How do you get them into the milking shed?

ISAAC: They know where the milking shed is—I stand there and tell them. I tell the leader. Then I wait, and they go in on their own.

ARIEL: That's a little hard to believe . . .

ISAAC: The goats have minds, and they are curious. Some are smart and active, others are lethargic. Some lead, others follow. I know each one, and I perceive their desires and intentions. Eventually the leaders go up the ramp and the others follow.

ARIEL: How long do you wait?

ISAAC: As long as it takes. There's no rush.

I asked Adva if she had seen how Isaac works with goats, and her face lit up. She confirmed that Isaac had a special bond with the goats and that

Fig. 16. Leading the goats at sunset

they followed his will without any yelling and waving of hands and that the operation ran smoothly despite this approach (Fig. 16). Isaac called this "inaction in action" and claimed that it could work anywhere, in any work environment. The key was not to impose your will but to allow others to recognize the objective conditions and act on their own. This approach clearly resonated with Shmuel's equanimity in the winery; both appear to be aspects of work that is performed with the insights of Self-inquiry.

The milking was easier to carry out than the herding because the goats had their heads in locks. But both jobs were revealing in terms of showing me the (internal) obstacles confronting the new volunteer and student at the Neot Smadar school. For in working with goats you must confront your own injured self-worth. As a professor I am accustomed to standing in front of my subjects, not behind them. As I stand before a class, thirty pairs of eyes lock on mine, awaiting my words. Here it's thirty pairs of tits and half that number of upraised tails, not even bothering to tell me what they think of me as it's so obvious. In the classroom I am also in the practice of disseminating things to the subjects—information, knowledge—important things. Here I am on the receiving end of the transaction. The milk I don't see, but the pellets that drop at eye level I do. The milk goes into an unseen tank, and Nurit will later haul it behind a tractor—named after one of the goats—to the dairy. The shit drops right there on the platforms, and later, on Rachel's instruction, I shall climb up with a broom in hand and sweep and scoop it all into a dustpan.

I could not help thinking how different all of this—the noise, dust, and shit—was from the place where the milk ended up and where I had worked on another occasion. The cheese factory was everything the goat pen was not. It was virtually silent and disinfected and was run by only two men who hardly ever spoke. One (in 2013) was Gadi, the biggest man in Neot Smadar, who never stops wisecracking—but not at work. The other was Abdo, a worker from Darfur, sophisticated in a subtle way and shy. The day at the factory begins in a bourgeois-style lobby with a couch, coffee table, three chairs, and nice artwork on the walls—sketches of goats on what appears to be goat parchment with attractive frames. Gadi gave me a sheet of instructions to study and handed me over to Abdo, who softly whispered work instructions.

I was told to wear a special hair cover, wash my hands carefully, and sanitize them. Before entering the sealed and chilled workroom, I stepped into white rubber boots and donned a white rubber apron. The cheese work consisted of stacking blocks of goat cheese in three rows of six pieces in several stacks, pouring brine over this, and pasting labels that marked this as Bulgarian cheese. Most of my work had little to do with cheese but was cleaning up after Abdo: soaping and washing the tables, rinsing buckets and crates and grates—some by hose and others in the large dishwasher. It was a white, soapy day punctuated by short stretches of conversation. Abdo had arrived in Israel a few years earlier—he was in severe violation of Somali law and would have to find a way to conceal his whereabouts upon returning home. Abdo supported a family, to which he sent money in a labyrinthine way that concealed its origins in Israel. In Neot Smadar Abdo was able to communicate in Hebrew, English, and Arabic and was highly respected—although he did not participate in the school regimen like other residents or even volunteers.

Rachel and Maya did not seem to mind the madness of the milking shed, or even notice it—they were both immersed in and flowing with the work, and there was nothing for them but what came next: a series of tasks, all performed with quick competence. What was I getting out of the experience? Decades earlier, Gurdjieff had written that people need to be jolted out of complacency, out of their comfort zones, in order to attain a higher level of self-awareness.[11] Yossef, in his Jerusalem and Neot Smadar teachings, echoed this idea. It's nice to get compliments, to do work that the world considers important and that everyone praises. But we learn little from that; novelty and humility are better teachers. In discomfort we truly awaken to what is going on right now: how the body is reacting, how the self we cultivate so carefully is threatened, how the things we cling to slip away at this very moment. We learn what is real and what has been carefully constructed out of illusions.

Was I seeing any of that while sweeping goat shit? Perhaps a little bit. I wasn't really suffering; after all, I was on a mission. Furthermore, whatever shock the work is designed to induce can take time to register; my ego never really left. Some goats, as noted, will kick, while others are tame. After fifteen minutes of milking, I developed the illusion that I had something to do with the difference. I began to believe that if I handled the udder with feeling—the way I touched my cat, say—the goats responded with love. Or at least they would stay relaxed. A few weeks later, when I discussed this with Maya, she confirmed that there were different ways of touching goats (her two favorite goats were Chama and Wodjack) and that the animals could tell the difference. That seems sensible, but I still doubt I could have developed a feel so quickly and under frantic conditions. Still, at the time I thought I was a goat whisperer, but only when the goats had their asses toward me and their necks locked down.

After a short break, the goats were sent out to pasture with Amir guiding them and me tending to the rear of the herd. Amir was a twenty-year old boy who looked like a Bedouin or North African—especially when he was handling the goats. He had opted for national service instead of going into the army, so this was his duty to Israel: loping up a dirt road while hollering and whistling while two hundred goats followed him, kicking up dust that I, trying to keep up at the rear, inhaled. The goats left the pen eagerly and noisily, and they now attacked a two-acre grass patch with great passion. Several fought for space around three plastic troughs and bunted or grabbed the hose I used to add water. The goats ate furiously moving forward the whole time, like lawn mowers locked into forward gear. They never finished the patch they were working on before moving to the next. They were four-legged metaphors for what religious literature everywhere decries as greed, not to mention gluttony. Only when they reached the end of the pasture—where Amir and I turned them back—did they reverse direction.

Work and Young Leadership

Later on, before lunch, Adva called a meeting. We sat under a thatch roof on chairs and pillows, and there was tea, coffee, and dates on a low round table. Everyone except Maya (and me) lit cigarettes and blew smoke at everyone else. I felt the familiar sweet nausea of cheap cigarettes in one hundred–degree heat. Adva reclined on something that looked like an old couch, and as everyone drank in silence she had a mysterious smile on her lips. She looked tired, perhaps as a result of the late meeting the night before. A young woman joined the group, later introducing herself as Hadar. She came from the art center, where she spent the day making ceramic pots for the community to sell. We sat there for about ten minutes then briefly introduced ourselves—I was the only unfamiliar face. Adva said: "The question I would like to raise—and take your time answering it—is as follows: what does this meeting, the one we are having right now, mean to you? I shall leave the question wide open so you can answer it any way you wish."

A long silence followed, and it didn't look as if anyone would say a thing. Adva kept her smile and lit a second cigarette. Maya seemed angry, and Nurit hid her face under a hat, though we were sitting in the shade. Michael looked as if he was struggling hard not to say something—I got the impression he did most of the talking in this group. Finally Hadar said that she appreciated the meeting, being with people, because her own work was isolated and she felt alone. She was in her late twenties and attractive, and I thought she spoke because the silence felt uncomfortable and Adva needed some support. Her answer was anecdotal, and I believed that Adva was hoping to hone a sensitivity or self-awareness that involved giving attention strictly to the present moment. Two years later I would ask her if such questions emerged from the conversations that took place in the more advanced Self-inquiry group to which she belonged. She denied that this was the case and told me that she could not say precisely where these questions came from.

Now Michael felt free to express himself, at length but without focus. He was somewhat older than the rest, in his thirties. He was striking looking, with intensely sad eyes and flowing black hair. He had signed up for the construction seminar, having left his job as a theater director in Germany under sad personal circumstances. Now he spoke about connecting with other people and breaking the barriers of loneliness, but he seemed to use too many words, and, although no one interrupted, his listeners appeared to lose their concentration. As he spoke I tried to read Adva's expression— would she interrupt Michael's rambling?—but she gave away nothing. The meeting was going nowhere, and since she had set an agenda, she had to be sizing up this poor performance. And she was. After another long silence, Adva announced that she wanted these meetings to be a shared responsibility. Both listening and speaking were incumbent on all of us as members of a community, and she did not wish to carry the entire load. "I'm not in charge; I'm not your boss or your teacher; this is about all of us."

This seemed to work, and people, all but Nurit, took turns sharing their thoughts about the meeting. Adva gently coaxed Nurit into saying something but let it go after a couple of futile attempts. This lasted for thirty minutes, and then we dispersed and went to eat lunch. I left thinking that Adva had to be a bit disappointed—the young members of her crew had not relished the mandatory conversation circle as anything other than a place for smoking. But then I remembered that expectation and its flip side, disappointment, were frowned upon, so I wondered instead whether Adva was able to check her feelings or whether she even cared.

What struck me most deeply was the contrast between work and talk. These young women moved fluidly through the chores of running a goat farm, completely immersed in every act and connecting with each other almost telepathically. But as soon as the work ended and they sat down to reflect on their inner worlds they lost their desire to communicate, perhaps even their words. Could it be that work was a better "spiritual" school than the conversation circle? Did they learn something from their competence and the joy of working, and did this carry over into other areas of their lives?

Two years later I got some answers, from Adva herself. In the summer of 2014 she had been chosen to lead the immense summer project (in which I participated), and the year after that she shared her feelings about work and leadership with me, and also gave me the report she had composed at the end of the summer project.[12] She wrote: "When Alon and Dagan asked me to lead the project I was stunned. I thought they were confused and meant for me to lead just one of the work groups. I did not understand how they could be so irresponsible." Adva added in her report: "The moment I said yes was beyond my control. Something in the stars, in God." She tried to get out of the position, even sent in a letter of resignation—which was ignored.

The report continues: "I started the project wondering, 'Why me?' I felt they had decided to torture me—assign to me a task that was two sizes too big for me. I felt frustrated, anxious, angry. . . . The task of leading both the project and the goat farm was huge, and I felt no one understood what it meant to actually run that goat operation alone."

However, Adva then described a dramatic turnaround in her feelings about leading the summer project and attributes the change to the older members of the community who supported her. The support of the leadership crew (Avigdor, Nadav, Amnon) eventually changed her entire frame of mind. For example, they arranged for extra help at the goat farm: they took over the afternoon milking, when Adva had to focus on the communal project. The young woman's gratitude flows out of her report: "Thank you for the shared journey. The start was hard. One clash with Nadav. Second clash with Avigdor. Then, a conversation—opening things up. Coming closer together. An encounter with that which is other than me—without trying to change it and learning to observe myself." Meeting the crew from the project of the previous summer, Adva learned that they were constantly together. She discovered the paradoxical flavor of being and working as a group of people: "In one way or another we were together in this event. A lot of mutual empathy gave us the foundation and allowed each one to remain true to himself. There was no need to push anyone or promote anything. No need for ambition—only presence. There is so much freedom and space in a shared intention and a joint movement. . . . I would describe the energy of the project as a gentle energy. I experienced a project whose heart was relationships, and the work only supported that. I experienced leadership without attachment."[13]

As I look over my notes today, it strikes me that Adva had to have learned an extremely valuable lesson about communication (especially listening to others) and work. The path of Self-inquiry runs through both, but the school at Neot Smadar forces one to refine attentive relationships before work itself can become a place of self-observation. What I saw as a great workplace (the goat operation) was efficient, but the young women working there had a long way to go before working with goats became something more significant in terms of inner work. I wonder what sorts of questions Adva might bring to her conversation circle at the goat farm in order to make the connection between communication and work a true learning experience.

The Lesson of the Bolt

On July 4 I was sent to work in the garage. The date was a mere coincidence, but in my mind the garage is the most American area in Neot Smadar. It is situated at the western end of the long structure that used to be an enormous chicken coop. The space around the garage is a paradise for junk collectors. Old cars that had been parted out stand shimmering in the hot sun: several Japanese and European models that will never be restored. The most impressive useless car, the jewel in the crown of junk, is undoubtedly an early 1990s model VW minibus perched on the roof of a storage shed. There's even a fire truck with its sad red paint faded into the desert beige background. Black plastic pipes lie rolled up near an old air conditioning unit that sits on the grease-saturated soil with its exposed wiring sticking out, as though seeking a power source. Near the fire truck stands a cement mixer surrounded by several piles of worn tires. Two functional trailers stand together like stranded brothers with their rear ends toward a football field–sized area of scrap metal, machinery parts, steel beams—in short, twenty-six years of accumulated debris. This is the underbelly of Neot Smadar, the place where the pristine southern desert must tolerate the refuse of a gorgeous ecological project.

The inside of the garage is not much neater. There is a grease pit and a hydraulic lift, like every other garage. But the place is a mess of unfinished projects, overburdened tables along the back wall, and a plethora of items hanging on the walls with no observable pattern—although there is a surprisingly large collection of timing belts. The real tools, inside two professional tool kits, are kept stored in a separate room that has its own lock. There are two offices, and in the corner stands a coffee table surrounded by four comfortable chairs with filthy cushions. The place reeks of cheap cigarettes, the smell of which made me nauseous as soon as I walked in.

In 2013, when I worked there, the garage was run by Samuel—the most American of all the community members. Actually Samuel is an American, or at least was one. An immigrant from New York who had moved to Israel, he had studied Hebrew and settled in Neot Smadar a few years earlier. Samuel had left an orthodox Jewish life in the States, but he carries himself like a true American male—a bit perhaps like Steve McQueen. He dresses like an off-duty Marine and drives a 1956 Jeep that appears to have barely survived the Korean War. Though fluent in Hebrew, he enjoyed gabbing with me in slangy American English—the two of us violating all the norms of careful and minimalistic Neot Smadar discourse.

When I arrived that Thursday, Samuel was getting ready to leave.

"I'm off to see the doctor," he said and then cursed.

"What's wrong?" I asked.

"Same old, same old," he said, holding up his thumb.

Sometime earlier—maybe a year or two—Samuel had accidentally severed his thumb while doing carpentry work. The thumb was placed on ice and transported, along with Samuel, to Beer Sheva for reattachment. It was now in its rightful place and was somewhat functional, but something had gone wrong because it was turned about 15 degrees. That is, the thumbnail was pointing too far away from proper alignment.

Samuel said: "I'm going to have that piece of shit fixed, by a real surgeon this time."

"You mean today?" I asked.

"Nah, no way," he replied. "I'm just having it looked at right now. Anyway, I'll be back in two or three hours."

"OK, then," I said. "What should I do while you're gone?"

The previous day Samuel had disassembled the two hydraulic pistons that moved the lift on an old Manitou forklift. One was fine but required servicing. The other was disassembled, and Samuel showed me the two-inch bolt that ran up its center. It appeared that the threads had become damaged near the bottom and needed repair. This was not a major problem if the garage had the proper tools: a Murray thread-repair kit or a thread file.

"We don't have the right tools," Samuel said, looking around, "but here, try working with this file."

He handed me a smallish three-sided file from a Nicholson set, and it seemed too big. The bolt was already held in a table clamp, and Samuel pointed at the trouble area. I thought the thread was shot.

"See if you can fix it," he said. "I know you can. When I get back we'll screw it back into the piston and zip it all up. I'm outta here."

And he was gone.

I spent the next three hours wasting time with that bolt,[14] knowing from the very start that there was no way to fix the thread without proper tools. I could have taken my bicycle over to the Pundak—the restaurant—and spent three pleasant hours over a cup of coffee and a piece of cake under a shady tree—with a book or my diary. But I stayed at the garage trying to look busy. Most people find it virtually impossible to report what goes through their minds in any given quarter-hour, let alone three hours. But I had my diary, and there was little else to do except observe my thoughts and feelings, and so the lifeless bolt became my spiritual teacher—and I can report on the bolt now.

There was no reason I should have been concerned about fixing the threads on that bolt, but, as usual, I made things harder than they needed to be. I cared what Samuel would think when he got back. I used him as my scorekeeper. A few weeks earlier, when I had first gone to work in the garage, Samuel had patted my shoulder and said smilingly (after I confessed to knowing little about auto mechanics), "Don't worry, pal, none of us here are real mechanics." There was nothing surprising about that. Samuel had only recently been assigned to run the garage, and Ofer, his chain-smoking assistant, had also joined recently. Like all the people who ran different facilities in the community (such as Adva in the goat pen, Guy in the fruit-processing area, and others), they were not selected based on being experts in their work. Early in the life of Neot Smadar, Yossef had declared experts off limits and insisted on self-reliance and on learning on the job. The leader's position rotated every few years, and the new leader would be someone who had assisted the previous one—but did not necessarily possess specialized knowledge.

The garage had come into existence in the early years of the community thanks to Eitan and Guy (the older one). Neither one of these men was a mechanic by trade, but they turned themselves into competent mechanics who could service and repair automobiles, farm machinery, forklifts, Caterpillar machines, and Bobcats. They occupied this position for several years until they decided to pass it on to someone else, and now Eitan ran the solar panel project while Guy handled special projects and troubleshooting around Neot Smadar. When stumped by some mechanical issue, Samuel would call one of those men, and if the job was especially difficult (or a car or tractor was under warranty), a certified mechanic would come to the garage or the vehicle would be taken to the dealership an hour away.

That first day for me, a 2008 Mazda pickup truck sat near the lift with a new radiator leaning against its fender and a new thermostat in a box on its hood. I asked Samuel about them, and he said that the thermostat needed to be replaced, but he was not sure where it belonged. I went into the office, and after a quick search on the internet found a diagram of the Mazda's engine with a clear illustration of where the part went—that is, where the radiator hose entered the engine bloc. We raised the truck, and sure enough—that's where it was. An hour later I had the old thermostat in my hand and I was flush with waves of pride, despite signals from my brain telling me to cool it: now Samuel would expect me to demonstrate competence on a regular basis.

Later that morning my ego became inflated one more time. After breakfast Isaac told me that the car he used to carry workers to the Pundak, a beat-up old Renault, had a flat. Putting on the spare tire was an easy job— the easiest there is. But I was dressed like a mechanic, and the car was sitting in front of the main office, where too many people who knew me passed by. It's one thing to be a professor who volunteers to work in a meshek, to wash dishes and pick fruit—anyone can do that; but a mechanic? So I got approving looks and favorable clickings of tongues with a compliment here and there: "A mechanic too? What next? What can't you do?"

That morning I made the implicit decision to keep a scorecard, and why not? I was up 2:0, with two successes and no failures. In truth, I reflected as I examined the damaged bolt on July 4, I have always had a scorecard running in my head. Everything was always graded on a scale from "great for me" to "this is really hurting me." Nothing was ever neutral, or, if it was, it was only because of my preoccupation with another matter just then. The very same day that I worked on the Mazda truck I failed to get the new thermostat into its housing because of an obstruction. The only way to get it in was to move the air conditioner unit out of the way, which required loosening the belt and pulling the alternator forward. The work was not conceptually difficult but required muscle and patience. I found out the next day that Dani—Anat's nephew, the kid with the Mohawk hairdo—spent all afternoon working on it until he got it done. Does his achievement take any points off of my scorecard? Is anyone (besides me) keeping score?

The file I had been given to work on the bolt with was hopelessly big. And it was far too coarse. I ran the narrow edge along the thread a few times and looked closely. Nothing seemed different. So I went looking for the mechanic's flashlight—the kind that has a hook at the end for hanging under the car—and peered even more closely. Then I ran the file a few more times, and again, nothing about the thread seemed to change. I took off my reading classes and went to wash and dry them, then started all over again. The threads, looked at closely, were mesmerizing, like op art. The more closely you looked, the deeper the vertigo you experienced. But I kept going, filing a few times and examining the result and seeing nothing. I ran through this routine for half an hour, and then I realized why I wasn't seeing anything. I wasn't paying attention!

To an outside observer it looked as though I was. After all, I was bending over the bolt, I was moving a file back and forth, blowing on the bolt, holding a light close to it, gesturing with my head, and perhaps making significant sounds with my mouth. But that was just an impression—an ape could have done the same things. Meanwhile, my mind was elsewhere.

Ofer was puttering with some job nearby, Shay had just brought in a temping machine and was servicing it, and other people came and left looking for tools and whatnot. I was paying more attention to those things, wondering if anyone had real tools, whether they knew what an idiot I was for using that file. I wondered whether Samuel, with his macho desert boots (the only lace-up boots in the whole kibbutz) and his off-center thumb, knew this job was impossible and that's why he had given it to me (and not to Ofer), to set me up for failure or to avoid it himself. I suddenly realized that if I didn't stop thinking and worrying and being elsewhere in my mind, I could never truly see the thread—not really *see* it. So for a few moments I actually stopped all that noise in my head and looked.

And then I actually exclaimed, "Holy shit! What did I do?"

I had made things worse—a lot worse. One of the threads, two-tenths of an inch from the bottom, had been both bent and flattened, but my filing had made the ones closer to the end of the bolt just as bad. The file was too big, and I hadn't been seeing its damage properly. So what should I do now? Samuel knew the bolt was damaged, but not this badly.

I needed an alibi. So I left my workstation and began a noisy search for a smaller file. "What are you looking for, Ariel?" asked Ofer, the assistant. He knew very well that I was wasting time with that bolt and what I really needed. "I need a smaller file," I said. "The one I'm using is doing more harm than good." Ofer took my file and made a thoughtful sound. I followed him into the inner sanctuary of the garage where the good tools were kept, and he puttered around until he found a box with several round files. Some were small but round—useless. "See if you can use any of these." Then he snapped his thumb and forefinger and went back into the workshop, to a table next to the back wall. He found a box with Murray threaders, but they were all too small. "I have a few bigger ones at home," he said, and I waited for him to continue, thinking, "Will you get them?" But he said nothing and went back to his work, and I was left with the round files.

Shay left his work with a mechanical tamper and came over to look at my project. "Do you mind if I have a look?" he asked. He picked up the three-sided file and bent down until his nose was virtually touching the bolt. He moved the file slowly, concentrating like a surgeon above an open heart, his long black hair dangling over the bolt. After a few moments he said: "Let's try to screw it into the piston as it is." The two of us used considerable force, then stopped and unscrewed the bolt. Shay ran his finger against the inner thread of the piston and blew into it, then reattached the bolt to the clamp and resumed filing. He repeated this three times, for about fifteen minutes, and felt he was making progress.

"See, you need to alternate filing—real slow and easy—with screwing the bolt into the thread, until you work your way through."

"Right," I thought, "and any minute the Messiah will arrive and serve us all espresso." But I said, "Thanks, Shay, I appreciate your help."

Shay laughed at that formal thank you—it was an awkward gesture in the community where the formalities of hello, goodbye, please, and thank you were discarded. But I really was grateful—or rather I felt a lot better because of the splendid alibi he had given me: no one could do this job.

In my four or five days in the garage that summer, I handled several jobs and my scorecard was roughly even. The glow of success never lasted very long—there was always failure, and sometimes reminders of my incompetence waited just around the corner. On the other hand, no one cared about my failures—or even noticed them. This was a significant fact, but at that early stage I still had no idea.

There had been an old Subaru Justy that wouldn't start. It turned over, but there was no spark, or something like that. I was on my own again with that job—no one had asked me to look at the car; I had seen it standing uselessly for a week and wanted to fix it. It was David's car, used for getting around when he did his troubleshooting work in the community. After some time Raviv joined me—he was a young volunteer who was considering the possibility of staying in Neot Smadar. Raviv was rugged looking, with gleaming white teeth behind a permanent smile, and he knew as much about cars as I did—not a lot. We looked at the ignition coil, cables, spark plugs, and distributor.

But you can't fake your way out of a broken car. You can reason through a mechanical malfunction, or you can get lucky—but rarely. In any case, you have to know the basics: the systems, their components and function, and the logic of sorting out likely causes for distinct symptoms. This is called diagnostics. I understood the logic of it, but I also knew my own limits: "It's probably the distributor, and there's no way I'm taking *that* apart," I told Raviv. Here's what Matthew Crawford says in one of my favorite books about working with your hands, *Shop Class as Soulcraft:* "The fasteners holding the engine covers of a 1970s era Honda are Phillips head, and they are *always* rounded out and corroded. Do you really want to check the condition of the starter clutch, if each of the screws will need to be drilled out and extracted, risking damage to the engine case? Such impediments can cloud your thinking."[15] So the problem was not one of logic but one of physical circumstances and my own weakness (laziness) relative to a reasonably clear goal. I reflected that Dani, he of the replaced thermostat, would probably take the distributor apart and deal with the consequences if he had to. I just quit and moved to another job.

I also quit another task: repairing a John Deere lawnmower that wouldn't start even after Ofer had replaced the entire electrical harness of the ignition system. He concluded that one of the wires linking the starter to the battery—running through the innards of the small tractor—had been cut.

"If you're interested in that job," he said when he caught me looking at the mower, "you need to trace the wiring and find the break."

"What do you mean by 'trace the wiring'?"

"You need to follow it with your eyes and your finger." He sounded pissy. Ofer often sounded angry, even when he wasn't, and his constant smoking irritated me.

"But you can't—it runs inside the machine."

Now he really raised his voice: "So open it up! Pull the wiring out."

I knew that was not realistic. There were too many wires, and they were mostly wrapped together in black protective sleeves before disappearing into the underbelly of the tractor. Still, I began to unscrew the panels that could be removed and saw nothing but glimpses of the black sleeves running in and out of greasy components. Before I went any further it suddenly occurred to me that perhaps the starter switch was faulty. I found a red electrical wire somewhere in the garage and attached small clamps at both ends. One end went on the positive terminal of the battery, and the other I attached at the electrical panel to what I surmised was the ignition contact. The tractor started right up.

The rest of the morning until lunch I spent wasting time with the rusty screws of the tractor panels, which covered years of improvised repairs.

Just before lunch I told Ofer that I could not find the problem and showed him how I had hotwired the tractor. Ofer sucked on his cigarette and said nothing. He had to be thinking I was a lowly poseur and should not be in that garage. A few days later I saw the lawnmower doing its work around the lawns of Neot Smadar with the clamped red wire dangling on its right side, where the battery was. I felt a tiny spike of satisfaction, but I was also embarrassed. I was embarrassed for me and a little bit for Neot Smadar.

My biggest flop had been private, and it really hurt. One day Samuel showed me a brand-new injector pump for the diesel engine of that same old Manitou forklift. He himself had disassembled the old one, and now he asked if I could bolt on the new one. It was a simple job—glue on the new replacement gasket and screw three bolts. But of course nothing is as simple as it seems. The three bolts form a triangle, and the inner one goes between the injector pump and the engine body—about an inch apart. That's hardly enough space to get a wrench into, and besides, to get started you need to use your hand, which does not fit into that space. Meanwhile, all of this takes place as your body suffers. You have two alternative approaches: you can lie on the ground holding up the twelve-pound part with your right hand, precisely lining it up with the holes while trying to screw the bolts with your left hand. But the inner hole is not accessible to your hand, and you can't get it started with the wrench. You're basically blind. A better option is to climb the forklift, squeeze between the radiator and the engine, and reach down and hold the heavy part with your right hand while working the bolts between your left thumb and forefinger as your body twists and your hand sweats because it's a hundred degrees in the shade.

I spent about thirty minutes on the floor before conceding that this would never work because I could not reach the inner bolt. Then I moved to the top, climbing over the large wheel and crouching behind the radiator. The first two bolts were fairly easy to get started, despite my twisted back and the sweating. The third bolt—the inside one—took me ninety minutes to get right. How could that be? Every time I thought I had found the hole with the bolt—my body shaking from the effort of keeping the part lined up (the first two bolts were not fully tightened yet), holding the bolt gently between thumb and forefinger, as though looking for the Voice of America on an old Soviet AM radio—the damn thing dropped to the ground. I kept count: twenty-three drops. Twenty-three times the bolt slipped out of my hand and landed under the forklift, and twenty-two times I uncoiled my body, set my foot on the hub of the large wheel, stepped down, retrieved the bolt, climbed back up, and started all over.

It could have been sweat or grease, maybe weak fingers or lack of concentration—I don't know—possibly all of these or none. Once again, I discovered that the difference between failure and success was attention so refined that I could detect—without seeing it, of course—the difference between a true twist and one that was off by a hundredth of an inch at the first thirtieth of a twist. That tiny difference was where salvation could be found—the razor's edge. If only I could shut out the fear of dropping the bolt—or the rage and frustration of the last drop.

No one saw my grotesque odyssey; they all seemed busy with their own quiet battles. So what was the flop, and how was it private? On my eighteenth or nineteenth descent—I was probably swearing at myself—I missed the wheel hub after I had already committed all of my momentum downward. My right leg slipped against the axle, and my left leg rushed backward to compensate and hit the ground too far forward, and I hit the cement with the left cheek of my butt, twisting myself clockwise—the same direction I had been crouching while supporting the heavy injector pump. Naturally I wrenched my spine and pelvis and spent the rest of the summer in pain and limping like an old man who could not get the job—any job—done. That was my flop, a couple of weeks before July 4.

Standing now over the bolt with the file in hand—it had been over two hours—shifting my weight constantly to ease my backache, I reflected on my situation. There was my obvious lack of experience in the garage, but that was extenuated by the absence of tools. More to the point, to be honest, I cared too much about being evaluated. Hell, I was constantly judging myself, and harshly. But I now realized that this, too, was not the more basic problem. No, underneath was a deeper issue. It seemed that everything I did—filing a bolt, replacing a part, even making coffee at the garage, all of it—was chained to the idea of a goal. I enslaved myself to the end-means mindset, to the path and its destination. I surrendered whatever freedom might be available in any action done for its own sake, in the true present time, by coupling the act with a consequence. I thought: "It's not whether

Samuel will be pissed off or not . . . *I'm* the one who's upset because my filing has to lead somewhere, but it cannot." My dilemma, the paradox here, was of my own making. If only I could play with the bolt, or with anything else—the sort of game that does not have a winner or loser. Just like kittens wrestling. But consequences held me by the throat—long before I worried about judgment.

When Samuel came back, we tried to screw the bolt into the piston and assemble the hydraulic mechanism. We were only off by a fraction, and we discussed the possibility of sawing the bolt by a quarter of an inch or so. But then I was sent to another location, and I never did find out what Samuel did (the simplest solution would have been to buy a replacement bolt for about three dollars). After returning from the doctor, Samuel said nothing at all about the filing, and I saw no evidence that he gave it a thought. He just hit the ground running—no gathering of historical information, no looking back.

The drama had been entirely my own production. The bolt was trying to teach me a lesson, and it took the painful recollection of my back-flop to wake me up to the fact that this was not a garage at all but a classroom in a school. That, I believe, is how Yossef understood Neot Smadar as a school, although it is hard to be certain ten years after the man passed away. I decided to continue this sort of study and to observe how others in Neot Smadar are doing on this path. It doesn't matter how old you are, how well educated; this study is extremely hard to do—that is, to remain perfectly naïve in the present moment and to treat work as a noninstrumental activity, even when it is essential. The term in religious literature is "mindfulness," or perhaps "presence." It depends on honest inner observation and a willingness to confront the mind's hyperactive meandering and exaggerated attention to the self. And I believe that Yossef, who was following in the footsteps of Gurdjieff, understood that it's the daily task and the routine experience that offers the best path for Self-inquiry to the modern student.

The Extended Family:
Sociality in Neot Smadar

IN 2015, A FEW DAYS AFTER THE FESTIVAL of Shavuot, the holiday that cele-
brates crops and the giving of the Torah on Mt. Sinai, I heard the following:
according to Jewish tradition, when Moses came down the mountain there
were six hundred thousand Israelites waiting for him below. Each one of
these Israelites was expected to give himself wholeheartedly to the new
Torah, and each one of them had to be completely certain that every one
of the others also gave himself to the Torah and supported all the others
entirely. These were the conditions for receiving the whole Torah, and that
was also a description of the perfect community. I heard this from Omri,
who in the summer of 2015 was one of the two secretaries of the school at
Neot Smadar, and I took it as a parable for what Neot Smadar can be as a
community.[1] Interestingly, Omri did not point out that, given the fulfill-
ment of these two conditions, the Torah, or at least the commandments,
would become superfluous from the legal and social point of view.

For a historian of religion who works with religious traditions, denom-
inations, congregations, sectarian groups, and so forth, it is not easy to
determine where Neot Smadar belongs on the spectrum of "religious" communities. The subject is usually dominated by sociologists and anthropologists under the heading of sociality and includes such areas of research as
charisma, communitarianism, renunciatory or monastic organizations, natural versus intentional communities, new religious movements (NRMs),
and, in Israel, kibbutz studies (socialist utopias). The category of NRMs,

previously "cults," is where most sociologists would situate Neot Smadar, and the concept of charisma would dominate their analysis of its sociality. There is no doubt that Weber's theory of charisma has influenced the way that NRMs have been analyzed, and the concept has transferred neatly from sociology to religious-historical research, for example, in explaining the ways Jesus may have communicated his vision to others and empowered his followers.[2] Charisma is a familiar answer to the dilemma of social cohesiveness, and it is a religious, perhaps magical, solution, though it remains subject to reductive sociological theorizing.[3] The Weberian understanding of charisma as reputational authority would appear to apply to the leadership function of Yossef as Neot Smadar was established. And, in keeping with the theory, after Yossef's passing, the question of maintaining authority also appears to point toward bureaucratization or rule-making in response to the loss of charisma. In Neot Smadar, as in other religious communities, Weberian theorists may seek to identify the way that both charisma and institutions enable groups to overcome a basic structural conflict between social needs and individual impulses by means of distinctly religious factors.

However, other types of scientific theories have sought to account for the way that religion is implicated in the formation and solidarity of communities. For instance, in the past two decades, "rational choice theory" has actually pursued such a task in biological (and economic) terms, and several researchers have looked for evolutionary ways of explaining the factors that account for social cohesiveness and the perceived benefits of such values as altruism in the face of selfish interests.[4]

How can such reductive theories (including that related to charisma) be reconciled with the conscious reflection of community members (men like Omri or Alon) on the nature of their own sociality? After all, many residents are somewhat familiar with academic theories while rejecting their applicability to the school and the community of Neot Smadar. The Shavuot story Omri told me is about the intentional personal acceptance of a value and a vigilant trust in others to do the same. Should we ascribe such trust to the magnetism of a charismatic leader (Weber did not regard Moses as such a man) or to the genetic inheritance of successful evolutionary forces—both of these theories deploying mechanistic causal factors? What should we make of the conscious and often skeptical thinking of the community members concerning sociality and their ever-present vigilance about their own unity? The very conflict identified at the core of all community existence—the centrifugal and centripetal tug and pull of competing forces—represents one of the tasks of Self-inquiry in facing objective conditions at the school in Neot Smadar.

For example, it is an inescapable aspect of a working economy (meshek) with communal features that some individuals do more than others. As a result, those who happen to manage the work (the secretary or work coordinator) experience and even embody the internal stress that comes with trying to promote fairness. In 2010 that individual was Anat G. (the secretary at that time), who read a critical report to the group of veterans in which she openly shared her deepest feelings. The report was not merely an exercise in venting frustration; it was an impressive demonstration of the self-awareness that runs through Neot Smadar as a spiritual but working community.[5]

In order that a distorted picture not emerge from the emphasis of this meeting, I will begin by saying—and this is a subterranean stream that runs through this report—I have been privileged to receive trust and support, to try the unknown, that is, this challenge from one moment to the next. I have encountered love; I am surrounded by love. I have grown and become wiser, and I empty and meet myself in a naked mirror that is uncompromising. . . . This love is with me all the time, and there is a deep gratitude, but at the same time I need help, personally and professionally, I need help from the cosmos, from existence, from humans, and from the depths of my heart.

What is my problem? I ask what are we doing here, what is this togetherness, for what? Activity and more activity and then what? Why do I ask? Because in the crossroads of my position I encounter in a stark way the disintegration [of our world].

The reality, as it is, the separation, so to speak, strikes forcefully. It brings out individual ambition, lack of support, territoriality, and gossip—all of these accompanied by strong feelings. This is due to the fact that it is expected of me, in my capacity as secretary, that I help maintain an atmosphere that will enable us to work and live together. But say I had amazing charisma and I could unify all these contradictions and conflicts through my charisma, unite everyone—after all, that is what Yossef did. But this cannot work on the basis of someone else's charisma, and the fact is that he is gone. And so—where do we proceed from here?

In a sense Anat appeared to implicitly conform to Weber's theory of individual charisma as a solution to the problem of sociality. But if she truly had done so, she would have proposed strengthening the institutions that were meant to replace the role of Yossef. She would have offered rules and suggested that certain offices would receive greater authority.[6] Instead she offered the following:

> According to Kabbalistic terms, harmony is expressed by the statement Love thy neighbor as thyself. As I understand this, there can be no meaningful Self-inquiry without humility, and this subject is out of focus. We can talk about it a great deal and with great sophistication, but in reality, on the ground, in the flesh, when the ego is swollen, in my view, there is no Self-inquiry, and all the verbal display and the intellect—and even actions—are a mere illusion.
>
> Today I see the disintegration in me and in others. In other words, disintegration is the profane—that which is not sacred—grains and grains of sand and the intensity of our life emphasizes and reflects that situation because there is no energy to hide the truth. And my job, as secretary, is super-intensive and I am not immune to negative emotions.

This remarkable statement reveals that the true value of Yossef was not his personal charisma but something that he pointed at for others to see, something sacred, accessible via Self-inquiry and something that acts as the root of harmony. According to Victor Turner, reflecting on maintaining charisma in the absence of the charismatic leader, the key is celebrating "anti-structure" in order to maintain *communitas* and doing so with celebrations, festivals, and other performances.[7] In pointing to the absence of Yossef's vital influence, Anat also hints that charisma is accessible, but only if Self-inquiry holds sway. So what is it? What is the communal force generated by Self-inquiry? In order to capture this elusive reality, Yossef called Neot Smadar "an extended family" (mishpaha murhevet). Today, too, that is where the answer to the community's sociality should be sought and where we should look.

The Extended Family

The Israeli kibbutzim, in their early years of the early 1920s, never called themselves families. They used the word "*kvutzah*," sometimes "*kehilah*," which is an excellent translation of "community" (*Gemeinschaft*). These were their charismatic years, soon giving way to "kibbutz" and its institutions and rules.[8] Neot Smadar started out as an extended family, and so it remains today.

Early on Yossef insisted on monastic-style separation of the sexes: couples spent the nights in separate housing, and families were temporarily split up. This lasted for about six months, a period long enough for people to reflect on the limitations of family- and couple-based islands of attachment within the larger community. According to Carmela, who recently reflected on Yossef's intentions, Self-inquiry is individualistic in the same way that consciousness is personal. Coupling can diminish this individual focus, and the intimate couple represents the weakened agendas of two individuals who have forgotten why they came to Neot Smadar.[9] However, ironically, Self-inquiry is also a joint venture, and the life together of all the individuals who choose this path invites one to "cross the boundaries" of personal needs and attachments.

The first general principle of the school is that it exists as an "extended family." This implies that a way of life and systems of relationships of an extended family create a necessary foundation for the community, whose essence is Self-inquiry (see Chapter 10). The condition of the school is deep cooperation, mutual accountability, respect, trust, and friendship. But this is not the ordinary and familiar family-oriented community. It is a condition that invites the opportunity to touch (and challenge) basic elements of human existence, such as absolute identification with one's own family and children, defense of the boundaries of "mine," and acceptance of the obvious in relationships. The individual is invited to expose and deeply explore the array of prejudices and conditioning in this field. At the same time, due to the very existence of such a community, some needs arise that are not directly related to the school, namely, needs in the areas of health, education, and finances. Even these mundane concerns need to be addressed under the canopy of the school.

Today the extended family concept plays out in many ways both subtle and obvious. The clearest example is the mutual warmth and physical closeness on constant display in Neot Smadar. Warm embraces are commonplace, men and women demonstrate spontaneous physical affection, people are generous with their time and show attentiveness to others; they avoid cliques and always make room for others to join in on conversations. According to Ilana, the most illustrious demonstrations of the extended family concept are Shabbat dinner and Saturday breakfast—festive affairs at which "family tables" are open to others, when song circles open up for all to join, and when sharing food and conversation feels natural. In Neot Smadar children run about, and the young ones are picked up by and snuggle against adults who are not their parents—everyone is an uncle or an aunt. Moreover, young members of the community are attached as "uncles" to families with children in order to create new relationships, to mix populations, to help and be helped. Even the children going through their "dreadful twos," when babies fear strangers, interact with no drama. The extended family manifests itself in the rotation of homes or, better yet, in the easy willingness to share space with others (including visitors like myself) and the absence of possessiveness with regard to property, food, or honor. As Ilana put it to me, the extended family is about the *feeling* of being together, not the idea. "It comes from the heart."[10]

At the same time, with the rare exception of a young volunteer couple, married couples avoid showing any physical intimacy in public, holding hands, whispering, or carrying on private conversations. A novice would have a hard time trying to identify the actual couples and the families— who is paired up with whom. I asked several members of the community about intimacy and the absence of even a tame gesture like the holding of hands, and the answers I received (from Avigdor, Isaac, Galit, Shlomit, Shmuel, Carmela, Iris L., and others) were consistent: "The gesture is a demonstration of attachment—he is mine, I belong to her, we are some- how different, or separate, from the others in the way we are together." It is important to bear in mind, as we read such an explanation, that the goal of Neot Smadar's sociality is not social cohesion but individual Self-inquiry. So the point my informants are conveying is not that intimacy disrupts an ideal but that it may distort the simple but difficult practice of Self-inquiry: "If I identify myself with my wife or my children (the words of Avigdor), I am strengthening an aspect of cognitive self-awareness which Self-inquiry seeks to illuminate and transcend."

I asked my informants: "What about private intimacy? Is there any emotional space reserved just for my partner, when we are alone together?"

Carmela, who is married to Rony, confessed that this was a difficult question to answer—due to the difficulty in discriminating and isolating those emotions reserved for just one person. On the subject of intimacy she explained: "What is the intimacy of a couple, and what is the intimacy of a group of people? Certainly Neot Smadar allows for the couple's intimacy, but there is also a special sort of intimacy among people in general. A person feels the closeness and trust that usually characterizes a family or a few old friends. A special sort of language has formed here that allows people of different backgrounds, or those who have just arrived, to open up and share with confidence. This is a special situation that encompasses those who arrive almost immediately."

In some respects, then, Neot Smadar is a complicated monastery with the appearance of a commune. Multiple generations of well-adjusted individuals share a life in a beautiful place where romantic intimacy takes its place in a broader context of unusual public caring. But the picture, naturally, is more complicated. Young members of the community—unlike the older informants I have cited—sometimes experience loneliness and unfulfilled desire. Straight or gay, it can be very difficult for some members of such a small community to find love, perhaps marry and raise children. The young families in Neot Smadar (Guy and Vered, Dagan and Eleanor, Natalia and Doron, and others) arrived as families, and many formed in Neot Smadar (Maya and Dani, Noam S. and Sivan, Sharon and Nadav, Shirley and Adi, Carmela and Rony, Arturo and Karen, etc.). Most of these couples and the single men and women in their twenties and thirties did not study with Yossef, and they may be reflecting the ever-changing aspect of Self-inquiry as a rigorous practice. Will this younger generation, whether their emotional needs are met or not, change the nature of Neot Smadar's sociality? However, to return to the main issue at hand, what is the theory behind this sort of paradoxical togetherness, where neither charisma nor institutions hold sway and Self-inquiry promotes empathy?

To put this in more religious terms, how can contemplative practice, which may undermine intimate emotional attachments, lead to a social existence of such high cohesiveness and affective satisfaction? Before attending in detail to the folk theory that accounts for this, I must look briefly at other examples of what may be termed "mystical sociality."

Mystical Sociality

Interestingly, this is a paradox that runs through postmodern social thought and postmodern liberation efforts—including the formation of intentional communities and other forms of mystical utopianism. Philip Wexler has carefully dissected this phenomenon in *The Mystical Society*: "We are forgetting the determinative power of organized social life, social structure, and technology to affect not only meaning and identity but also the conditions of experience and, perhaps most importantly, to set the terms for opposing, transforming, and transcending the social present."[11] Mysticism, according to Wexler, is where this paradox (it takes a group to break the hold of the group) can be overcome in order to salvage authentic being as it acts in a sublimated "de-repression" (the removal of what many in Neot Smadar call conditioning). Mysticism works in three ways: It enables a practical return of the sacred to social life. It provides interpretative categories for understanding social life. And finally, it provides the space for the social imagination to become actualized in practice.[12]

In seeking to perform all three functions, a community like Neot Smadar could serve as an isolated laboratory where we might eventually see the emergence of analytical categories that overcome the untenable paradoxes of individual versus society and contemplation versus action. At this point even the most advanced students at Neot Smadar are locked into the conceptual paradoxes I have described. The same students who reject ontological and analytical categories and promote a radical indeterminacy when it comes to Self-inquiry continue to abide by the concepts of individual and community, charisma and persuasion, contemplation and action as binary oppositions. Is there a way to honor that indeterminate epistemology and at the same time understand social and economic life in Neot Smadar as organically related to the school in conceptual and practical terms? If Wexler is correct and the secret is mysticism, we need to look at the way that mysticism combines contemplation with action and the way that it promotes sociality while rejecting society as a conceptual category.

In Chapter 7 I defined mysticism as a particular approach to the construction of cultural maps and the systematic reading of the maps in a way that undermines their validity. Considered from the perspective of discourse, this was an auroboric activity, both self-referential and self-contradictory. However, throughout the twentieth century mysticism was understood in a variety of far more concrete ways, as, for example, direct knowledge of God or Ultimate Reality, a special philosophical epistemology, a set of contemplative practices, and so forth. Those who identify today an implied conflict between mysticism and daily work are demonstrating the influence of those theories that regard mysticism as a subjective phenomenon, be it spiritual or psychological. As Ruffing puts it: "The increasing privatization of religion in general during the modern period has tended to separate mysticism, often referred to historically as the contemplative or inner life, from the worldly life of politics, commerce, academics, and public life."[13]

I have repeatedly encountered members of Neot Smadar who think about mysticism as an altered state of consciousness or as access to some other nonordinary reality that may or may not conform to the ordinary life of work and community. One member reminisced sadly about the day she realized that "this is all there is," that years of Self-inquiry did not lead to illumination or a radical transformation of consciousness and she noted that it was too late to turn back.[14] Such an expectation, or judgment, is both a personal and an academic straightjacket that limits the historical record of mystical action to just one dimension.[15] My own institution—Georgetown University, which is Jesuit in its origins and ostensible ideology—draws on the thought and actions of Ignatius of Loyola as an example of the possible interplay between mystical introspection and sociopolitical action. A relationship with God, directly obtained, is about performing actions in the world as servants of a "Royal Household" and is not an exclusive and intimate moment: "Love," Ignatius says laconically, "manifests itself in deeds. . . . This priority of action, and so the need to be good at what one does . . . is the most characteristic feature of Ignatian spirituality. It is a mysticism of effective and transformative action in a world, undertaken as a mission from a beloved sovereign."[16]

But even the less institutionally active mystic, Meister Eckhart (whom Rudolf Otto used as an example of pure introspection) demonstrated that the highest form of contemplation leads to "truly just and efficacious work."[17] Bernard McGinn clearly summarizes this relationship: "Although . . . the goal . . . of mysticism may be conceived of as a particular kind of encounter between God and the human, between Infinite Spirit and the finite human spirit, everything that leads up to and prepares for this encounter, as well as all that flows from or is supposed to flow from it for the life of the individual in the belief community, is also mystical, even if in a secondary sense."[18]

A familiar modern example of this relationship can be seen in the life and writings of Thomas Merton. According to Philip Sheldrake, this relationship was not a compromise or an extension of one reality (the spiritual) to another (society). Although Merton began his spiritual career with the understanding that an opposition had to be overcome between God and the world, by the 1960s, as his spiritual understanding deepened, Merton saw the matter differently: "It was like waking from a dream of separateness, of spurious self-isolation in a special world, the world of renunciation and supposed holiness. The whole illusion of a separate holy existence is a dream."[19] In fact "the self," the inner sprit of man, truly exists only in community and solidarity with others—it has no other reality.[20] As a result, mystical contemplation itself must be radically reevaluated: "The spiritual life is not a life of quiet withdrawal, a hothouse growth of artificial ascetic practices beyond the reach of people living ordinary lives. It is in the ordinary duties and labours of life that the Christian can and should develop his spiritual union with God. . . . Christian holiness in our age means more than ever the awareness of our common responsibility to cooperate with the mysterious designs of God for the human race."[21]

These evocative words ("the dream of self-isolation") remind us that underlying the ostensible conflict of mysticism and everyday life is not just a theology of separation but also an individualistic psychology that posits the empirical reality of a separate self and the abstract reality of society or community as the aggregate of such selves. This is a historical construction, and I return to it shortly when I discuss sociality.[22] It bears stating what may be obvious to many readers, namely, that socially proactive (indeed, reforming) mysticism is widespread in Judaism, Islam, Hinduism, and Buddhism, as well as Christianity. The social mysticism of Hasidism and its contemporary philosophical expression in Buber's *I and Thou* are familiar to everyone in Neot Smadar. Less known are the devotional mystics of early modern India, such as Sri Caitanya or the Aghori mystics (followers of Baba Kinaram) of Varanasi today and, in Buddhism, the broadly conceived concept of the Bodhisattva or the political spirituality of Tibetan Buddhism.[23]

In a place like Neot Smadar the distinction between Self-inquiry (contemplation) and social action—vital as it may be—is a practical matter and therefore visible. Underlying it, however, is that more subtle and insidious obstacle to well-being. This is the historicity of our intuition of selfhood as an individual matter. We see this even in the observations of people like Yoram about social conditioning. If Self-inquiry is ultimately about unraveling this conditioning, there is the risk of enshrining the view that individuality and sociality are antagonistic and in the very act of contemplation strengthening a different illusion and creating a new obstacle. For example, underlying this assumption about personhood is the notion of interiority into which society "injects" its content via enculturation and socialization. This is pure ideology, of course, and a fairly recent (and western) conception, individual psychology.[24] So can that same contemplation—that is, Self-inquiry—lead to the insight that ontologically speaking the self is radically like the other and that sociality is not an aggregate but something more essential to the self's deepest aspirations?

Omri and the Extended Family

Over the past two summers I carried out detailed interviews with Omri, who today is one of the two secretaries of Neot Smadar. Omri is one of the older members of the community, a lean man with curly black hair who rarely speaks and tends to shut his eyes when listening to others. Omri struck me as one of the most dedicated practitioners of Self-inquiry, a man who tries to apply it throughout the day—without much fuss. The following is an abbreviated transcript of a 2015 conversation that begins with Omri explaining why he cannot necessarily repeat some of the things he had said the year before.

OMRI: I do not hold a conception of Self-inquiry in my head as a sort of discipline (*torah*). I do not hold onto knowledge in such a way. What I said last year changes according to context and circumstances, certainly my approach or perspective changes. The important subject is the classical one: what is a person's purpose (*yi'ud*)? Or rather, what is the most fitting social arrangement for a person, what is the most appropriate state of consciousness, state of existence?

ARIEL: Self-inquiry is a changing activity?

OMRI: Self-inquiry has two aspects. On the one hand, it is basic to humanity —at least ideally—but life is dynamic and ever changing, as the Buddhists have so insistently pointed out. Self-inquiry is about keeping awareness open to the fact of this impermanence. Man receives that which is essential by contact with the present, not contact with ideas.

ARIEL: So the role of the school is to provide the optimal conditions for a person who wishes to inquire about the nature of the self?

OMRI: On the one hand, it provides an opening in the system of mechanical, conditioned responses on which he depends. It provides the opportunity to stop and develop careful attention. On the other hand, the conditions make it possible for this attention to develop and grow, to renew itself and constantly break new ground.

ARIEL: Do the conditions include activities that are necessary for survival?

OMRI: Yes. We value the economy as an extraordinarily effective learning opportunity. It is one of the strongest features of the school here.

ARIEL: Why is that?

OMRI: We would like to see the Self-inquirer learning to meet himself as he is. There is no need to create artificial conditions (such as a monastery or ashram) because he encounters himself as a human being, and the point of departure is life itself.

It is easy to see how the individual is a forward-skipping creature, moving toward an idea, toward something sacred. But in the process he skips over the present moment. We want him to learn what there is, not what ought to be (that comes later and is special in its own way). Earning a living, work, economy, leading a work group—all of that is part of reality, and it is actually a gift.

We learn in our school as a sort of fine hothouse—not entirely disconnected from reality but in a sense separate so one could act calmly. It is all about acting calmly, now.

ARIEL: How does all of this translate into social relationships?

OMRI: That is a complicated matter, but it has to do with attention, with conversation, and with the absence of response. For example, the head of the date farm during an intermission organizes a conversation circle in which he invites his workers to learn how to participate in a conversation without response. When someone in a group speaks, we have an obsessive need to respond. Even if we don't speak, our minds manufacture a response. I listen, but if I suddenly respond the response becomes the main thing, not the listening. That is where attention comes in—it keeps us from this pattern.

ARIEL: Is this just a matter of running a conversation?

OMRI: No. It applies to every mechanical situation. Let's say I vowed to be silent but then I spoke. I vowed to avoid gossip and then I gossiped. Gossip has no intrinsic significance (good or bad). What is important is the attention to the fact that I strayed from a vow, that I lost my focus. It is not a moral issue but one of vision and wisdom. The heart itself is wise.

ARIEL: Last year you also mentioned compassion in this context.

OMRI: Compassion comes from the Self-inquirer's contact with sorrow to which he does not respond. This begins with suffering on a personal level, then it rises to a universal consciousness. Through prolonged training one learns to contain the suffering, study it, and elevate it to the level of sorrow. Then from the stage of sorrow, which he allows himself to experience without attempting to respond to it, the first stirrings of compassion emerge. (If all humans were attentive to this process, it would be the beginning of salvation.)

This process brings about a true change in the person, who is no longer just human (*ben-enosh*) but becomes fully actuated as a man (*ben adam*). From a cultural product he elevates himself to the level of the universal, like a Jesus or a bodhisattva. Here, too, is where authentic generosity is born—generosity goes together with compassion.

ARIEL: Does this generosity lead to altruism?

OMRI: It becomes possible to finally encounter authentic feeling, which is not sentimental. One acts from this motive rather than from a calculation of benefit. That is when we meet our purpose (*yi'ud*)—but it is not in time, and it is not about becoming someone or something. It is now.

At this point Omri narrated the rabbinic commentary on the episode of Moses and the Israelites under Mt. Sinai—the same narrative that opened this chapter. He was describing the sort of reality that could become manifest not if trust in others were an act of faith but if it were an act of keen mental attention. This is not a "theory" of sociality, clearly, but it implies one: contemplative attention to the ceaseless flow of reality—in the present moment—leads to a state of consciousness that is universal and in which compassion develops from the vision of the human condition. I believe that is the most accurate and concise way of describing the implicit theory on which Neot Smadar's sociality (and communal work) is based.

As a theory, this contemplative principle is subject to empirical testing and falsification. No one in Neot Smadar who has spoken to me believes that the "extended family" idea of sociality has been completely successful, and, as seen in Anat's report, it sometimes fails to excel. A more thorough study of this precise aspect of Neot Smadar's life may reveal where the flaws have been, whether in objective circumstances, psychological obstacles, or the very conception. But how is this folk theory different from an organizing principle like charisma, which utilizes religious elements but is reductive, or from a communitarian idea like the socialist kvutzah, which is nonreductive?[25] At the same time, how is it like the notion, articulated by Merton and others, that social engagement represents the field where the spirit does its holiest work?

The members of Neot Smadar, especially the more philosophically inclined individuals, try to avoid speculation and theorizing about their situation. The key to Omri's (and others') implied theory of sociality is remarkably simple: the routine world in its totality is a condition for Self-inquiry. The world is the school—its walls, desks, books, teachers, and everything else. There is no other place that is set aside for spiritual work; it must take place in the total reality we occupy. In that sense, community is like work: it is an objective necessity and therefore the place where vision is acquired. One could just as well do this in a city while unloading crates at the vegetable wholesale market. What is essential to Neot Smadar's sociality is that everyone else (even the children in a limited way) is also engaged in the same inquiry, and thus the parable of Mt. Sinai applies: one's actions are transparent to everyone else even if he or she is entirely unlike anyone in personality and disposition. I trust you to support my Self-inquiry as I support yours. The unifying force is not an idea, a moral principle, self-interest, or even faith; it is the shared task of Self-inquiry. The beneficial consequences, those that make Neot Smadar such a delightful community, grow out of the psychological fruits of that trust coupled with sharp insight into the nature of the self. This is what Omri was explaining in our conversations.

Working toward the Extended Family

One of the more remarkable aspects of the extended family and its relationship to contemplation is the reliance on difficult, even ascetic, objective conditions as ways of deepening the social bond. The communal projects today represent an example of this.

Several years ago Neot Smadar won a substantial grant after submitting plans for a complete overhaul of the community landscape. The plans called for retiling the decrepit paths in the old neighborhoods near the dining hall. Also included in the plans were several new paths, new gardens around many of the homes, painting of those homes, new parking lots, updating the underground water and sewage systems and the electrical grid, fixing up the old swimming pool, and other items. The project was planned for several summers: usually in July and August.

The normal daily routine would be changed: work would end at lunchtime (1:00 p.m.), and then members would take a break and reassemble at 4:15 p.m. for the project meeting before that work began. Routine tasks that had to continue (involving the Pundak, goats, kitchen, food processing, main office, and so on) would continue with rotating crews. Everyone else was expected at the project meeting—but the project was voluntary. In fact, the theme of these projects—often articulated by the pithy aphorism tacked in the entry hall to the dining room—was something along the lines of "Why should I join?" or "What is volunteerism?"[26]

The project organization followed the model established in the early days of Neot Smadar, when getting things done was a spiritual lesson. There were three coordinators, and the veterans made sure to pick a member of the younger generation (someone like Shirley in 2013 or Adva in 2014) to head the project, backed up by more experienced individuals (Nadav) and by a senior member of the kibbutz (Avi one year, Avigdor the next). Adva (2014) then divided the workers into groups (*huliot*) to perform the distinct jobs, each group with its own leader. Those leaders, too, were often younger members of the community, cutting their teeth in leadership roles and learning important lessons about their inner reality. The groups were to do jobs that included planning and measuring, paving (two groups), using heavy equipment, landscaping and gardening, painting, specialized work (electricity and plumbing), and steelwork. A few assignments required a large number of workers, most notably pouring cement, which was a sort of communal apotheosis.[27] There was some degree of flexibility among the groups, but workers mostly stayed in the same group and only rotated jobs within the group.

For example, the paving groups—in which I labored—had to perform

Fig. 17. The author at a landscaping project, 2014

the following tasks: dismantling the old path, assembling the paving bricks on loading platforms, setting down new paving sand, measuring the dimensions and direction of the path, smoothing out and plumbing the sand, cleaning the old bricks or bringing new ones, laying down the bricks in a distinct pattern, cleaning the space on either side of the path, and setting the steel rods before pouring the cement. If the path was not in the shade, which was usually the case, the work would commence with temperatures of a hundred degrees or higher. The bricklayer worked on his or her knees, bending over the slowly progressing edge of the path. Some of the bricks— or paving stones—weighed over twenty pounds, and the individuals who carried them from the loading platforms where they were being cleaned bent over, hauled them up, and then bent down to place them gingerly by the paver. The worker who prepared the sand was also on his or her knees, bending over with the wooden plank that graded the correct height (Fig. 17). The folks cleaning the bricks had it easier, as they sat and rubbed the bricks against each other, inhaling dust.

The head of my group (in the second summer) was a young man called Noam. He was a nerdy and tense-looking man of fair complexion who had no experience with paving or with leading work groups, and Alon joined us in order to support him. Alon was immensely experienced in this sort of work, but he was a control freak, and his micromanagement drove Noam to severe anxiety. During one of the work breaks, as he led a group discussion—one of the group leader's tasks—Noam confessed that he was worried that we were progressing too slowly. Meir interrupted and asked, "How do you know? Maybe we are going too fast?" This was a good point, of course, and could have alerted the young man to the struggles he was imposing on himself. Instead Noam clammed up and the discussion ended somewhat uncomfortably.

But then Noam had his moment of revelation. On a hot afternoon one of the workers asked another: "Do you feel the ecstasy? I'm getting a rush from this!" The other worker nodded and smiled. But Noam overheard this and barked at the man: "Are you serious, or are you being sarcastic?"

The man calmly responded: "Why would I be sarcastic? Are things so awful? I'm actually enjoying this!" Then he turned away.

The next day I asked Noam about this exchange, and he said: "What happened yesterday struck me like a lightening bolt. I suddenly realized that I was suffering for no reason, that people around me were having a totally different experience. It's like I snapped out of a dream." And indeed, from that day on Noam was a new man. He moved more slowly, stopped sweating so profusely, and actually seemed relaxed. He also smiled more easily at Alon's supervision.

The highlight of the project was pouring cement. While the project work normally ended at 8:00 p.m., dinnertime, the cement pouring lasted until it was finished late at night. The following description is from my diary entry of a year earlier (2013), when cement was poured in the old neighborhood paths:

Last night we poured the cement on the sides of the path we had paved earlier in the day and days before. Work started after dinner at 8:30 p.m., and floodlights had to be set up to illuminate the area. Amnon headed this group, which also included David, Dagan, Yehudit, Sigal, Maya, and later Dani. Several children joined the group, including Agam (Dagan's son, who

Fig. 18. Landscaping project, 2013

was eight years old), Atur (Noam C.'s son, who was ten) and Sigal's twins, who were then five. Cement was mixed by Raviv and Uriel off to the side and poured into the lowered shovel of a Caterpillar backhoe loader, which then sidled gently against the edge of the path. Several of us, including two of the little boys, grabbed plastic buckets and scooped up cement, which we then poured into the channels alongside the pavement tiles (Fig. 18). Yehudit and Sigal were on their knees with trowels, smoothing the cement (after it had been tamped). It was an intense scene of chaotic but joyful movement. People moved fast around one another, children running between our legs with buckets only a quarter full of heavy cement. Despite the high energy, progress was slow. No one showed irritation, and, as workers switched positions, they were transitioned into the new job patiently, with humor.

At some point little Agam grabbed my hand and called one of the twins, and the three of us marched to bring more steel rods. The two of them were chatting the whole time and gossiping (as eight-year-old boys might) about some of the workers there. We carried the long rods to the front of the group, where some of the channels were still being prepared for cement. Agam told me what to do, and I obeyed without complaining.

As the evening wore on, the work became increasingly difficult and I felt a pull in my left leg, but everything held up. The evening was cool and dry, with a slight breeze coming off the western hills. In time things quieted down a bit, and the group began to work as a more efficient unit and progress accelerated. The boys, however, remained loud and boisterous even as they kept up the work (scooping quarter-buckets, smoothing the cement, running around). They were completely thrilled, if not entirely efficient, and although they slowed the work down (or made doing it a bit more difficult), not a single adult showed any trace of impatience or irritation.

The area that was lit up included another site; the other group was paving a path, while ours was pouring the cement, and there was little contact between the two groups until the end of the evening. At 12:30 a.m. a circle was set up in a dusty patch of ground (by the cement mixer); drinks and ice cream appeared out of the darkness, and everyone was treated. Avi, who was supporting Shirley, the young woman in charge of the entire project, explained the history of the path—the "path of conflict," it was called—and the reason it was given that odd name (a disagreement over where it should run). Everyone laughed at Avi's wit, and at 1:00 someone brought a guitar and singing commenced. Sometime later I left.

These projects are extraordinary from a psychological and social point of view. They are physically demanding and extremely time-consuming. Between the morning work and the project in the evening, there is little time to accomplish anything else. At night the body aches and the hours of sleep are short. The task that needs to be completed dictates the duration and organization of the work—the project is no ritual but actual work. And yet, for participants who commit themselves to joining, who cross the threshold of resistance, the project is a liminal space indeed.

Conclusion

It remains extremely difficult to pin down a theory that accounts for Neot Smadar's sociality. Omri's theory, described earlier, seems best. From an academic perspective, observing the conditions of Self-inquiry with contemplative commitment, which leads to trust and compassion, resembles little of what one finds in sociological, let alone biological, theorizing. Instead there is the practice of the extended family. The extended family, as reported to me, is one of the central and most supportive conditions for Self-inquiry. But it also represents an attempt to shape an exemplary social arrangement. In the world of the extended family the individual emerges from the state of intimacy that characterizes the immediate family into a broader and collective sort of intimacy. There is no contradiction there but the addition of another dimension that enhances Self-inquiry. Self-inquiry can take place only where a nurturing freedom prevails, with each perspective nurtured in its own place.

The element of trust that runs through the extended family superficially resembles charisma (of persons or ideas). However, practicing Self-inquiry in the company of others may be closer to the ideas espoused by John Rawls about social justice (along with empathy and even intimacy) than to anything Weber and his followers wrote about charisma. At the same time, the uncompromising realism about objective conditions as the field of Self-inquiry nudges trust in the direction of evolutionary-psychological theories about groups. For example, those members of the community who have a difficult time accepting undesirable or "boring" jobs or who shirk the extra effort of special (and voluntary) projects clearly fail to understand the true meaning of Self-inquiry. However, there is no "official" view on this matter in Neot Smadar. After all, the place is a school and not a kibbutz. In fact, I should add that sociological or psychological theories about social cooperation are alien to the way members of Neot Smadar talk about their world. What truly matters is the development of conditions that enhance the community and Self-inquiry at the same time. But an evolutionary theory (simply put) might also suggest that recalcitrant workers present themselves as unworthy of trust because they fail to share the burden of the work that is essential for economic survival. The difference here is that members of the community, while recognizing the rather obvious evolutionary argument, do not abide by its predictable outcomes (such as ejecting the individual or setting up extraordinary tests). Instead, the difficulty of dealing with these individuals is a learning opportunity for everyone else—another condition of Self-inquiry.

The elderly, the weak, the ill, and the psychologically fragile can remain members of the community. They do not face expulsion for their failure to contribute work. They are, however, expected to engage in Self-inquiry, to study honestly in Neot Smadar's school for Self-inquiry. Because the community is first and foremost a school, why else would they wish to remain?

A Wedding Gift for Dani

A FEW DAYS INTO JUNE 2013, SOMEONE handed me a note that read: "You are invited this Thursday at 19:00 to the circle of fire behind the art center." For a couple of weeks everyone in Neot Smadar had been occupied with preparations for Maya and Dani's wedding. There had been other weddings in Neot Smadar, but not many, and as for those that had gone before, people were preparing to make it a special affair. This meant mostly offering musical and dance performances, so everyone was rehearsing, either in groups or individually. I saw someone practicing his cello in the middle of a field, and another person was blowing into a flute on top of a building in the late evenings. Shachar, at the fruit-processing plant, used the breaks to belt out an Arab song in front of YouTube while fingering a harmonium.

The note seemed unrelated to any of this, and I didn't make the connection until Anat told me that Thursday night—the night before the wedding—was "men's night" and that it would be best to wear boots because "you'll be out in the desert." That's all she said, so I put on my work boots—an extra pair of Alon's—and went down to the art center. On the southern side of the building, which is surrounded by an enormous garden of roses, spiny zilla, fagonbush, climbing grapes, and many other plants in a complicated design (with a fish pond tucked inside) was a stone circle enclosing the ash of old fires. Ten men were already sitting there, silently. All were casually dressed but not in work clothes, and all were wearing sandals.

By 7:20 thirty men had gathered. There was no chatting, although no one appeared solemn, either. There were young volunteers and veteran members, long hair on some and shaved, balding heads on others. Half the men looked around expectantly, and the other half appeared to smile in some hidden anticipation. Dani, the groom, was there, too, but no one paid him much attention. It did not seem to me that he knew what was going on. His intense dark eyes were focused inward. He was marrying Maya, a tall blond woman that I found severe—even ascetic. She had taught me to milk goats a few days earlier.

Then, just before the sun set, Avi stood, faced the group, and said: "This night is not just for Dani but for all of us men who are here. Tonight we shall learn a valuable lesson about manhood, about being true to what we all are. And this lesson consists of four parts." Then he took a sheet of paper, unfolded it, and began to read: "Fear is the first natural enemy a man must overcome on his path to knowledge. . . . And what can he do to overcome fear? The answer is very simple. He must not run away. He must defy his fear." He read these words slowly as the evening light softened and a cool breeze blew from the western hills. I couldn't think of why the subject of fear had come up, except as a joke about weddings. But there was seriousness in Avi's tone, and more in the long pauses between certain words, and he sounded sincere. "Tonight," he said, folding the paper and tucking it into the rear pocket of his jeans, "we shall know fear and we shall learn to overcome fear by confronting it and defying it." I looked around—this had to be a joke—but learned nothing from the men's faces. Avi was wearing a white shirt over his jeans, but his sandals were old and scruffy. In time, we would become friends; at this point I was just trying to read him.

The whole situation struck me as staged, almost theatrical. Yossef, I had been told repeatedly, was a stage director in his professional life, and the methods he employed at Neot Smadar had the flavor of stagecraft. I could see this later, as I looked into the matter. The theatrical philosophies and techniques that were most influential at the time of Yossef's work— those of Jacque Copeau, Antonin Artaud, Jean-Louis Barrault, and others—showed through. For example, the extended retreats into the countryside with an ensemble of actors for bonding and self-exploration, the improvisation exercises involving indeterminate starting situations ("*matzav efes*"), the relaxation of normal inhibitions, and others figured in Yossef's approach as they did in contemporary theatrical training.[1] But then again, isn't ritual as such a theatrical production?

"Here is what we're going to do," Avi continued. "Each of you will find a stick at least forty centimeters long," he held his hands apart to demonstrate. "And you will keep this stick with you as we go on a 'duration walk' into the desert. Later on you will find out what to do with it." I had no idea what a "duration walk" was, but I learned quickly that at the very least it consisted of a leader followed by a line of other walkers, none passing the person in front and each sticking carefully to the same path. And the walk was silent, always. I found a long stick (worrying that it was too thin; I was thinking about scenarios requiring self-defense . . .) and joined the line of walkers in the middle. I did not know the man walking in front of me or see the one who followed me. The line of walkers felt both vague and concrete, like the relationship you form with other passengers on a long-delayed flight. Avi led us, walking at an easy pace toward the lotus pond near the entrance to the community and then out the gate, which was already locked; we squeezed through a tight opening in the fence. The line of walkers slithered silently in front of me and behind, along the southern fence toward the west. The few evening clouds were a quickly fading crimson, and the golden hills to the south dissolved to a shade of Mojave beige before my very eyes. I reflected on how quickly the night falls in these latitudes, and I smelled a trace of smoke from the northwest. We walked through a harvested wheat field, along the furrows. Then we stopped and faced north. I was looking at the community fence and beyond at the apricot and apple orchards, blending in the deepening darkness with date palms, then a steep rocky hill on top of which I could barely identify a large structure, like a giant man.

We stood there silently. My back was starting to hurt, and I looked for ways to lean on the stick without breaking it. I could hear a few whispers from the younger men—speculations, I supposed, on what we were doing there. I felt awake with curiosity. After fifteen minutes another snake of men emerged from a hole in the fence straight ahead, and that group walked in our direction and the two groups became a single long line of silent walkers headed south, toward a wide and barren stretch of desert strewn with rocks and potholes. The men walked slowly along the field, then formed a huge circle and stopped when the circle was completed. There were about fifty men, all facing in, all carrying sticks. I began to feel nervous. Circles had a way of doing that to me. As long as we were just walking in line, the group seemed unreal. There was just the one man in front of me—I was safe in my private world. Circles threatened that.

Three men—I made out only Alon—left their spots and approached Meir, who, at seventy, was the oldest man there. He was holding by far the largest stick—it was a pole actually. The four men whispered, and Meir pointed to a point across the circle from where he was standing, directly to the west. The three men went to that spot and stood there, about fifty meters away. It was almost dark, but you could still make out the features of the men who were close at hand. The ground was a blur of dark shadows. Suddenly one of the three men tore away from the others and began to run. He also began to yell—a frightening nonhuman shriek that bounced off the hills and made my spine shudder. He ran and yelled like an injured being set on horrible revenge, and my eyes followed his every step, my heart beating madly, until the man launched himself and hit Meir's pole with his own stick and then came to a stop. I felt my stomach quiver and my knees felt wobbly, but I was so focused on the runner that these bodily feelings were a mere whisper, barely registering in my brain. Then the second man took off with an explosive roar. Suddenly, I felt real fear.

The man standing on my left, a shadow in the corner of my eye, doubled over and began to quiver. Then something in his throat gave way and he began to howl in laughter, a mad and liberated howl that set off the whole line of men on my right. The desert exploded in derisive merriment at the expense of the runners. And I realized what my fear was about: "I'm going to have to do this too—I'll be running with the goddamn stick in the air yelling and screaming and all these men—I don't know these guys—will howl in joy at my pathetic display!"

I never knew what I sounded like yelling with brutal abandon, shrieking and letting my lungs explode into my throat. No one really knows, and I had never really thought about it. And frankly, having now done it, I still don't know. I recalled the scene in *Cabaret* when Liza Minelli stood under a rail bridge and, when the train came, let out such a scream, which was drowned in the booming riot of the train above. How would such a cry sound in the silent desert, just as the last light of day was disappearing behind the western hills? And Liza's character brought a friend to impress; whom would I bring? What about fifty men—almost all of them strangers and all of them tough, with sharp, penetrating eyes, evaluating the abandon, the sincerity, the power of my primal scream? Could I truly join this coterie of men, or would I remain an outsider, as I've been all my life? My run would expose my heart; my standoffishness would finally be exposed as ridiculous. That's why my knees shook as I watched the others run.

It turns out that there are as many varieties of primal screams as there are fingerprints and running styles—so I discovered from watching those who went before me. Some exploded for the first twenty meters and then collapsed, only to return in a hoarse, dry whimper at the end of the run. Others shouted words—"I'm coming, I'm coming"—and still others found their inner castrato. One runner just growled (he also ran at a measured, even pace). Some voices broke in mid-yell, and some runners preferred to ululate instead of holding a steady note. There were rising pitches and descending bellows. Sometimes the screamer sounded as if he was possessed by three demons fighting an internal battle, and other runners emitted a pathetic beseeching sound, followed by a long bray.

The runners sprinted, skipped, lollopped, hopped, jogged, stumbled, rolled, limped—and some even exploded and leaped—young stags those. Fifty meters is a short enough distance for everyone to accomplish the mission, which was to hit the stick held up in the air by Meir, the wise elder who was spared the run. I can't exactly say what I sounded like and what I looked like. I had those boots on, so my ankles were spared the torture of flip-flops or flimsy sandals. The boots were heavy, but, to be honest, I felt as if I was flying. Bad knees, hurting back—these disappeared in the flood of adrenaline that saturated my terrified brain. I danced through the stones and floated above the ditch. I roared like a lion and blasted like thunder. I was the Indian god Indra, waving the thunderbolt and threatening the drought with a raging storm.

But I could be wrong. Maybe I looked wobbly and sounded like air leaving a balloon, who can say? I did hear some laughter (through the thunder in my ears) but no howls or knee slapping—as far as I could tell. The run ended with a lunge at Meir's pole, and walking back to the group I felt nothing in my body but burning fire in the throat—which remained sore for three days. But I was elated; how had I sidestepped all those rocks in the dark? And then I remembered where I had heard, or read, the words Avi had spoken about fear: of course this was all Don Juan stuff—the words belonged to Carlos Castaneda!

Like many of my friends in Israel and America, I had read every one of Castaneda's novels about the American anthropologist who learns the "ways of the sorcerer" from an old Yaqui Indian called Don Juan. The early ones, read when I was still in college, I took for the man's extraordinary spiritual experiences, that is, as real. In time, as other anthropologists and sociologists began to question Castaneda's truthfulness, I, too, began to doubt—and lost my passion for the continuing stream of spiritual adventures.[2] However, there is a passage in one of the early Castaneda novels about the American being forced to run down a desert slope in the darkness of a moonless night. At first he hesitates and, indeed, hurts himself on his overly deliberate descent. But as he finally lets go of fear and abandons himself to some greater force, he is able to hurl himself down the slope without stumbling, as though his legs had eyes of their own. That image blew into my head as the group tightened the circle and Avi took out a flashlight and the folded sheet of paper.

Then he began to read again: "Once a man has vanquished fear, he is free from it for the rest of his life because instead of fear he has acquired clarity—a clarity of mind which erases fear." That was the second part of the lesson Avi had promised earlier. I doubted anyone there (except for myself and perhaps one or two new volunteers) had experienced any fear around the run, and I also thought—smiling to myself—that nothing was clearer than fear. Except, perhaps, pain. I felt elation and immediately sought to explain it: either I was thrilled at having "passed a test" or I was simply enjoying a rush of beta endorphins and would have felt no different even if I had been the only person there. The sense of having passed a test was in my mind, I thought; the runner's high was in my brain. Which is it, Professor?

Most religious groups practice rites of passage or initiatory rituals for those who wish to join or for those who progress from the periphery to the inner circle. These are often tests of courage or of stoic acceptance of pain. I have studied these rituals for years and believe that they operate on multiple levels.[3] From a social and perhaps evolutionary point of view, the group needs to eliminate freeloaders from overburdening limited resources. From a psychological perspective, the initiate needs to "die" to his old self—that is, open himself to a new identity—and pain or extreme effort is an effective tool for achieving this.[4] Regardless of which precise ritual technique is used, as the anthropologist Roy Rappaport noted, the acts are generally not capricious but are modeled on some other source—broadly understood as culture. In other words, the ritual is a cultural performance that can be understood in different ways depending on what it does with the model or on which tools it uses. For example, Erving Goffman understood the ritual as an "expressive rejuvenation or reaffirmation of the moral values of a community."[5] Victor Turner, in contrast, understood ritual as the dramatic performance of deep social and psychological processes such as breach, crisis, redress, and reintegration. In a nutshell, ritual for Turner was social theater.[6] Still other scholars do not believe that ritual conveys meaning at all; rather it describes the manner in which any act can be performed—there is no generalizable social foundation or religious institution that is properly described by the term "ritual."[7]

But there, in the desert, the cultural link that I identified was not to Neot Smadar's own cultural life but to that of the Yaqui Indian fictionally depicted in the novels of Castaneda, which was entirely alien to the men gathered in the dark. Furthermore, I also believed that Carlos Castaneda was parodying (if not exploiting) this tradition in his early books. In the first volume, from which Avi had been reading, Don Juan told his aspiring new student that he would take him for a student only if he could identify the "power spot" on the old Indian's porch and that he should spend the entire night looking for it if need be. What follows is a comical search for some special physical location—the narrator squinting, crawling on hands and knees, peering through the corners of his eyes—all in pursuit of the numinous. He finally collapses in exhaustion, and Don Juan finds him curled up asleep in the morning and declares: "I see you found the correct spot!"[8]

It took me some time to realize that if Castaneda's novel is a sort of mockery, the performance in which I had just participated (and witnessed) was a parody of a mockery. And indeed, ritual in general does not merely display cultural facts; ritual is commentary. This is how the Sri Lanka scholar Bruce Kapferer put it: "Ritual reveals itself as essentially the hermeneutic of culture—a method whereby culture analyzes itself."[9] The ritualistic-theatrical genre of the silly warrior circle was a hysterical satire: a mimesis ad absurdum of the warrior ethos that almost cracked my ribs in laughter. It was a clever performance with shifting frames of references (ordeal, reading of scripture, military charge, wisdom of the elders), which suggested to me that the cultural allusions (Castaneda's) were just props, that the commentary concerned something far more essential and hidden.[10]

The circle opened up, and Avi led us quietly in the direction of the hill where I had seen the giant figure. As we climbed the rocky slope I began to experience some anxiety again: were they planning to go charging down the hill? It was steep and strewn with jagged rocks, but if you were crazy enough, who knows? I had no idea what these men were capable of doing. They looked tough—the older men did. They were lean and leathery from exposure to the sun and even in their best clothes looked no better than construction workers on a lunch break—their pain threshold, I surmised, had to be scary. Besides, they were bonded in a group, and who knows what groups can make an individual do, especially in rites of passage? I had seen scarification, mutilation, severe insect and ant bites, beatings, and desert marathons—all in the name of joining. Was this to be one of those situations? Was the dash in the circle a mere warm-up? Then I noticed the sandals on the man walking ahead of me, and the flip-flops on the man ahead of him. "No way these guys can run down this mountain—not without major injury," I thought. It was obvious. "And if they are that tough—or that committed—I'm not joining them in that adventure. Shit, I'm a visitor, a college teacher. No toppling down a mountainside for these old knees."

So it was decided, I'd be opting out—I could now give these thoughts a rest and focus on the climb. I felt free, myself, again. We reached the hilltop and walked along the dark edge toward the man-shaped figure, which turned out to be a stack of wood arranged like the Burning Man of the California desert. A strong wind blew from the northwest, behind our backs. As we stood in a large semicircle facing the Burning Man, Dani lit the wood, which exploded in a spectacular burst of orange against the black desert lowlands beyond. We leaned into its warmth and looked at one another in the new light. Everyone was calm and dreamy-eyed, not a trace of religious or group fanaticism. In the soft glow of the fire my fears of a cultish sprint down the slope seemed feverish and paranoid. "If the others knew what's going through my mind . . .," I thought. I looked around at those fifty strangers who had let me into their world for the evening. "I have to stop this, I'm thinking too much. Just enjoy the fire."

David interrupted this internal monologue—he had already been reading for a while—with this third part of the lesson, read from the same folded sheet from which Avi had previously read: " . . . but then he must defy clarity and use it only to see, and wait patiently and measure carefully before taking new steps. And thus he will have overcome his second enemy, and will arrive at a position where nothing can harm him anymore. It will be true power." I believe that Castaneda had been writing at UCLA for a generation of young people who sensed the decline of spiritual work as "work," that is, as a discipline that requires complete commitment and lifelong dedication. That was the sort of thing Gurdjieff had insisted on, but by the 1960s his enterprise was in tatters. What emerged instead were Krishnamurti weekends in Ojai or Zen retreats on top of Mt. Baldy (in the San Gabriel Mountains), Vedanta boutiques in L.A., and the captivating but merely voyeuristic literary works of Alan Watts, D. T. Suzuki, Aldous Huxley, John Lilly, Robert Bly, and a whole slew of others.[11] The Native American—better yet—the native Mexican sorcerer was the solution: exotic and autochthonous at the same time. Here is a hidden mystic, a man of astonishing spiritual power in our own backyard, perhaps even walking among us. A generation and a half later Dani was absorbing life lessons from the fictitious Yaqui mystic, his words translated into Hebrew.

But there was nothing here of the awe that Castaneda was trying to instill in his young readers. Most of these men had served in the military—many in elite units and with battle experience. They were dreamy but also joyful and enjoyed their play-acting, and the entire affair really seemed more like Burning Man than desert initiation. I do not mean that there was anything bacchanalian about the proceedings; rather there was a determination to fully enjoy the freedom of the fantasy. As Lee Gilmore put it in a recent book: Participants "ritualistically and self-consciously de- and reconstruct ad hoc frameworks in which to create and perform self-reflexive spiritual-

ities, which can become for many a profound and life-changing experience."[12]

Everyone watched the fire, which roared above Castaneda's musings. We
stood there for a while, then climbed down slowly, aided by the fire above
and a couple of flashlights someone had brought. Standing at the bottom
of the hill, waiting for the last in line, I saw that the mood had shifted. Men
were chatting and laughing in the darkness. Some were speculating on the
origin of the quote, and then someone let it out: "Dani loves Carlos Castaneda, so we decided to give him a Don Juan evening." A volunteer asked
who this Don Juan was, which was greeted with laughter. Voices began to
compare volumes and episodes, and no one bothered to answer the young
volunteer. He would have to find out for himself. Someone asked, "So
what else are you planning?" and I heard a comically conspiratorial "Wait
and see."

The final stretch of our walk was five minutes around to the front of the
lake. We sat on the rocks by a dock and waited. Out in the middle of the
lake was an island with trees and tall grass. We could see a fire going there,
and two people were beating drums in an unsteady rhythm that suggested
incompetence or drunkenness. We listened silently for about ten minutes
as the drumming continued to deteriorate, until a number of elder members of the group yelled from the shore, "Enough, quiet down!" This made
no difference, and two more people joined in, and then all of us called out
in tandem: "QUIET!" and the drumming stopped. A few moments of complete silence followed, with a light breeze rustling the bamboo leaves. Then
the frogs resumed their supercilious croaks, and as the breeze picked up
the canes of bamboo clacked together. My watch read 10:40—we had been
out for nearly four hours.

Then Amnon stood up and addressed the men: "The rest of the evening
will continue on the island. But only real men are invited." He snickered
theatrically and continued: "So those of you who are mere boys can stay
here, dry and comfortable. The men among you, leave your clothes in a
plastic bag—someone will bring it over to the island—and you know what
to do afterward." With this he quickly removed his clothes and his long
white body shot into the air, bent, and tore apart the inky water. What followed looked like the starting line of a nocturnal triathlon, with dozens of

naked male bodies lunging into the water followed by vigorous and inef-
fective strokes designed for warmth more than progress. I jumped in with
the rest. The water was cool and immediately ended my musings. I felt like
laughing—it was all so silly—but maybe I was just cold and laughter was
a warming response. The island was about sixty meters away, just over the
length of an Olympic-size pool, but all the splashing bodies made the going
slow.

On the island we were each handed a towel and we snuggled up to the
fire, waiting for our clothes to arrive by boat. The silence was now broken
as men looked at one another shivering and stomping their feet, and everyone laughed at everyone else. The inhibitions were now gone; we might
as well have been drunk. It was a party. A long table stood behind the fire,
set up with food—the same exact food served in the dining hall that night.
We dressed, then ate, and sipped hot tea. The ground around the fire was
covered with mats, blankets, and strewn pillows, and everyone got comfortable. Two men had brought their guitars and were strumming tunes I
did not recognize as men around me hummed along. The men closest to
the fire seemed most cheerful and were certainly the loudest, while those
sitting on the periphery, like myself, were more introspective and quiet.
Finally Avi stood near the fire, unfolded his crumpled paper, and read the
final (fourth) passage out of Castaneda: "This enemy too (power) will have
to be defeated, by defying it deliberately. The man will be by then at the end
of his journey of learning and almost without warning he will come upon
the last of his enemies: old age! This enemy is the cruelest of all, the one he
won't be able to defeat completely, but only fight away. This is a time when
a man has no more fears, no more impatient clarity of mind—a time when
all his power is in check, but also a time when he has an unyielding desire
to rest. . . . If a man sloughs off his tiredness, and lives his fate through, he
can then be called a man of knowledge."[13]

That was finally a bit of Castaneda I could applaud. Fighting the fatigue
of age, ha! We are all warriors, and all of us will certainly lose, if not sooner,
then later. I watched Dani, who was listening closely. To me he looked
about twenty-nine. What was he taking in from the reading? Was it as remote as a Homeric recitation in praise of the cunning of Odysseus, or was
it hitting home in some meaningful way? This was Dani's rite of passage;

we were just undergoing mock initiation for his sake, and many of us have already heard the early whispers of old age. What does he know? Granted, he loved Castaneda, as I did at his age, but is all of this mere talk and gesture, or is something moving in Dani's mind? After the wedding, Dani and Maya disappeared for several weeks; later I discovered that they had gone to Georgia—the former Soviet Republic—for their honeymoon. He came back with a thick black beard, which I thought had to do with this night with the men, or perhaps with the facial hair of Georgian men in Tbilisi cafés or bars. At any rate, growing a beard was a perfect masculine gesture for a man who had just given himself over in marriage to a woman. Not one other man in Neot Smadar sported a beard.

In retrospect I believe that what Dani got from this evening had little to do with fear, clarity, power, or old age. What he got was friendship and love. Those were his wedding gifts, and there was plenty of each. Some men offered him a song, others a poem, a joke, a funny toast. As the evening stretched into night, then into early morning, different men tended the fire as songs alternated with stories; wine glasses were raised, and I felt myself getting sleepy. I didn't know Dani, but I thought he was a lucky man. Was he exceptionally lovable, a friend of everyone in the community, or were all of these desert-hardened men—usually silent and introspective—just finally happy to be sentimental? And why had the evening been designed like a rite of passage? Dani was already inside! He was already accepted and loved and was old enough to be treated like a man, not a boy. Oh well, who can say? Years later, as I reflected on that evening with a deeper understanding, I understood that what it revealed was precisely the meaning of "extended family." Dani was no more loved than anyone else, but as his wedding gifts he received loving acts. I smiled thinking that maybe the entire episode had been my own secret rite of passage. It was I who overcame fear and surrendered my walls to become a member of this group of men. Well, almost a member; after all, I had nothing to give Dani as his wedding gift.

It took me months to realize what the ritualistic evening was about, what cultural values were deconstructed—even savaged—and which were somehow reaffirmed in the theatrical comedy. A friend was telling me about a wedding he had attended that same year, somewhere outside of Tel Aviv.

And then it struck me like some megawatt feedback surge at a rock concert: "Of course . . . the Israeli wedding! The desert run, the burning man, the swim, and especially the song-gifting by the fire—these were all the perfect reversal of that which passes for the sanctified union of man and woman in Jewish Israel today." Indeed, the norm now seems to dictate the spending of fifty thousand dollars or more for wedding halls or gardens, food and drink, live bands, dresses and flowers, transportation, and, not least, the rabbi. The gifts, too, are immensely expensive and figure in the way the couple's parents calculate their financial investment in the ritual. There are phone apps today that enable guests to calculate the "correct" amount to give as a wedding gift. The Israeli wedding has become the perfect realization of social union, not to say love, in a consumerist capitalistic age: profligate and hyperdemonstrative.[14] And calculating, too, with cash-based tit-for-tat as the currency of social exchange.

In Neot Smadar, in that dark desert night, there was running and stumbling, climbing, readings, naked bodies, guitars and drums, and storytelling. What Dani received as wedding gifts were performances. The whole night was a sly performance. And its power came not from the imitation of Yaqui culture, whatever that happened to be, but from its brutal contrast with Israeli culture. That was the subject of the play: there were other ways of coming together as a community besides spending and eating.

Later that night I found myself beginning to doze off, and then I needed to relieve my bladder but didn't wish to do it on the small island. So I hitched a ride on a boat that was going for more supplies at 12:30 a.m., then took a leak in the bushes away from the lake with my back to the faded light of the fire and the sounds of guitars and laughter. Then I turned east, into the dark night, and went off to bed. I was the first to leave, but the alarm would be going off at 5:00, as usual. In my case, old age won over power.

Conclusion: Looking Forward

NEOT SMADAR SHOWS ITSELF AS A RICH and textured picture: dozens of complicated men and women running a diverse economy all year long for twenty-six years now, telling hundreds of stories. This book captures a sliver, several quick glances within an epic. Do these glances capture anything essential? Does each moment encapsulate something valuable that the totality hides in infinite layers of detail? Perhaps. In this conclusion I try to simplify the picture even further and see what happens.

Imagine a twentieth-century man, an atheist, coming into contact with Nagarjuna's *Mulamadhyamikakarika* and falling in love with it. He falls in love with Buddha's teaching (in that text) that all of dependent arising is empty, but he also understands that conventional reality is important for grasping ultimate truth. If one takes emptiness too strictly, the entire Buddhist edifice collapses and one loses hope for liberation. Hence one must accept the notion that "what is co-arisen is empty" is also empty and that (an apparent paradox) is called the middle way and allows one to move forward in practice (karika 14).

Now imagine that this man, who does not buy into the specific Buddhist terminology, gains insight into the emptiness of co-arising, or what he calls the utter disorder of phenomenal experience. At times he feels liberated and energized, but he steadfastly refuses to describe those brief instants of insight in any substantive terms. Instead he decides to create a school. What would the school teach? It would not teach about God, Dhamma,

Torah, Christ, or any such thing. In fact, this man would not transmit in-formation as such. Instead he would hold conversations in which he would ask those present what they wished to discuss. And then he would punc-ture these people's presumptions and show them how he observes—within himself—what is going on at the precise moment of the exchange. He would try to show how he sees while shunning "content."

Then this man seeks to move the school to the desert, where it will be isolated and free of distractions. That's a smart and rather conventional move—like setting up a monastery in the mountains. But his students are family people, some with children. And they cannot live on charity or funds raised by a roof organization—a sangha or the Catholic Church. They will have to work for a living and create a functioning community. So what does the school teach about community, and what does it teach about work? Well, the school will not legislate moral rules (about stealing, lying, forni-cating, and the rest), and it will not issue commands about work and hard effort and self-sacrifice. It will not even promise that work will make one a better person.

The basic and simplest goal of the school—to put it in terms of Nagar-juna's "Middle Way"—is to realize the nature of dependent co-arising as emptiness without surrendering to the nihilistic and counterproductive denial of the world as a place of learning (and work and community). This man understands that in order to realize truth you do not need to depend on meditation, on reading the sutras or listening to sermons. He also un-derstands you do not have to renounce your family and put on the robes of a monk (just as the Buddhist householder Vimalakirti understood this in the *Vimalakirti Sutra* or as Krishna taught Arjuna in the *Bhagavad Gita*). Instead, every single act that one performs while living in this community is a chance for learning the simple truth about the nature of the self. This includes the work that supports the community, the conversations and re-lationships with others in the community, the shared meals, holidays, and weddings and all the rest. In this place life in its totality is a set of con-ditions for learning, for Self-inquiry, as long as one remembers that this does not involve a doctrine—or any other content—but rather a refined and ever-evolving willingness to observe the self as a process.

Yossef did not study Buddhist (or Hindu) philosophy, though he was impressed with the teachings of Krishnamurti. His constant goal and repeated mantra was "Let's be naïve." In other words, in order to cut through the clutter of the self (the Buddhist dependent co-arising) one cannot possibly rely on Krishnamurti, on Gurdjieff, or anyone else. Either you see what is going on directly or you are mistaking conventional knowledge (the lesser of Buddha's two forms) for what is real. Today veteran members of Yossef's school, men and women in their sixties and seventies, have often excelled at being naïve and sharp. But this has come at an enormous cost and continues to try them every single moment. One never reaches a place where a goal has been reached, where one can rest, knowing the job is done.

The simple truth of emptiness can be harsh and depressing when it is accepted as an idea that overrides experience. Yossef taught his version of emptiness for a long time, and some have discovered that they needed to "shatter Yossef" (kill the Buddha, in Neot Smadar parlance). That is what Yossef demanded, and they finally took the step. At that moment, they abandoned the intellectual aspect of Self-inquiry in favor of the experience it makes possible. The intellectual aspect posits this opposition: if you take emptiness seriously, either nothing matters (or is worth doing) or everything is meaningful in a sublime way, and therefore one must be a failure for not fully realizing this. The second option was the vicious cycle of spiritual ambition and existential failure. As long as Yossef was alive it was possible to bring up the matter of failure (in achieving the ostensible goal of Self-inquiry) over and over again and listen to his biting insights ("You are failing because of your own goal-oriented ambition") and regain some motivation. The death of Yossef removed this crutch, and something else had to replace the dilemma of understanding the teaching while failing to apply it. The intellectual approach to spiritual work had to give way to something else. This replacement is provided by an attitude that looks like a subtle attentiveness. It is not a prescription, a rule of conduct, or an institution.

In conclusion, today's Neot Smadar of the older members is just fine. It is alive and dynamic precisely because no one knows where it is going— no one has answers, but most are willing to live open to what is offered.

That is the lesson I have heard from my friends, the veterans. Here is how Krishnamurti put the matter of reaching a goal or a conclusion: "The moment one has reached a conclusion, a position of achievement, of knowledge, from which one starts examining, one is finished, then one is translating every living thing in terms of the old."[1] The younger members of Neot Smadar, those who did not know Yossef and have not struggled with his version of emptiness, present another case. Theirs is another book altogether.

NOTES

Introduction

1. Aran Patenkin, *Neot Smadar—First Days,* documentary film, 1989.
2. The term "Self-inquiry" is my translation of "limud atzmo shel ha'adam" (the study of one's own self), in which study (limud) must be distinguished from the study of some subject.
3. Smadar was Yossef's wife, who had been killed in a car accident a few years earlier. "Neot" means "oasis."
4. Meeting in the sukkah, Hanukkah, third candle, December 15, 1998, in "Collected Sukkah Talks," 1998–1999, Neot Smadar Archive.
5. Talal Asad, *Formations of the Secular: Christianity, Islam, Modernity* (Stanford, CA: Stanford University Press, 2003), 192.
6. Ibid.; Jose Casanova has disputed this theory, arguing that the resurgence of public religion in contemporary life undermines the dialectic implied (as an ostensible product of the Enlightenment) between religion and secular rationality. See "Secularization Revisited: A Reply to Talal Asad," in *Powers of the Secular Modern: Talal Asad and His Interlocutors,* ed. David Scott and Charles Hirschkind (Stanford, CA: Stanford University Press, 2006), 12–30. Casanova's position seems to hold the upper hand currently, after 9/11. See, for instance, Lance Gharavi, ed., *Religion, Theater and Performance* (New York: Routledge, 2012).
7. S. N. Eisenstadt, "Israeli Identity: Problems in the Development of Collective Identity of an Ideological Society," *Annals of the American Academy of Political and Social Science* 370, no. 1 (1967): 116–123.
8. Forming an "intentional community" signifies, essentially, "voting with one's feet" in withdrawing from society at large to reestablish more authentic human bonds, according to Susan Love Brown, ed., *Intentional Community: An Anthropological Approach* (Albany, NY: State University of New York, 2002), 5–6.

9. Philip Wexler, *The Mystical Society: An Emerging Social Vision* (Boulder, CO: Westview, 2000), 11. Clearly, this is an unusual way of understanding the term "mysticism." See Chapter 7.

10. Several informants attributed the song to Iris T., but I could not verify this. All the translations from Hebrew in this book are my own.

11. Anat G., "Sedakim," received by email January 17, 2015.

12. P. D. Ouspensky, *In Search of the Miraculous: The Teachings of G. I. Gurdjieff* (San Diego: Harvest, 2001). Ouspensky and Gurdjieff, who played a role in the work of Yossef, are discussed in Chapter 4. The psychological concept of "presence" ("the faculty of voluntarily bringing back a wandering attention") was first explored by William James, quoted here from *Psychology: Briefer Course* (New York: Harper Torchbooks, 1961), 424.

13. Peter B. Clarke, *New Religions in Global Perspective: A Study of Religious Change in the Modern World* (London: Routledge, 2006); Timothy Miller, "The Evolution of American Spiritual Communities," *Nova Religio: The Journal of Alternative and Emergent Religions* 13, no. 3 (February 2010): 14–33.

14. See www.Tamara.org/what-is-tamara/about-us, accessed April 2, 2015. The classic in this field is still Benjamin Zablocki, *Alienation and Charisma* (New York: Basic, 1980), which predates the communitarian debates with liberalism widely discussed by Amitai Etzioni. See also George Lunddskow, *The Sociology of Religion: A Substantive and Transdisciplinary Approach* (Los Angeles: Pine Grove, 2008), 49–52, for the continuing influence of Ferdinand Toennies.

15. Amitai Etzioni, *The Spirit of Community: Rights, Responsibilities and the Communitarian Agenda* (London: Fontana, 1993).

16. Lev Vygotsky, *Thought and Language* (Cambridge, MA: MIT Press, 1997).

17. John Rawls, *A Theory of Justice* (Cambridge, MA: Harvard University Press, 1999).

18. See Chapter 4.

19. Eliezer Ben-Rafael, Yaacov Oved, and Menachem Topel, "Introduction: A Difficult Question," in *The Communal Idea in the 21st Century*, ed. Eliezer Ben-Rafael, Yaacov Oved, and Menachem Topel (Leiden: Brill, 2013), 1.

20. See St. Augustine's rules for monastic life: "The main purpose for you having come together is to live harmoniously in our house, intent upon God in oneness of mind and heart. . . . Call nothing your own, but let everything be yours in common." Quoted in *Regular Life: Monastic, Canonical, and Mendicant Rules*, ed. Daniel Marcel La Corte and Douglas J. McMillan (Kalamazoo, MI: Medieval Institute Publications, 2004), 53.

21. Excluded are "natural" groups like clans, tribes, or castes, which are not intentional. Furthermore, charisma seems to conflict with intention (Susan Brown Love); according to Weber, it acts as a sort of magnet. See Charles Lindholm, ed., *The Anthropology of Religious Charisma: Ecstasies and Institutions* (New York: Palgrave Macmillan, 2013).

22. Janja Lalich, *Bounded Choice: True Believers and Charismatic Cults* (Berkeley: University of California Press, 2004).

23. The most appropriate context is a free-flowing one. See, for example, Nicholas J. Demerath III, "Social Movements as Free-Floating Religious Phenomena," in *Blackwell Companion to Sociology of Religion,* ed. Richard K. Fenn (Oxford, UK: Blackwell, 2001), 229–248.

24. See Miroslav Volf, *Work in the Spirit: Toward a Theology of Work* (New York: Oxford University Press, 1991). Away from Christian models of "sacred" work, one may consult A. D. Gordon (familiar to many in Neot Smadar), *Ha'avoda* (Tel Aviv: Hapoel Hatza'ir, 1923), and, nearly as familiar, M. K. Gandhi, *Bread Labour: The Gospel of Work,* ed. Ravindra Kelekar edited (Ahmedabad, India: Navajian, 1960). For the relationship between work and community in the United States, see Robert Bellah, *Habits of the Heart: Individualism and Commitments in American Life* (New York: Harper & Row, 1985).

Chapter 1. A Search for Religious Experience

1. On Israel Vipassana Trust (a meditation center) and self-identification in postsecular globalized Buddhism, see Joseph Loss, "Explicit Non-religious and Implicit Non-secular Localization of Religion" *Nova Religio: The Journal of Alternative and Emergent Religions* 13, no. 4 (2010): 84–105.

2. Many of them were feeding on the labor mysticism of Aharon David Gordon. On A. D. Gordon, see Anita Shapira, *Hapoel Hatzair* (Tel Aviv: Am Oved, 1967).

3. E. Valentine Daniel, *Fluid Signs: Being a Person in the Tamil Way* (Berkeley: University of California Press, 1987).

4. Ibid., 269.

5. The methodology in this sort of research contrasts sharply with the cognitive-evolutionary program of researchers like Whitehouse, who are more interested in the function of religious pain than in its experience and its discursive form. See Harvey Whitehouse and James Laidlaw, *Ritual and Memory: Toward a Comparative Anthropology* (Walnut Creek, CA: Altamira, 2004). The ideas in this work were based on earlier research: Harvey Whitehouse, "Rites of Terror: Emotion, Metaphor and Meaning in Melanesian Initiation Cults," *Journal of the Royal Anthropological Institute* 2, no. 4 (December 1996): 703–715.

6. Susan Kwilecki, *Becoming Religious: Understanding Devotion to the Unseen* (Carnbury, NJ: Associated University Presses, 1999).

7. Ibid., 77.

8. Ibid., 80.

9. See Wayne Proudfoot and Phillip Shaner, "Attribution Theory and the Psychology of Religion," *Journal of the Scientific Study of Religion* 4, no. 4 (1975): 317–330. For a more recent study, see Ann Taves, *Religious Experience Reconsidered: A Building-block Approach to the Study of Religion and Other Special Things* (Princeton, NJ: Princeton University Press, 2009), "Introduction."

10. I am referring to the phenomenological act described by Edmund Husserl as the subject's conscious relationship to the object (content) of consciousness. See, for

instance, *Ideas: General Introduction to Pure Phenomenology* (New York: Routledge Classics, 2012), 170 ff.

11. A sampling of the most obvious candidates includes Rudolf Otto, *Mysticism East and West: A Comparative Analysis of the Nature of Mysticism* (New York: Macmillan, 1970). See also Evelyn Underhill, *Mysticism: A Study in the Nature and Development of Spiritual Consciousness* (London: Methuen, 1977). A far more recent and sophisticated version of such a position was developed by Robert K. C. Forman in *Mysticism: Mind, Consciousness* (Albany: State University of New York, 1999). The vast literature and its fundamental position are surveyed and undermined in a series of publications, beginning with Steven T. Katz, *Mysticism and Philosophical Analysis* (New York: Oxford University Press, 1978).

12. Russell T. McCutcheon, "Introduction," in *Religious Experience: A Reader*, ed. Craig Martin and Russell T. McCutcheon (Sheffield, UK: Equinox, 2012), 15. The reference here, and everywhere else, to maps and territory is a recognition of the preeminent position of Jonathan Z. Smith's critique of Eliade's failure to draw the proper ontological distinction between symbol-making and unmediated experience. See especially Smith's *Map Is Not Territory: Studies in the History of Religions* (Chicago: University of Chicago Press, 1978), perhaps the single most influential work on the study of religion in the past fifty years. For its influence, see Tyler Roberts, *Encountering Religion: Responsibility and Criticism after Secularism* (New York: Columbia University Press, 2013), Chapter 1.

13. McCutcheon, "Introduction," 10.

14. Charles Taylor, *Sources of the Self: The Making of the Modern Identity* (Cambridge, MA: Harvard University Press, 1989), 477.

15. Ibid., 472. The decisive influence on the constructivists was not Nietzsche but Wittgenstein and, following him, Gilbert Ryle, who had a significant influence on anthropologists like Clifford Geertz. In Geertz's emphasis on thick description as the narrative of anthropological description the key was not detail for its own sake but the tacit recognition that the description can never reach into the essential experience and must instead communicate structures of signification, or what Ryle had called "established codes." See Clifford Geertz, *The Interpretation of Cultures* (New York: Basic, 1973), 9. The reference in Ryle is to his *Collected Essays: 1929–1968* (New York: Routledge, 2009), 489–490. This is how Ryle assessed Wittgenstein's famous position on meaning ("Don't ask for the meaning, ask for the use" in *Philosophical Investigations*, vol. 1, 43): "The use of an expression, or the concept it expresses, is the role it is employed to perform, not a thing or person or event for which it might be supposed to stand." Ibid., 377.

16. Mircea Eliade, *Images and Symbols: Studies in Religious Symbolism* (Princeton, NJ: Princeton University Press, 1961).

17. Ann Taves writes that "religious experience meant something very different in 1750 and in 1900 in the Anglo-American context." See her *Fits, Trances and Visions: Experiencing Religion and Explaining Experience from Wesley to James* (Princeton, NJ: Princeton University Press, 1999), 351.

18. Recent writings in anthropology have sought to enrich the domain of experience (subjective, embodied) in relation to the social and political practices of power—by means of phenomenological methods. See Kalpana Ram and Christopher Houston, eds., *Phenomenology in Anthropology* (Bloomington: Indiana University Press, 2015).

19. Ariel Glucklich, in *Sacred Pain* (New York: Oxford University Press, 2001), analyzes the experience of South Indian pilgrims in terms of the neurodynamic benefits of self-induced pain.

20. McCutcheon, "Introduction," 4.

21. Peter Berger, *The Sacred Canopy: Elements of a Sociological Theory of Religion* (New York: Anchor, 1990).

22. Mark Johnson, *The Body in the Mind* (Chicago: University of Chicago Press, 1987,) x. For application to the subject of religious experience, see David Yamane, "Narrative and Religious Experience," *Sociology of Religion* 61, no. 2 (Summer 2000): 171–189.

23. Johnson, *The Body in the Mind*. These ideas were developed in several further publications, including George Lakoff and Mark Johnson's *Metaphors We Live By*, 2nd ed. (Chicago: University of Chicago Press, 2003). In the words of Clifford Geertz, the empirical passage between cultural productions and personal experience is "treacherous," and this is where I must go next. See Geertz, "Making Experiences, Authoring Selves," in *The Anthropology of Experience*, ed. V. Turner and E. Bruner (Urbana: University of Illinois, 1986), 377–378. Cited in Yamane, "Narrative and Religious Experience," 173.

24. According to Vygotsky, "The mechanism of social behavior and the mechanism of consciousness are the same . . . we are aware of ourselves, for we are aware of others." See Lev Vygotsky, "Consciousness as a Problem of Psychology of Behavior," *Soviet Psychology* no. 17 (1979): 29–30. See also his *Thought and Language* (Cambridge, MA: MIT Press, 1997), xxiv. See in addition Mary B. McVee, Kailonnie Dunsmore, and James R. Gavelek, "Schema Theory Revisited," *Review of Educational Research* 75, no. 4 (Winter 2005): 531–566. The sociocultural view in its contemporary constructivist variations has been ridiculed by Steven Pinker in several publications, not least *The Language Instinct* (New York: Harper Collins, 1994). Linguists following Noam Chomsky's theories of a universal grammar; evolutionary cognitive psychologists working on the modular property of the brain (with "innate knowledge"), which Chomsky called "mental organ"; and researchers in several other fields reject the constructive reduction of human knowledge and experience. See Pinker, *The Language Instinct, and* David J. Buller, *Adapting Minds: Evolutionary Psychology and the Persistent Quest for Human Nature* (Cambridge, MA: MIT Press, 2005).

25. Johnson, *The Body in the Mind*, 14.

26. Stanley A. Mulaik, "The Metaphoric Origins of Objectivity, Subjectivity, and Consciousness in the Direct Perception of Reality," *Philosophy of Science* 62, no. 2 (June 1995): 283–303.

27. Francisco Santibáñez, "The Object Image-Schema and Other Dependent Schemas," in *Atlantis* 24, no. 2 (December 2002): 183–201.

28. The "Stanford Prison Experiment," for example, conducted by Philip G. Zimbardo, displays the ease and rapidity with which cultural personas disintegrate. See Zimbardo, *The Lucifer Effect: Understanding How Good People Turn Evil* (New York: Random House, 2007), and Kent L. Brintnall, *Ecce Homo: The Male-Body-in-Pain as Redemptive Figure* (Chicago: University of Chicago Press, 2011). Tyler Roberts argues that theology itself can create disruptions in the self and in social formations. See his *Encountering Religion*, 20.

29. The cybernetic and bidirectional relationship between society (or culture) and the body generates meanings that are most clearly visible in the domain of emotions. "Love" is just one example, of course. This topic is discussed in a later chapter. See M. L. Lyon and J. M. Barbalet, "Society's Body: Emotion and the 'Semantization' of Social Theory," in *Embodiment and Experience*, ed. Thomas J. Csordas (Cambridge: Cambridge University Press, 1994), 48–68.

30. For the former, see Whitehouse, "Rites of Terror" 714; for the latter, see I. M. Lewis, *Ecstatic Religion: A Study of Shamanism and Spirit Possession* (New York: Routledge 2003), 49, and Thomas J. Csordas, *The Sacred Self: A Cultural Phenomenology of Charismatic Healing* (Berkeley: University of California Press, 1997), 119.

31. That was the central thesis of the phenomenological research in Glucklich, *Sacred Pain*, and earlier in *The Sense of Adharma* (New York: Oxford University Press, 1994).

32. Wexler, *The Mystical Society*, 8.

33. "Jerusalem Files," April 4, 1986, "Conversations (Yossef Words)," July 7, 1995.

34. The conversations discussed in these chapters took several hours and occupy over twenty pages. I have reduced these by over 90 percent but have tried to retain the central points.

35. In this paragraph Yossef implicitly reprises the entire history of Indian (Hindu, Buddhist) psychology without a single reference or citation; all of it appears to be based on his own self-observation.

36. See *Yoga Sutra* 1.2 and Edwin Bryant's commentary, *The Yoga Sutras of Patanjali* (New York: North Point, 2009), 21–23. See also *Bhagavad Gita* 5.21–22.

37. The conversation also reveals interesting social dynamics (such as teacher-student), but this is discussed elsewhere.

38. The subject of "mechanistic thinking" and the ego feature in a later chapter on mysticism. Despite his unmistakable indebtedness to Asian and Western mystical ideas, Yossef refused to acknowledge sources and operated in a "naïve" manner, that is, as a strict introspectionist. This is still true for residents of Neot Smadar.

39. I use the term "ruse" purposefully because there is something mischievous, not to say devious, about verbal paradoxes such as "childless mother" and "pool full of nothing" in Kabir (fifteenth century); "sound of one hand clapping" in Zen; and the occult spiritual meanings in the eroticism of the Song of Songs according to Origen (third century).

40. A sociological way of putting this is "sharing their constructions." See Ole Riis and Luigi Berzano, eds., *Annual Review of the Sociology of Religion*, vol. 3: *New Methods* (Leiden: Brill, 2012), 129. A great deal of scholarly attention is currently devoted to the epistemology of field researchers' "experience" with informants, with their notes, and with the narrative that emerges in their books. See, for example, Judith Okely and Helen Callaway, *Anthropology and Autobiography* (London: Routledge, 1992), and Helwon Chary, *Autobiography as Method* (Walnut Creek, CA: Left Coast, 2008). See also the introduction to the present work.

41. The method of the observer-participant, now being challenged in many ways, owes its origin to the hermeneutics of Gadamer, Habermas, and Ricoeur. But see Clifford Geertz, *Works and Lives: The Anthropologist as Author* (Stanford, CA: Stanford University Press, 1988), 90–92. Geertz is commenting on the Malinowskian diary-writing tradition as exemplified by Rabinow, Crapanzano, and Dwyer—all writing about Morocco (using the authorial "I")—and they appear to be the targets of Bourdieu's "narcissistic" comment.

42. Pierre Bourdieu, "Participant Objectivation," *Journal of the Royal Anthropological Institute* 9, no. 2 (June 2003): 281–294.

43. Robert Tyler, *Encountering Religion: Responsibility and Criticism after Secularism* (New York: Columbia University Press, 2013), 16. "Disciplined suspension" applies not to the adherence to a scholarly worldview but to the act of applying it as a tool to reduce the other.

44. C. Taylor, *Sources of the Self*, 47.

45. See David Yamane's discussion (following S. Chase) in "Narrative and Religious Experience," 183.

Chapter 2. Washing Dishes

Chapter 2 is a personal narrative and has no notes.

Chapter 3. The Oasis of Neot Smadar

1. The system includes natural sewage purification and water re-use for irrigation. See www.neot-smadar.com/environment.

2. See Chapter 8 on the asceticism of communal projects.

3. Israeli law requires businesses in remote locations to allow the free use of restrooms.

4. Over the years Neot Smadar has employed a small number of paid workers in a number of capacities (e.g., construction, agriculture, heavy equipment operation, dairy work). These have included Sudanese, Palestinians, Thais, Chinese, and others.

5. However, the economy must adapt to the needs of the school in some special ways: the various branches need to accommodate a constant stream of young volunteers, the crews need to be flexible and allow for relatively quick rotation, the

work must be local and ethical (organic, humane, ecological), the arrival of new workers must be monitored, and so on. See the school's document: "What Is the Economy of a School?"

6. The distinction between *kvutza* (lit. "group") and kibbutz resembles that of *Gemeinschaft* and *Gesellschaft*. See Ferdinand Toennies, *Community and Society (Gemeinschaft and Gesellschaft)* (New Brunswick, NJ: Transaction, 1988).

7. This is based on a written report by Alon dated August 17, 2011.

8. See J. R. Blasi, *The Quality of Life in a Kibbutz Cooperative Community* (Cambridge, MA: Institute for Cooperative Community, 1977); E. Cohen, "The Structural Transformation of the Kibbutz," in *The Sociology of the Kibbutz: Studies of Israeli Society*, ed. E. Krausz, vol. 2 (New Brunswick: Transactions, 1983) 75–114; Henry Near, *The Kibbutz Movement: Crisis and Achievement, 1939–1995* (Oxford, UK: Littman Library, 1997).

9. It is virtually impossible to translate *"sharat"* in the sense that Yossef intended it. It appears in various forms in biblical Hebrew in the sense of serving, ministering, waiting upon, and so forth. The word "servant" in modern Hebrew is the closest meaning, but no one in Neot Smadar would accept this as a proper translation. The vagueness or ambiguity of Yossef's intended meaning is maintained by sticking to his own word, "sharat," without a translation.

10. This honesty of Yossef is a common theme in his methodology as the sharat of the school. See Monica's words in Chapter 4, on the school.

11. Ilana's report, April 1, 2015, 3.

12. This material and the triangular imagery come from a conversation with Alon in June 2014. The same material is presented with greater subtlety in the report Alon wrote upon leaving the position of secretary (April 1, 2015). Unlike Ilana, Alon focuses on the more technical aspects of joint leadership and the tasks they confronted immediately after assuming the role.

Chapter 4. A School for Self-Inquiry

1. Terrence G. Kardong, *Pillars of Community: Four Rules of Pre-Benedictine Monastic Life* (Collegeville, MN: Liturgical Press, 1991); Charles S. Prebish, *Buddhist Monastic Discipline: The Sanskrit Pratimoksa Sutras of the Mahasanghikas and Mulasarvastivadas* (Delhi: Motilal Banarsidass, 2002); William B. Helmreich, *The World of the Yeshiva: An Intimate Portrait of Orthodox Jewry* (Jersey City, NJ: Ktav, 2000).

2. Anat G. has recalled that, according to Yossef, "all that currently exists is just a preparation for the school."

3. I heard this from Rony M., from David, from Monica, and from many others—in separate conversations with each.

4. Gurdjieff writings. See G. I. Gurdjieff, *Meetings with Remarkable Men* (New York: E. P. Dutton, 1963), and G. I. Gurdjieff, *Transcripts of Gurdjieff's Meetings, 1941–1946* (London: Book Studio, 2008).

5. John Welwood, "Reflection and Presence: The Dialectic of Self-Knowledge," *Journal of Transpersonal Psychology* 28, no. 2 (1996): 107–128.

6. P. D. Ouspensky, *In Search of The Miraculous: The Teachings of G. I. Gurdjieff* (San Diego: Harvest Book, 2001).

7. Ibid., 105.

8. Ilan Amit, *Gurdjieff and the Inner Work* (Tel Aviv: Mapa, 2005).

9. Ouspensky, *In Search of the Miraculous*, 15; the Sanskrit word for this discernment, *viveka*, especially in its Advaita Vedanta usage, would be especially appropriate here.

10. Rony O., interview with the author, September 9, 2014.

11. The consequence was a sort of shock or "dissonance," which in Hebrew is called *za'azua*. The concept harkens back to Gurdjieff, where it is taken from the world of musical notes and the shock that melodic dissonance creates. Some of the school's early work is discussed by Yoram Harpaz in an article published in *The City Paper (Ha'Ir)* of Jerusalem (March 31, 1989), and more systematically in David Maliniak's unpublished paper "Neot Smadar: The Story of a Building, The Story of Builders" (May 2015).

12. See Chapter 11.

13. The topic of the self-denying teacher or master in the religious life (Tibetan Buddhist, Hindu Yogi, Zen master, or even Greek philosopher) is immense. It was clearly a central theme in the talks of Krishnamurti. A superb analysis of this phenomenon can be found in Nigel Tubbs, *Philosophy of the Teacher* (Malden, MA: Blackwell, 2005), especially in Part II (57–150).

14. There is nothing systematic here, however tempting it might be to relate this to continental phenomenology (Husserl), Indian metaphysics (Vedanta), or even transpersonal psychology. Yossef simply saw how conscious experience proceeded as a process.

15. One such incident included Gil, as Gil and Avi ignored Yossef in obtaining construction material from retired aqueduct parts.

Chapter 5. The School after the Death of Yossef

1. See Ronald L. Grimes, *Deeply into the Bone: Re-inventing Rites of Passage* (Berkeley: University of California Press, 2000). Grimes's observations on the necessity of making such rituals meaningful (embodied) also apply to Dani's wedding ritual, described in Chapter 11.

2. Anat's report, May 14–21, 2003.

3. Ramana Maharshi realized early in his life that the fear of death was the fear of losing the ego or self. He used this insight to discover his true inner self. See Arthur Osborne, *Ramana Maharshi and the Path of Self-Knowledge* (Tiruvannamalai, India: Sri Ramanasraman, 2004), 9.

4. Mark Juergensmeyer, *Radhasoami Reality: The Logic of a Modern Faith* (Princeton, NJ: Princeton University Press, 1991), 43. The subject of the death of the

religious teacher and the succession that must take place as a result is universal, not limited to charismatic groups. For an introduction to the issues involved in the context of Jewish Hasidism and Islamic Sufism, see C. Lindholm, ed., *The Anthropology of Religious Charisma: Ecstasies and Institutions* (New York: Palgrave Macmillan, 2013). The succession questions raised tend to focus on authority and the legitimacy of new knowledge. See, for example Jacqueline Ilyse Stone, *Original Enlightenment and the Transformation of Medieval Japanese Buddhism* (Honolulu: University of Hawai'i, 1999).

5. Omri recently illustrated this notion by means of the distinction between "ben-adam" (the fully actualized human) and "ben-enosh" (the merely human). However, the subtlety of this point, I am told, is lost in the translation from the Hebrew terms.

6. The subject of theoretical and ontological reduction is immense and is not discussed here. In the domain of mind and brain, see Patricia Smith Churchland, *Neurophilosophy: Toward a Unified Science of the Mind/Brain* (Cambridge, MA: MIT Press, 1998). In the domain of religious experience, see Ann Taves, *Religious Experience Reconsidered: A Building-block Approach to the Study of Religion and Other Special Things* (Princeton, NJ: Princeton University Press, 2009). For religion and brain science, see Eugene D'Aquili and Andrew Newberg, *The Mystical Mind: Probing the Biology of Religious Experience* (Minneapolis: Fortress, 1999).

7. See Robin Waterfield, trans., *The Theology of Arithmetic: On the Mystical, Mathematical and Cosmological Symbolism of the First Ten Numbers* (Grand Rapids, MI: Phanes, 1988); Christopher Bamford, ed., *Homage to Pythagoras: Rediscovering Sacred Science* (Hudson, NY: Lindisfarne, 1994); Adela Yarbro Collins, *Cosmology and Eschatology in Jewish and Christian Apocalypticism* (Leiden: E. J. Brill, 1996); Sophia Wellbeloved, *Gurdjieff: The Key Concepts* (London: Routledge, 2003).

8. Sukkah meeting, Wednesday, May 2, 1990.

Chapter 6. The Art of Listening

1. Hanina Ben-Menahem, Neil S. Hecht, and Shai Wosner, eds., *Controversy and Dialogue in the Jewish Tradition* (New York: Routledge, 2005). Recall Reb Sanders's silent treatment of his brilliant but haughty son in Haim Potok's *The Chosen*.

2. Yajnavalkya is featured in the *Brihadaranyaka Upanishad*, while Uddalka Aruni is in the *Chandogya Upanishad*.

3. John J. Holder, *Early Buddhist Discourses* (Indianapolis: Hacket, 2006). See especially "Discourses on Noble Quest" (*Ariyapariyesana Sutta*). See Richard F. Gombrich, *How Buddhism Began: The Conditioned Genesis of the Early Teachings* (London: Routledge, 2006). For Zen, see Shoyo Roku, *Book of Serenity: One Hundred Zen Dialogues* (Boston: Shambala, 2005).

4. Quote from *Yoga Sutra* 1.3.

5. See Jiddu Krishnamurti's famous dictum on freedom from the desire for an answer: "Freedom from the desire for an answer is essential to the understanding of

a problem." See *Commentaries on Living*, Series 1, Chapter 41: "Awareness" (New York: Quest, 1956).

6. Avigdor in conversation with the author, December 20, 2015.

7. One of the persistent themes of Self-inquiry is observing the images we project about others whom we encounter and our blindness to how we construct such images out of our own material. Several informants discussed this subject with me in great detail. While Buddhists and Hindus discuss the form we give to emptiness or impermanence in all things, the emphasis in Neot Smadar is on encounters with other people.

8. Jon Frederickson, in discussing psychodynamic listening, quotes Henri Bergson: "Our personality is precisely that: the continuous melody of our inner life." "Psychodynamic listening" refers to our feelings and thoughts as psychic forces moving in a "field" that includes speaker and listener. See Frederickson, *Psychodynamic Psychotherapy: Learning to Listen from Multiple Perspectives* (Philadelphia: Taylor & Francis, 1999) 7.

9. Milan Kundera, *The Book of Laughter and Forgetting* (New York: Harper Perennial, 1999) 110.

10. "Truth cannot be given to you by somebody. You have to discover it; and to discover, there must be a state of mind in which there is direct perception. There is no direct perception when there is a resistance." See J. Krishnamurti, *Total Freedom: The Essential Krishnamurti* (San Francisco: HarperSanFrancisco, 1996), 60.

11. Andrew Newberg and Mark Robert Waldman, *Words Can Change Your Brain* (New York: Plume, 2013), 4–5.

12. See Chapter 10 on the extended family.

Chapter 7. Everyday Mysticism

1. See Chapter 1 on religious experience. See also Bernard McGinn, *The Foundations of Mysticism: Origins to the Fifth Century* (New York: Crossroads, 1995), xiv.

2. Swami Ramdas, *In Quest of God: The Saga of an Extraordinary Pilgrimage* (San Diego: Blue Dove, 1994), 141.

3. Augustine, "Homily on Psalm 41.9"; quoted in McGinn, *The Foundations of Mysticism*, 239–240.

4. See Philip Wexler in *The Mystical Society* and Philip Wexler and Jonathan Garb, eds., in *After Spirituality: Studies in Mystical Traditions* (New York: Peter Lang, 2012). I return to Wexler's work later in this chapter. I am unable to rule out (or verify) what one member of Neot Smadar referred to as "private moments of illumination" in the community.

5. Steven T. Katz, ed., *Mysticism and Philosophical Analysis* (New York: Oxford University Press, 1978); Steven T. Katz, ed. *Mysticism and Religious Traditions* (New York: Oxford University Press, 1983).

6. Robert K. C. Forman, *Mysticism: Mind, Consciousness*. Albany: State University of New York Press, 1999.

7. Thich Nhat Hanh, "New Heart Sutra Translation by Thich Nhat Hanh," http://plumvillage.org/news/thich-nhat-hanh-new-heart-sutra-translation, accessed August 11, 2016.

8. The "hybrid" here is the linking of western jargon (mystical) with a radically different religious culture. But see Paul Mommaers and Jan van Bragt, *Mysticism Buddhist and Christian: Encounters with Jan van Ruusbroec* (New York: Crossroads, 1995), 31 ff.

9. Richard H. Robinson and Willard L. Johnson, *The Buddhist Religion: A Historical Introduction* (Belmont, CA: Wadsworth, 1997), 87.

10. The philosopher Nagarjuna (ca. 150–250 CE) states in *Samyuta Nikaya* XII.15: "When one sees the arising of the world [sensory phenomena] as it actually is with right wisdom, 'non-being' with reference to the world does not occur to one. When one sees the cessation of the world as it actually is with right wisdom, 'being' with reference to the world does not occur to one." Quoted in Robinson and Johnson, *The Buddhist Religion*, 88.

11. Quoted without attribution from *Zen Notes* 1, no. 5 (New York: First Zen Institute of America), 1. See Huston Smith and Philip Novak, *Buddhism: A Concise Introduction* (San Francisco: HarperSanFrancisco, 2003), 100.

12. Barbara Stoler Miller, *Yoga: Discipline of Freedom* (Berkeley: University of California Press, 1995).

13. *Sankhya Karika* LXII, quoted in Edwin F. Bryant, *The Yoga Sutras of Patanjali* (New York: North Point, 2009), xlvi.

14. Barbara Miller makes a similar point about desire: the same psychological drive that makes us cling to false permanence is essential for motivating us to practice discipline (yoga) and attain samadhi. See Miller, *Yoga*, 4. This is a problem every college freshman perceives, but, as we shall see, is a major obstacle to actual practice.

15. Bryant, *The Yoga Sutras*, 307.

16. Arthur Osborne, *Ramana Maharshi and the Path of Self-Knowledge* (Tiruvannamalai, India: Sri Ramanasramam, 2004), 10.

17. Rik van Nieuwenhove, Robert Faesen, and Helen Rolfson, eds., *Late Medieval Mysticism: Of the Low Countries* (New York: Paulist, 2008), 145.

18. Ibid. 145.

19. Ruusbroec, *The Spiritual Espousals* (*Opera Omnia* III.c.19–33), quoted in Mommaers and van Bragt, *Mysticism*, 21.

20. The prophetic figures prominently in the next chapter, but see David Tracy, "Recent Catholic Spirituality: Unity amid Diversity," in *Christian Spirituality III: Post-Reformation and Modern*, ed. L. Dupré and D. Saliers (New York: Crossroad, 1989), 143–173, and Johan Baptist Metz, *A Passion for God: The Mystical-Political Dimension of Christianity*, trans. and ed. J. Matthew Ashley (Mahwah, NJ: Paulist, 1998).

21. Don Cupitt, *Mysticism after Modernity* (Malden, MA: Blackwell, 1998). See especially Chapter 4: "Mysticism Is a Kind of Writing."

22. According to Mark McIntosh, Bernard McGinn prefers "consciousness" to "ex-

perience" in order to emphasize both the cognitive dimension of the mystical moment and the influence of context. See Mark McIntosh, *Mystical Theology* (Malden, MA: Blackwell, 1998), 31.

23. P. Sheldrake, "Contemplation and Social Transformation: The Example of Thomas Merton," in *Acta Theological Supplementum* 11 (2008): 181–197; Janet Ruffing, ed., *Mysticism and Social Transformation* (Syracuse, NY: Syracuse University Press, 2001).

24. In Vedanta this would be the distinction between a conception of Brahman that possesses qualities (saguna) and is potentially subject to knowing as opposed to a conception of Brahman that transcends all qualities (nirguna) and cannot be known. Only the latter is ultimately "real."

25. I do believe Yossef displayed great skill in *viveka*, which is a special sort of discrimination between different states of consciousness.

26. Alex Watson, "The Self as a Dynamic Constant: Ramakantha's Middle Ground between a Naiyayika Eternal Self-Substance and a Buddhist Stream of Consciousness-Moments," *Journal of Indian Philosophy* 42 (2014): 173–193.

27. This is a decisive factor in the conception of Neot Smadar as an "extended family." See Chapter 10.

Chapter 8. Constructing the Art Center

1. Lobsang P. Lhalungpa, *The Life of Milarepa* (Boston: Shambala, 1977).

2. For example, Foucault, in The *History of Sexuality*, vol. 2 (New York: Vintage, 1990), understands asceticism as an aspect of the ethical formation of the subject; Geoffrey Harpham, in *The Ascetic Imperative in Culture and Criticism* (Chicago: University of Chicago Press, 1987), sees asceticism as that which enables communication within a culture; it is the fundamental operating ground of culture as a shared entity.

3. Quoted in Richard Valantasis, "A Theory of the Social Function of Asceticism," in *Asceticism*, ed. Vincent L. Wimbush and Richard Valantasis (New York: Oxford University Press, 1995), 547. See also Gavin Flood, *The Ascetic Self: Subjectivity, Memory and Tradition* (Cambridge: Cambridge University Press, 2004), 252–254.

4. Harpham, *The Ascetic Imperative in Culture and Criticism.*

5. Contemporary work on organizational psychology focuses on the inefficiency in a project or on rewards, on the difference between intrinsic and extrinsic motivation, and on communication in groups such as work teams. See, for example, Alfie Kohn, *Punished by Rewards: The Trouble with Gold Stars* (New York: Houghton Mifflin, 1999); Caron Sansone et al., *Intrinsic and Extrinsic Motivation: The Search for Optimal Motivation and Performance* (San Diego: Academic Press, 2000). Neot Smadar projects represent an excellent laboratory for studying such issues, but it is important to emphasize that whatever wonderful consequences emerge from the work, these are always subsidiary to Self-inquiry. This is a novel concept that requires separate study (see Chapter 11).

6. According to one report, he was usually wrong about people not showing up: if they were not at the worksite it was because they were needed elsewhere.

7. Valantasis, "A Theory."

Chapter 9. At Work in Neot Smadar

1. This is not because work (say, peeling carrots) resembles meditation or may sometimes produce mildly euphoric states of consciousness such as those described by Courtney Bender in *Heaven's Kitchen: Living Religion at God's Love We Deliver* (Chicago: University of Chicago Press, 2003), 76.

2. Miroslav Volf, *Work in the Spirit: Toward a Theology of Work* (New York: Oxford University Press, 1991) 10–11.

3. Ibid., 13, 79, 89, et passim. For these comments I am indebted to Jürgen Multmann's *Theology of Hope: On the Ground and the Implications of a Christian Eschatology* (New York: Harper & Row, 1967).

4. Quoted in Terrence E. Kardong, *Four Rules of Pre-Benedictine Monastic Life* (Collegeville, MN: Liturgical Press, 2010) 57. For a fascinating Jewish contrast, see Shimon Hatzadik on torah, avodah, and *gmilut chasadim* (Torah, work, and charity) as the three foundations of the world, which must be joined together. *Mishnah* Nezikim, Masechet Avot, Chapter A, mishnah B.

5. A. D. Gordon often rejected ideologies in favor of practical work with the soil. But he rhapsodized that it was this work under the sun and the land of Israel that created a new human being (*"tipus adam chadash"*), about whom the school in Neot Smadar is silent. See Aviva Opaz, *Sefer Hakevutzah* (Jerusalem: Yad Ben Tzvi, 1996), 31–32; Anita Shapira, *Hapoel Hatzair* (Tel Aviv: Am Oved, 1967), 151.

6. The literature on Zen and dish washing alone is substantial and popular, with the theme of the paradoxical value of the merely mundane as spiritual discipline playing a key role. See Philip T. Sudo, *Zen 24/7* (New York: HarperCollins, 2005). Many in Neot Smadar have read Thich Nhat Hanh and would approve of his take on dish washing (see "The Zen of Dish-Washing" at www.speakingtree.in, March 9, 2013). When Alon posted "What is complete work (avoda shlema)?" on the dining room bulletin board, most comments focused on mindfulness.

7. Mihaly Csikszentmihalyi, *Flow: The Psychology of Optimal Experience* (New York: Harper Perennial, 1991).

8. August Turak, *The Business Secrets of the Trappist Monks: One CEO's Quest for Meaning and Authenticity* (New York: Columbia University Press, 2013).

9. Avigdor, interview with the author, May 17, 2015.

10. Shmuel, email to the author, December 26, 2016 (forwarding the information provided by Natasha Biran).

11. Jacob Needleman and Goerge Baker, eds., *Gurdjieff: Essays and Reflections on the Man and His Teachings* (New York: Continuum, 2004) 117. Gurdjieff's ideas related to shock are complex and include the notion of a gap between the notes mi and fa and the implications of this in terms of developing constant and dis-

passionate self-observation. See Jeanne De Salzmann, *The Reality of Being: The Fourth Way of Gurdjieff* (Boston: Shambala, 2011).

12. Adva's report, August 5, 2014.

13. Adva's report can serve as a detailed case study on the effect of "shock" (discussed earlier) on Self-inquiry.

14. "A person who scorns the little things has no place in the school. An undertaking one has assumed is more important than one's self-image." From the guidelines of the school at Neot Smadar.

15. Matthew Crawford, *Shop Class as Soulcraft: An Inquiry into the Value of Work* (New York: Penguin, 2009), 26.

Chapter 10. The Extended Family

1. Omri, interview with the author, May 27, 2015.

2. Pierluigi Piovanelli, "Jesus' Charismatic Authority: On the Historical Applicability of a Sociological Model," *Journal of the American Academy of Religion* 73, no. 2 (June 2005): 395–427; Bruce J. Molina, *The Social World of Jesus and the Gospels* (London: Routledge, 1996).

3. According to Max Weber, "charisma" applies to a "certain quality of an individual personality by virtue of which he is considered extraordinary and treated with supernatural, superhuman, or at least specifically exceptional powers or qualities." See Weber, *Economy and Society: An Outline of Interpretive Sociology* (Berkeley: University of California Press, 1978), 241. Over the decades since Weber's work was published, charisma has been redefined many times over, but it remains vague and misleading in common usage—as seen in the comments by Anat below.

4. Laurence R. Iannaccone, "Religious Participation: A Human Capital Approach," *Journal for the Scientific Study of Religion* 29 (1990): 297–314; Rodney Stark and Roger Finke, *Acts of Faith: Explaining the Human Side of Religion* (Berkeley: University of California Press, 2000). On the biology of altruism and religious-social values, see Sarah Coakley and Martin Nowak, *Evolution, Games, and God: The Principle of Cooperation* (Cambridge, MA: Harvard University Press, 2013), or, alternatively, David Sloan Wilson, *Darwin's Cathedral: Evolution, Religion and the Nature of Society* (Chicago: University of Chicago Press, 2002).

5. Anat G.'s report, July 2010.

6. See C. R. Hinings and Royston Greenwood, "Disconnects and Consequences in Organization Theory?" *Administrative Science Quarterly* 47, no. 3 (September 2002): 411–421, for the Weberian theory on charisma, bureaucratization, and their limits.

7. Victor Turner, ed., *Celebration Studies in Festivities and Rituals* (Washington, DC: Smithsonian Institution Press, 1982). See also Gretchen Siegler, "In Search of Truth: Maintaining Communities in a Religious Community," in *Intentional Community*, ed. Brown, 41–66.

8. Ferdinand Toennies, *Community and Society (Gemeinschaft and Gesellschaft)* (New Brunswick, NJ: Transaction, 1988). Charisma is embedded not only in persons but also in ideas, as seen in the writings of the early kibbutz settlers. See Aviva Opaz, ed., *Sefer Ha-Kevutzah: Kevutzat Hasharon 1922–1936* (Jerusalem: Yad Ben Tzvi, 1996), and Henry Near, *The Kibbutz Movement: Crisis and Achievement, 1939–1995* (Oxford: Littman Library, 1997), 268.

9. Carmela, interview with the author, July 2015.

10. Ilana, interview with the author, July 2015.

11. Philip Wexler, *The Mystical Society: An Emerging Social Vision* (Boulder, CO: Westview, 2000), 11.

12. Wexler's main focus is post-modernity and contemporary globalized social media. Although the case of Neot Smadar is illuminated by his analysis it is interesting to note that until very recently the community was almost completely isolated: no television, radio, computers (internet). The main source of external information were the two copies of the daily Ha'aretz that arrived at the main office in the morning.

13. J. Ruffing, *Mysticism*, 2.

14. Iris L., interview with the author, May 2013.

15. See Chapter 7 on mysticism as a cultural phenomenon and the demise of "pure consciousness" in the academic study of mystical experience.

16. Robert J. Egan, S.J., "Ignatian Spirituality and Social Justice," address given in Toronto at Regis College, 1991, 34. See also Janet K. Ruffing, "Ignatian Mysticism of Service: Ignatius of Loyola and Pedro Arrupe," in *Mysticism*, ed. Ruffing, 104–128. The Georgetown University mission statement includes both the Catholic/Jesuit identity of the school and a wide-ranging ethical and educational agenda in the Jesuit tradition for the "glory of God." In another vein, see Dorothy Day, *House of Hospitality* (New York: Catholic Worker, 1939).

17. Amy Hollywood, "Preaching as Social Practice in Meister Eckhart," in *Mysticism*, ed. Ruffing, 84.

18. B. McGinn, *The Foundations of Mysticism*, xvi.

19. Thomas Merton, *Conjectures of a Guilty Bystander* (Garden City, NY: Doubleday, 1966), 140–141.

20. Philip Sheldrake, "Contemplation and Social Transformation: The Example of Thomas Merton," in *Acta Theological Supplementum* 11 (2008): 183. According to the Greek Orthodox theologian John D. Zizioulas, Christ ought to be taken as an absolutely relational entity and, of course, as the goal and measure of the spiritual life. The individual person is alienated from that state. See Zizioulas, *Being as Communion: Studies in Personhood and the Church* (Crestwood, NY: St. Vladimir's Seminary Press, 1997), 42–43.

21. Thomas Merton, *Life and Holiness* (New York: Doubleday Image, 1964), 9–19.

22. See the discussion on Amitai Etzioni and John Rawls (communitarianism and liberalism) in the introduction to this book.

23. Naturally I am glossing over significant differences: In Buddhist mysticism "what

is annihilated is the 'I,' the individuality, the 'person.' . . . On the other hand the Christian, who values the person, is obliged to formulate a delicate distinction . . . what is annihilated is not the person as such, with its unique capacity of self-presence, but the distorted preoccupation with oneself." See Paul Mommaers and Jan Van Bragt, *Mysticism Buddhist and Christian: Encounters with Jan van Ruusbroec* (New York: Crossroad, 1995), 95.

24. Christina Toren, "Imagining the World That Warrants Our Imagination: The Revelation of Ontogeny," in *Sociality: New Directions*, ed. Nicholas J. Long and Henrietta L. Moore (New York: Berghahn, 2013), 46. The best place to explore the origins and outlines of this conception is in Charles Taylor, *The Sources of the Self: The Making of the Modern Identity* (New York: Cambridge University Press, 1992).

25. Charisma theory is reductive in the sense of fully explaining cultural and psychological processes that may, in fact, account in reverse for the effectiveness of a particular individual's power. See Philip Smith, "Culture and Charisma: Outline of a Theory," *Acta Sociologica* 43, no. 2 (April 2000): 101–111.

26. Alon composed most of these. My favorite during the weeks of the project was this: "What is complete work?" The ambiguity is lost in translation, where *avoda shlema* can mean "complete" but also "perfectly executed" or "executed with attentiveness or mindfulness."

27. This replicated seasonal fruit picking, especially of dates, or the togetherness of holiday rituals and the occasional wedding, as Chapter 11 shows.

Chapter 11. A Wedding Gift for Dani

1. Antonin Artaud, *The Theater and Its Double* (New York: Grove, 1958); Jean-Louis Barault, *Reflections on the Theater* (London: Rockcliff, 1951); Robert Cohen and John Harrop, *Creative Play Direction* (Englewood Cliffs, NJ: Prentice Hall, 1974), 169–215. According to Hannah (interview with the author, June 8, 2013), Yossef may have been influenced (a bit later) by Keith Johnstone, who was famous for connecting theatrical technique with worldly wisdom. See Keith Johnstone, *Impro: Improvisation and the Theatre* (London: Faber and Faber, 1979).

2. See Stephen O. Murray, "Review: The Scientific Reception of Castaneda," *Contemporary Sociology* 8 (March 1979): 189–192.

3. There are numerous ways of defining and understanding rituals, and most reflect the task that researchers are pursuing. Roy Rappaport has a nicely condensed definition: Ritual is "the performance of more or less invariant sequences of formal acts and utterances not entirely encoded by the performers." See Roy Rappaport, *Ritual and Religion in the Making of Humanity* (Cambridge: Cambridge University Press, 1999), 24. For more expansive definitions of ritual, see Ronald L. Grimes, *The Craft of Ritual Studies* (New York: Oxford University Press, 2014), 185–197.

4. The figurative language of dying comes from Mircea Eliade's work on rites of passage (which were popular, along with Joseph Campbell, when Castaneda was

writing), but the more empirical work from that era was Victor Turner's on liminality—that in-between ritual state that initiates undergo as they transition. See Victor Turner, *The Ritual Process: Structure and Anti-Structure* (New Brunswick, NJ: Aldine Transaction, 2011).

5. Erving Goffman, *Presentation of Self in Everyday Life* (Garden City, NY: Doubleday Anchor, 1959), 35.

6. Victor Turner, *The Ritual Process: Structure and Anti-Structure* (Chicago: Aldine, 1969.)

7. Caroline Humphrey and James Laidlaw, *The Archetypal Actions of Ritual: An Essay on Ritual as Action Illustrated by the Jain Rite of Worship* (Oxford: Oxford University Press, 1994), Chapter 3.

8. Carlos Castaneda, *The Teachings of Don Juan: A Yaqui Way of Knowledge* (Berkeley: University of California Press, 1972), 24.

9. Bruce Kapferer, *A Celebration of Demons: Exorcism and the Aesthetics of Healing in Sri Lanka* (Bloomington: Indiana University Press, 1983), 177.

10. Marcia S. Calkowski, "A Day at the Tibetan Opera: Actualized Performance and Spectacular Discourse," *American Ethnologist* 18, no. 4 (November 1991): 643–657.

11. Some of this (in California) is covered in Jeffrey J. Kripal's *Esalen: America and the Religion of No Religion* (Chicago: University of Chicago Press, 2007) and, more broadly, in Timothy Miller, *America's Alternative Religions* (Albany: State University of New York, 1995). For an assessment of Castaneda's value and cultural influence, see Robert J. Wallis, *Shamans/Neo-Shamans: Ecstasy, Alternative Archaeologies and Contemporary Pagans* (New York: Routledge, 2003), 39–44.

12. Lee Gilmore, *Theater in a Crowded Fire: Ritual and Spirituality at Burning Man* (Berkeley: University of California Press, 2010), 5.

13. Castaneda, *The Teachings of Don Juan*, 60.

14. The literature on gift exchange and its role in social life is immense, much of it following Emil Durkheim and Marcel Mauss. There is widespread agreement that the replacement of pure gift exchange ("social capital") with monetary calculations reflects profound changes in the nature of social arrangements and relationships. See Marcel Mauss, *The Gift: The Form and Reason of Exchange in Archaic Societies* (Oxon, UK: Routledge, 2002). For a recent example of such work, see Ilana Krausman Ben-Amos, *The Culture of Giving: Informal Support and Gift Exchange in Early Modern England* (Cambridge: Cambridge University Press, 2008).

Conclusion

1. J. Krishnamurti, *Talks and Dialogues* (Berkeley, CA: Shambala, 1970), 67.

BIBLIOGRAPHY

Aanibanez, Francisco. "The Object Image-Schema and Other Dependent Schemas," *Atlantis* 24, no. 2 (December 2002): 183–201.

Amit, Ilan. *Gurdjieff and the Inner Work*. Tel Aviv: Mapa, 2005.

Artaud, Antonin. *The Theater and Its Double*. New York: Grove, 1958.

Asad, Talal. *Formations of the Secular: Christianity, Islam, Modernity*. Stanford, CA: Stanford University Press, 2003.

Bamford, Christopher, ed. *Homage to Pythagoras: Rediscovering Sacred Science*. Hudson, NY: Lindisfarne, 1994.

Barault, Jean-Louis. *Reflections on the Theater*. London: Rockcliff, 1951.

Bellah, Robert. *Habits of the Heart: Individualism and Commitments in American Life*. New York: Harper & Row, 1985.

Ben-Menahem, Hanina, Neil S. Hecht, and Shai Wosner, eds. *Controversy and Dialogue in the Jewish Tradition*. New York: Routledge, 2005.

Ben-Rafael, Eliezer, Yaacov Oved, and Menachem Topel. "Introduction: A Difficult Question." In *The Communal Idea in the 21st Century*, ed. Eliezer Ben-Rafael, Yaacov Oved. and Menachem Topel. Leiden: Brill, 2013.

Berger, Peter. *The Sacred Canopy: Elements of a Sociological Theory of Religion*. New York: Anchor, 1990.

Blasi, J. R. *The Quality of Life in a Kibbutz Cooperative Community*. Cambridge, MA: Institute for Cooperative Community, 1977.

Bourdieu, Pierre. "Participant Objectivation." *Journal of the Royal Anthropological Institute* 9 no. 2 (June 2003): 281–294.

Brintnall, Kent L. *Ecce Homo: The Male-Body-in-Pain as Redemptive Figure*. Chicago: University of Chicago Press, 2011.

Brown, Susan Love, ed. *Intentional Community: An Anthropological Approach*. Albany, NY: Bryant, Edwin, trans. *The Yoga Sutras of Patanjali*. New York: North Point, 2009.

Buller, David J. *Adapting Minds: Evolutionary Psychology and the Persistent Quest for Human Nature.* Cambridge, MA: MIT Press, 2005.

Calkowski, Marcia S. "A Day at the Tibetan Opera: Actualized Performance and Spectacular Discourse." *American Ethnologist* 18, no. 4 (November 1991): 643–657.

Casanova, Jose. "Secularization Revisited: A Reply to Talal Asad." In *Powers of the Secular Modern: Talal Asad and His Interlocutors,* ed. David Scott and Charles Hirschkind. Stanford, CA: Stanford University Press, 2006, 12–30.

Castaneda, Carlos. *The Teaching of Don Juan: A Yaqui Way of Knowledge.* Berkeley: University of California Press, 1972.

Chary, Helwon. *Autobiography as Method.* Walnut Creek, CA: Left Coast, 2008.

Churchland, Patricia Smith. *Neurophilosophy: Toward a Unified Science of the Mind/Brain.* Cambridge, MA: MIT Press, 1998.

Clarke, Peter B. *New Religions in Global Perspective: A Study of Religious Change in the Modern World.* London: Routledge, 2006.

Coakley, Sarah, and Martin Nowak. *Evolution, Games, and God: The Principle of Cooperation.* Cambridge, MA: Harvard University Press, 2013.

Cohen, E. "The Structural Transformation of the Kibbutz." In *The Sociology of the Kibbutz: Studies of Israeli Society,* ed. E. Krausz, vol. 2. New Brunswick: Transaction, 1983, 75–114.

Cohen, Robert, and John Harrop. *Creative Play Direction.* Englewood Cliffs, NJ: Prentice Hall, 1974.

Crawford, Matthew. *Shop Class as Soulcraft: An Inquiry into the Value of Work.* New York: Penguin, 2009.

Csikszentmihalyi, Mihaly. *Flow: The Psychology of Optimal Experience.* New York: Harper Perennial, 1991.

Cupitt, Don. *Mysticism after Modernity.* Malden, MA: Blackwell, 1998.

Daniel, E. Valentine. *Fluid Signs: Being a Person in the Tamil Way.* Berkeley: University of California Press, 1987.

D'Aquili, Eugene, and Andrew Newberg. *The Mystical Mind: Probing the Biology of Religious Experience.* Minneapolis: Fortress, 1999.

Davis, Leesa S. *Advaita Vedanta and Zen Buddhism: Deconstructive Modes of Spiritual Inquiry.* London: Continuum, 2010.

Day, Dorothy. *House of Hospitality.* New York: Catholic Worker, 1939.

de Certeau, Michel. *The Mystic Fable: The Sixteenth and Seventeenth Centuries.* Chicago: University of Chicago Press, 1992.

Demerath, Nicholas J., III. "Social Movements as Free-Floating Religious Phenomena." In *Blackwell Companion to Sociology of Religion,* ed. Richard K. Fenn. Oxford, UK: Blackwell, 2001, 229–248.

De Salzmann, Jeanne. *The Reality of Being: The Fourth Way of Gurdjieff.* Boston: Shambala, 2011.

Egan, Robert J., S.J. "Ignatian Spirituality and Social Justice." Address given at Regis College, Toronto, 1991.

Eisenstadt, S. N. "Israeli Identity: Problems in the Development of Collective Identity of an Ideological Society." *Annals of the American Academy of Political and Social Science* 370, no. 1 (1967): 116–123.

Eliade, Mircea. *Images and Symbols: Studies in Religious Symbolism*. Princeton, NJ: Princeton University Press, 1961.

Etzioni, Amitai. *The Spirit of Community: Rights, Responsibilities and the Communitarian Agenda*. London: Fontana, 1993.

Flood, Gavin. *The Ascetic Self: Subjectivity, Memory and Tradition*. Cambridge: Cambridge University Press, 2004.

Forman, Robert K. C. *Mysticism: Mind, Consciousness*. Albany: State University of New York Press, 1999.

Frederickson, Jon. *Psychodynamic Psychotherapy: Learning to Listen from Multiple Perspectives*. Philadelphia: Taylor & Francis, 1999.

Freud, Sigmund. *Civilization and Its Discontents*. New York: Norton, 2005.

Gandhi, M. K. *Bread Labour: The Gospel of Work*. Ed. Ravindra Kelekar. Ahmedabad, India: Navajian, 1960.

Geertz, Clifford. *The Interpretation of Cultures*. New York: Basic, 1973.

———. *Works and Lives: The Anthropologist as Author*. Stanford, CA: Stanford University Press, 1988.

Gharavi, Lance, ed. *Religion, Theater and Performance*. New York: Routledge, 2012.

Gilmore, Lee. *Theater in a Crowded Fire: Ritual and Spirituality at Burning Man*. Berkeley: University of California Press, 2010.

Glucklich, Ariel. *Sacred Pain*. New York: Oxford University Press, 2001.

Goffman, Erving. *Presentation of Self in Everyday Life*. Garden City, NY: Doubleday Anchor, 1959.

Golitizin, Alexander. "Suddenly Christ: The Place of Negative Theology in the Mystagogy of Dionysius Areopagites." In *Mystics: Presence and Aporia*, ed. Michael Kessler and Christian Sheppard. Chicago: University of Chicago Press, 2004, 8–37.

Gombrich, Richard F. *How Buddhism Began: The Conditioned Genesis of the Early Teachings*. London: Routledge, 2006.

Gordon, A. D. *Ha'avoda*. Tel Aviv: Hapoel Hatza'ir, 1923.

Gregory, R. L. *Eye and Brain: The Psychology of Seeing*. Princeton, NJ: Princeton University Press, 1997.

Grimes, Ronald L. *Deeply into the Bone: Re-Inventing Rites of Passage*. Berkeley: University of California Press, 2000.

———. *The Craft of Ritual Studies*. New York: Oxford University Press, 2014.

Gurdjieff, G. I. *Meetings with Remarkable Men*. New York: E. P. Dutton, 1963.

———. *Beelzebub's Tales to His Grandson*. New York: Two Rivers, 1993.

———. *Transcripts of Gurdjieff's Meetings, 1941–1946*. London: Book Studio, 2008.

Gyatso, Janet. "Healing Burns with Fire: Facilitation of Experience in Tibetan Buddhism." *Journal of the American Academy of Religion* 67 (1999): 113–147.

Hanh, Thich Nhat. *The Heart of Understanding: Commentaries on the Prajnaparamita Heart Sutra*. Berkeley, CA: Parallex, 2009.

Harpham, Geoffrey. *The Ascetic Imperative in Culture and Criticism.* Chicago: University of Chicago Press, 1987.

Helmreich, William B. *The World of the Yeshiva: An Intimate Portrait of Orthodox Jewry.* Jersey City, NJ: Ktav, 2000.

Hinings, C. R., and Royston Greenwood. "Disconnects and Consequences in Organization Theory?" *Administrative Science Quarterly* 47, no. 3 (September 2002): 411–421.

Holder, John J. *Early Buddhist Discourses.* Indianapolis: Hacket, 2006.

Humphrey, Caroline, and James Laidlaw. *The Archetypal Actions of Ritual: An Essay on Ritual as Action Illustrated by the Jain Rite of Worship.* Oxford: Oxford University Press, 1994.

Husserl, Edmund. *Logical Investigations.* London: Routledge, 2001.

———. *Ideas: General Introduction to Pure Phenomenology.* New York: Routledge Classics, 2012.

Iannaccone, Laurence R. "Religious Participation: A Human Capital Approach." *Journal for the Scientific Study of Religion* 29 (1990): 297–314.

James, William. *Psychology: Briefer Course.* New York: Harper Torchbooks, 1961.

Johnson, Mark. *The Body in the Mind.* Chicago: University of Chicago Press, 1987.

Johnstone, Keith. *Impro: Improvisation and the Theatre.* London: Faber and Faber, 1979.

Juergensmeyer, Mark. *Radhasoami Reality: The Logic of a Modern Faith.* Princeton, NJ: Princeton University Press, 1991.

Kapferer, Bruce. *A Celebration of Demons: Exorcism and the Aesthetics of Healing in Sri Lanka.* Bloomington: Indiana University Press, 1983.

Kardong, Terrence G. *Pillars of Community: Four Rules of Pre-Benedictine Monastic Life.* Collegeville, MN: Liturgical Press, 1991.

Katz, Steven T. *Mysticism and Philosophical Analysis.* New York: Oxford University Press, 1978.

———, ed. *Mysticism and Religious Traditions.* New York: Oxford University Press, 1983.

Kohn, Alfie. *Punished by Rewards: The Trouble with Gold Stars.* New York: Houghton Mifflin, 1999.

Krausman Ben-Amos, Ilana. *The Culture of Giving: Informal Support and Gift Exchange in Early Modern England.* Cambridge: Cambridge University Press, 2008.

Kripal, Jeffrey J. *Esalen: America and the Religion of No Religion.* Chicago: University of Chicago Press, 2007.

Krishnamurti, Jiddu *Commentaries on Living.* Series 1, Chapter 41: "Awareness." New York: Quest, 1956.

———. *Talks and Dialogues.* Berkeley: Shambala, 1970.

———. *This Matter of Culture / Think on These Things.* New York: Harper Perennial, 1989.

———. *Total Freedom: The Essential Krishnamurti.* San Francisco: HarperSanFrancisco, 1996.

Krishnamurti, J., and Dr. David Bohm. *The Ending of Time.* San Francisco: Harper San Francisco, 1985.

Kundera, Milan. *The Book of Laughter and Forgetting.* New York: Harper Perennial, 1999.

Kwilecki, Susan. *Becoming Religious: Understanding Devotion to the Unseen.* Carnbury, NJ: Associated University Presses, 1999.

La Corte, Daniel Marcel, and Douglas J. McMillan, eds. *Regular Life: Monastic, Canonical, and Mendicant Rules.* Kalamazoo, MI: Medieval Institute, 2004.

Lakoff, George, and Mark Johnson. *Metaphors We Live By,* 2nd ed. Chicago: University of Chicago Press, 2003.

Lalich, Janja. *Bounded Choice: True Believers and Charismatic Cults.* Berkeley: University of California Press, 2004.

Leighton, Taigen Dan. "Zazen as an Enactment Ritual." In *Zen Ritual: Studies in Zen Buddhist Ritual in Practice,* ed. Steve Heine and Dale S. Wright. New York: Oxford University Press, 2008, 167–184.

Lewis, I. M. *Ecstatic Religion: A Study of Shamanism and Spirit Possession.* New York: Routledge, 2003.

Lhalungpa, Lobsang P. *The Life of Milarepa.* Boston: Shambala, 1977.

Lindholm, Charles, ed. *The Anthropology of Religious Charisma: Ecstasies and Institutions.* New York: Palgrave Macmillan, 2013.

Loss, Joseph. "Explicit Non-religious and Implicit Non-secular Localization of Religion." *Nova Religio: The Journal of Alternative and Emergent Religions* 13, no. 4 (2010): 84–105.

Lunddskow, George. *The Sociology of Religion: A Substantive and Transdisciplinary Approach.* Los Angeles: Pine Grove, 2008.

Lyon, M. L., and J. M. Barbalet. "Society's Body: Emotion and the "Semantization" of Social Theory." In *Embodiment and Experience,* ed. Thomas J. Csordas. Cambridge, UK: Cambridge University Press, 1994, 48–68.

Mauss, Marcel. *The Gift: The Form and Reason of Exchange in Archaic Societies.* Oxon, UK: Routledge, 2002.

McCutcheon, Russell T. "Introduction." In *Religious Experience: A Reader,* ed. Craig Martin and Russell T. McCutcheon. Sheffield, UK: Equinox, 2012, 1–16.

McGinn, Bernard. *The Foundations of Mysticism: Origins to the Fifth Century.* New York: Crossroads, 1995.

McIntosh, Mark. *Mystical Theology.* Malden, MA: Blackwell, 1998.

McVee, Mary B., Kailonnie Dunsmore, and James R. Gavelek. "Schema Theory Revisited." *Review of Educational Research* 75, no. 4 (Winter 2005): 531–566.

Merton, Thomas. *Life and Holiness.* New York: Doubleday Image, 1964.

———. *Conjectures of a Guilty Bystander.* Garden City, NY: Doubleday, 1966.

Metz, Johan Baptist. *A Passion for God: The Mystical-Political Dimension of Christianity.* Trans. and ed. by J. Matthew Ashley. Mahwah, NJ: Paulist, 1998.

Miller, Barbara Stoler. *Yoga: The Discipline of Freedom.* New York: Random House, 2009.

Miller, Timothy. *America's Alternative Religions*. Albany: State University of New York, 1995.

———. "The Evolution of American Spiritual Communities." *Nova Religio: The Journal of Alternative and Emergent Religions* 13, no. 3 (February 2010): 14–33.

Molina, Bruce J. *The Social World of Jesus and the Gospels*. London: Routledge, 1996.

Mommaers, Paul, and Jan van Bragt. *Mysticism Buddhist and Christian: Encounters with Jan van Ruusbroec*. New York: Crossroads, 1995.

Mulaik, Stanley A. "The Metaphoric Origins of Objectivity, Subjectivity, and Consciousness in the Direct Perception of Reality." *Philosophy of Science* 62, no. 2 (June 1995): 283–303.

Multmann, Jürgen. *Theology of Hope: On the Ground and the Implications of a Christian Eschatology*. New York: Harper & Row, 1967.

Murray, Stephen O. "Review: The Scientific Reception of Castaneda." *Contemporary Sociology* 8 (March 1979): 189–192.

Near, Henry. *The Kibbutz Movement: Crisis and Achievement, 1939–1995*. Oxford, UK: Littman Library, 1997.

Needleman, Jacob, and Goerge Baker, eds. *Gurdjieff: Essays and Reflections on the Man and His Teachings*. New York: Continuum, 2004.

Newberg, Andrew, and Mark Robert Waldman. *Words Can Change Your Brain*. New York: Plume, 2013.

Noblitt, James Randall. *Cult and Ritual Abuse: Narratives, Evidence and Healing Approaches*. Santa Barbara: Praeger, 2014.

Okely, Judith, and Helen Callaway. *Anthropology and Autobiography*. London: Routledge, 1992.

Opaz, Aviva. *Sefer Hakevutzah*. Jerusalem: Yad Ben Tzvi, 1996.

Osborne, Arthur. *The Collected Works of Ramana Maharshi*. York Beach, ME: Red Wheel / Weiser, 1997.

———. *Ramana Maharshi and the Path of Self-Knowledge*. Tiruvannamalai, India: Sri Ramanasramam, 2004.

Otto, Rudolf. *Mysticism East and West: A Comparative Analysis of the Nature of Mysticism*. New York: Macmillan, 1970.

Ouspensky, P. D. *In Search of the Miraculous: The Teachings of G. I. Gurdjieff*. San Diego: Harvest, 2001.

Palgi, Michal. "Organizational Change and Ideology: The Case of the Kibbutz." *International Review of Sociology* 12 (2002): 389–402.

Palgi, Michal, and Shulamit Reinarz. *One Hundred Years of Kibbutz Life: A Century of Crises and Reinvention*. New Brunswick, NJ: Transaction, 2014.

Patanjali. *The Yoga Sutras of Patanjali*. Trans. Edwin Bryant. New York: North Point, 2009.

Phillips, Stephen H. *Classical Indian Metaphysics: Refutations of Realism and the Emergence of "New Logic."* Chicago: Open Court, 1995.

Pinker, Steven, *The Language Instinct*. New York: Harper Collins, 1994.

Piovanelli, Pierluigi. "Jesus' Charismatic Authority: On the Historical Applicability of a Sociological Model." *Journal of the American Academy of Religion* 73, no. 2 (June 2005): 395–427.

Potter, Karl. *Encyclopedia of Indian Philosophies*, vol. 3: *Advaita Vedanta up to Samkara and His Pupils*. Delhi: Motilal Banarsidass, 2008.

Prebish, Charles S. *Buddhist Monastic Discipline: The Sanskrit Pratimoksa Sutras of the Mahasanghikas and Mulasarvastivadas*. Delhi: Motilal Banarsidass, 2002.

Proudfoot, Wayne, and Phillip Shaner. "Attribution Theory and the Psychology of Religion." *Journal of the Scientific Study of Religion* 4, no. 4 (1975): 317–330.

Ram, Kalpana, and Christopher Houston, eds. *Phenomenology in Anthropology*. Bloomington: Indiana University Press, 2015.

Ramdas, Swami. *In Quest of God: The Saga of an Extraordinary Pilgrimage*. San Diego: Blue Dove, 1994.

Rappaport, Roy. *Ritual and Religion in the Making of Humanity*. Cambridge: Cambridge University Press, 1999.

Rawls, John. *A Theory of Justice*. Cambridge, MA: Harvard University Press, 1999.

Riis, Ole, and Luigi Berzano, eds. *Annual Review of the Sociology of Religion*, vol. 3: *New Methods*. Leiden: Brill, 2012.

Robinson, Richard H., and Willard L. Johnson. *The Buddhist Religion: A Historical Introduction*. Belmont, CA: Wadsworth, 1997.

Roku, Shoyo. *Book of Serenity: One Hundred Zen Dialogues*. Boston: Shambala, 2005.

Ruffing, Janet, ed. *Mysticism & Social Transformation*. Syracuse, NY: Syracuse University Press, 2001.

Ryle, Gilbert. *Collected Essays: 1929–1968*. New York: Routledge, 2009.

Sansone, Caron, and Judith M. Harakiewicz. *Intrinsic and Extrinsic Motivation: The Search for Optimal Motivation and Performance*. San Diego: Academic Press, 2000.

Shapira, Anita. *Hapoel Hatzair*. Tel Aviv: Am Oved, 1967.

Sharma, Arvind. *The Experiential Dimension of Advaita Vedanta*. Delhi: Motilal Banarsidass, 1993.

Sheldrake, P. "Contemplation and Social Transformation: The Example of Thomas Merton." *Acta Theological Supplementum* 11 (2008): 181–197.

Shirley, John. *Gurdjieff: An Introduction to His Life and Ideas*. New York: Torcher/Penguin, 2004.

Shulman, David. *Dark Hope: Working for Peace in Israel and Palestine*. Chicago: University of Chicago Press, 2007.

Smith, Huston, and Philip Novak. *Buddhism: A Concise Introduction*. San Francisco: HarperSanFrancisco, 2003.

Smith, Jonathan Z. *Map Is Not Territory: Studies in the History of Religions*. Chicago: University of Chicago Press, 1978.

Smith, Philip. "Culture and Charisma: Outline of a Theory." *Acta Sociologica*. 43, no. 2 (April 2000): 101–111.

Spiro, Melford E. *Kibbutz: Venture in Utopia*. Cambridge, MA: Harvard University Press, 1956.

Stark, Rodney, and Roger Finke. *Acts of Faith: Explaining the Human Side of Religion*. Berkeley: University of California Press, 2000.

Stone, Jacqueline Ilyse. *Original Enlightenment and the Transformation of Medieval Japanese Buddhism*. Honolulu: University of Hawai'i Press, 1999.

Sudo, Philip T. *Zen 24/7*. New York: HarperCollins, 2005.

Talmon, Yonina. *Family and Community in the Kibbutz*. Cambridge, MA: Harvard University Press, 1974.

Taves, Ann. *Fits, Trances and Visions: Experiencing Religion and Explaining Experience from Wesley to James*. Princeton, NJ: Princeton University Press, 1999.

———. *Religious Experience Reconsidered: A Building-Block Approach to the Study of Religion and Other Special Things*. Princeton, NJ: Princeton University Press, 2009.

Taylor, Charles. *Sources of The Self: The Making of the Modern Identity*. Cambridge, MA: Harvard University Press, 1989.

Thomson, Garrett. *On Gurdjieff*. South Melbourne, Australia: Wadsworth, 2003.

Toennies, Ferdinand. *Community and Society (Gemeinschaft und Gesellschaft)*. New Brunswick, NJ: Transaction, 1988.

Toren, Christina. "Imagining the World That Warrants Our Imagination: The Revelation of Ontogeny." In *Sociality: New Directions*, ed. Nicholas J. Long and Henrietta L. Moore. New York: Berghahn, 2013, 43–60.

Tracy, David. "Recent Catholic Spirituality: Unity amid Diversity." In *Christian Spirituality III: Post-Reformation and Modern*, ed. L. Dupré and D. Saliers. New York: Crossroad, 1989, 143–173.

———. "Afterword: A Reflection on Mystics; Presence and Aporia." In *Mystics: Presence and Aporia*, ed. Michael Kessler and Christian Sheppard. Chicago: University of Chicago Press, 2004, 239–244.

Tubbs, Nigel. *Philosophy of the Teacher*. Malden, MA: Blackwell, 2005.

Turak, August. *The Business Secrets of the Trappist Monks: One CEO's Quest for Meaning and Authenticity*. New York: Columbia University Press, 2013.

Turner, Victor, ed. *Celebration Studies in Festivities and Rituals*. Washington, DC: Smithsonian Institution Press, 1982.

———. *The Ritual Process: Structure and Anti-Structure*. New Brunswick, NJ: Aldine Transaction, 2011.

Tyler, Robert. *Encountering Religion: Responsibility and Criticism after Secularism*. New York: Columbia University Press, 2013.

Valantasis, Richard. "A Theory of the Social Function of Asceticism." In *Asceticism*, ed. Vincent L. Wimbush and Richard Valantasis. New York: Oxford University Press, 1995, 544–552.

van Nieuwenhove, Rik, Robert Faesen, and Helen Rolfson, eds. *Late Medieval Mysticism: Of the Low Countries*. New York: Paulist, 2008.

Volf, Miroslav. *Work in the Spirit: Toward a Theology of Work*. New York: Oxford University Press, 1991.

Vygotsky, Lev. "Consciousness as a Problem of Psychology of Behavior." *Soviet Psychology* 17 (1979): 5–35.

———. *Thought and Language*. Cambridge, MA: MIT Press, 1997.

Wallace, B. Allan. *Contemplative Science: Where Buddhism and Neuroscience Converge*. New York: Columbia University Press, 2009.

Wallis, Robert J. *Shamans/Neo-Shamans: Ecstasy, Alternative Archaeologies and Contemporary Pagans*. New York: Routledge, 2003.

Waterfield, Robin, trans. *The Theology of Arithmetic: On the Mystical, Mathematical and Cosmological Symbolism of the First Ten Numbers*. Grand Rapids, MI: Phanes, 1988.

Watson, Alan. "The Self as Dynamic Constant: Ramakantha's Middle Ground between a Naiyayika Eternal Self-substance and a Buddhist Stream of Consciousness-Moments." *Journal of Indian Philosophy* 42 (2014): 173–193.

Weber, Max. *Economy and Society: An Outline of Interpretive Sociology*. Berkeley: University of California Press, 1978.

Wellbeloved, Sophia. *Gurdjieff: The Key Concepts*. London: Routledge, 2003.

Welwood, John. "Reflection and Presence: The Dialectic of Self-knowledge." *Journal of Transpersonal Psychology* 28, no. 2 (1996): 107–128.

Wexler, Philip. *The Mystical Society: An Emerging Social Vision*. Boulder, CO: Westview, 2000.

Whitehouse, Harvey. "Rites of Terror: Emotion, Metaphor and Meaning in Melanesian Initiation Cults." *Journal of the Royal Anthropological Institute* 2, no. 4 (December 1996): 703–715.

Whitehouse, Harvey, and James Laidlaw. *Ritual and Memory: Toward a Comparative Anthropology*. Walnut Creek, CA: Altamira, 2004.

Wilson, David Sloan. *Darwin's Cathedral: Evolution, Religion and the Nature of Society*. Chicago: University of Chicago Press, 2002.

Yamane, David. "Narrative and Religious Experience." *Sociology of Religion* 61, no. 2 (Summer 2000): 171–189.

Yarbro Collins, Adela. *Cosmology and Eschatology in Jewish and Christian Apocalypticism*. Leiden: E. J. Brill, 1996.

Zablocki, Benjamin. *Alienation and Charisma*. New York: Basic, 1980.

Zimbardo, Philip G. *The Lucifer Effect: Understanding How Good People Turn Evil*. New York: Random House, 2007.

INDEX

A Mirror of Perfection, 123, 126–127
Abhidharma, 124
Accountant, 56
Achievement, 72
Adorno, T., 19
Adva, 61, 98, 165, 168–169, 172–175, 200
    On leadership, 174–175
Advaita Vedanta, 130
Agam, 203
Aghori, 128–129, 196
Alon, 24, 34, 62–63, 150–151, 202, 214, 232
    On cement work, 153
    On dining practice, 62
    On school and kibbutz, 55
Ambition, 72
Amish, 7
Amit, Ilan, 68
Amnon, 50–51, 98, 215
Amos, 99, 130–133
Anat G., 5, 38–39, 42, 77, 109–112, 136, 143
    On community, 188–189
    On death of Yossef, 82–88
Anat S., 146, 149, 150
Animals, 92
Apophetic, 126–127
Apple trees, 47

Apricots, 42, 47, 50
Arava, 1, 48–49
Arjuna, 155, 220
Arkadi, 162
Arnon, 57
Art center, 47, 51, 55, 141–156, 152, 206
Artaud, A., 207
Arts and crafts, 51
Arturo, 162
Arunachala, 15
Asad, T., 4
Asceticism, 10, 141–156,
    Defined, 142
Ascription, 17–18
Ashram, 8
Attachment, 15, 55, 70
    Yossef on, 153–154
Attention, 108, 113, 197–198
    And empathy, 114
Attribution, 17–18
Atur, 203
Authority, 96, 106, 148, 187
Autonomy, 140
Avi, 144, 200, 204, 207, 211, 233
    As project manager, 147–148
Avigdor, 109, 150, 154, 162, 191, 200
Ayyapan, 16

Banaras, 48
Barrault, J. L., 207
Barthes, R., 27
Becoming Religious, 16–17
Beer Sheva, 12, 176
Berger, P., 20
Bhagavad Gita, 107, 138–139, 155, 162, 220
Bly, R., 214
Boddhisattva, 124, 198
Body, 21–22, 84–85
Bohm, D., 14
Bolt, 175, 177, 184
The Book of Laughter and Forgetting, 113
Bomb shelter, 51
Boots, 31, 206
Bourdieu, P., 27
Brahman, 130, 134–135
Brain, 99
Bread, 32
Breakfast, 32, 37
Bruner, J., 28
Bryant, E., 125–126
Buber, M., xi, 14, 107, 196
Buddha, 219
Buddhism, 107, 114, 136, 196, 240–241
    Monks, 77, 99
Budget director, 56
Bulgarian cheese, 36, 49, 170
Burning Man, 213–214

Cabaret, 209
Cabernet, 163, 164
Campbell, J., 241–242
Cancer, 83, 86
Canola oil, 36
Carmela, 190, 192
Casanova, J., 225
Castaneda. C., 14, 211, 214
Caterpillar backhoe, 203
Causality, 26
Cement, 145, 153
    Pouring, 151, 200, 202–204

CEO, 52
Charisma, 8, 187, 199, 226, 240
    And persuasion, 193
    Weber on, 239
Charity, 98
Cheese, 49, 166, 170
Chicken coop, 58, 175
Children, 33, 52, 53–54, 117, 152
    In projects, 202–203
    During Shabbat, 191
Chinese workers, 145
Chomsky, N., 229
Christianity, 3, 77, 107, 122, 195
Circles, 60, 98
    Dance, 100
Clinic, 51
Code of conduct, 63
Coffee table, 105
Commitment, 152–153
Committee, 61, 91
Communication, 114, 175
Community, 1, 3, 61–62, 186, 190
    Collective, 56
    And conversation, 173
    Economy and school, 59
    Intentional, 4, 193, 225
    And Self-inquiry, 96
    Theories of, 187
    Types, 7–8
    And work, 220
Compassion, 98, 99, 198
Conflict, 93, 149–150, 152
    And suffering, 156
Connectedness, 142
Consciousness, 24, 88–89, 93, 123
    And cancer, 86
    And culture, 22, 128
    And thought, 99
    Universal, 198
    Yoga on, 125
Consensus, 91, 95
Constructivism, 19, 21, 122–123, 128
Contemplation, 1, 9, 159, 193, 198

Conversation, 23–25, 26, 43–44,
　104–120
　　Circle, 173
　　Goal, 61
　　In Jerusalem, 71
Cooling stack, 47
Copeau, J., 207
Couples, 192
Courage, 65–66
Cracks (song), 6
Crawford, M., 182
Crites, S., xi
Csikszentmihalyi, M., 161
Culture, 21

Dagan, 98
Dairy, 49, 50
Daliah, 165
Dalit, 55, 58, 91, 148
Dance, 100
Dani, 206–218
　　And Maya, 217
　　Rite of passage, 216–217
Daniel, E. V., 16–17
Date farm, 49, 62, 104
Dates, 37, 49
Daumal, R., 14
David, 101, 214
Dawn, 31
De Salzman, Jeanne, 69
Death, 25
Decision making, 57, 89–95
Desert, 1, 3, 12–13, 15, 220
Desire, 107–108, 136
Dialogue, 42–43, 107, 109
Diary, xiii, 106
Dining room, 30–44, 62
　　Crew, 32, 39
　　New, 33
　　Preparation, 33–34
Discipline, 126, 139–140
Dishes, washing, 32, 41
Disorder, 139

Don Juan, 211
Doors, 143
Doron, 37
Duality, 24
Duration walk, 110–111, 208
Durkheim, E., 142
Dying, Yossef, 83–85

Eck, D., x
Eco-village, 7
Economy, and community, 76, 197
Effort, 150–152
Eggs, 36, 39
Eilat, 12, 51
Eitan, 97, 178
Eleanor, 98
Elementary school, 52
Eli, 109–112
Eliade, M., 14, 18, 20, 228, 241
Emotions, 73–74
Empathy, 114, 116, 192
Emptiness, 23, 28, 123, 219–220, 222–223
Encounter, 27
*Encountering God: A Spiritual Journey
　from Bozeman to Banaras*, x
Error, 133
Ethanol, 163
Etzioni, A., 226
Everyday Mysticism, 121–140, 143
Experience, 22, 131, 133
Experiments, 70–71, 129
Experts, 178
Extended family, 54, 186–205, 217
　　As a principle of the school, 190
　　And Self-inquiry, 204

Families, 190, 192, 220
Fatigue, 145
Fear, 207, 209, 211
Feelings, 111, 118
File, 177, 179
Fire, 214, 215–216
Fish, 51

Floor, 145
Flow, 161
Fluid Signs, 16–17
The Flutes, 33
fMri, 99
Forman, R.C., 123
Foucault, M., 237
Foundation, 144
Freedom, 58, 78
Friendship, 217
Fruit, deciduous, 49
Funeral, 85–87

Gadi, 50, 98, 170
Galit, 117–118, 153
Garage, 52, 175–185
Garden, 48, 50
Gate, 208
Geertz, C., 27, 228, 229
Genesis, 107
Georgia, Republic, 217
Germany, 53
Gil, 47, 88, 144, 148, 150, 233
Gilmore, L., 214–215
Gimello, R., 123
Glasses, 34
Goal, 72, 108, 156
Goats, 49, 165–172
    And love, 171
    Milking, 166–167
    Products, 3, 166, 170
God, 16–17, 22, 116–117, 122, 126, 132, 195
    And work, 158
Goffman, E., 212
Gordon, A. D., 128, 159, 227, 238
Grapes, 164
Grasping, 136
Gravel, 145
Greeting, 40–41
Groups, 8, 23–24, 59–60, 97, 112
    Natural, 226
    Ritual, 213
Guest rooms, 52

Guitars, 216
Gurdjieff, G., 14, 65, 100, 149, 155, 171, 214, 221
    Influences on, 67
    In Israel, 68
    On shock, 233, 238
    And Yossef, 66–69
    On Zen, 159
Guy, 178
Guy B., 49, 61, 98

Hadar, 172–173
Hagar, 91–92
Hannah, xiii, 88
Harei Edom (wine), 160
Harpham, G., 143, 237
Harvard University, ix
Hasidim, 3, 195–196
Hatchery, 161, 163
The Heart Sutra, 123–124
Heat, 150
Hebrew Bible, 107
Heidegger, M., 28
Hendrik Herp, 123, 126–127
Herbs, 34, 165
Hertzel, 144
Hierarchy, 35, 61
Hinduism, x, 123, 136, 221
Holy, 15, 18
Holy Spirit, 127
Home, rotation, 55, 191
Householders, 16
Humility, 189
Husserl, E., 227
Huxley, A., 14, 214

I, 25–26
Identification, 70, 74–75, 153, 190
Ignatius of Loyola, 194
Ignorance, 95, 130
Ilana, 65–66, 95, 98, 100–103, 232
Illumination, 126
Impermanence, 197

Improvisation, 207–208
In Quest of God, 121–122
In Search of the Miraculous, 68
Inaction, 169
Individual, 7–8, 96, 193
Indra, 210
Ineffability, 27
Initiation ritual, 211–212
Intimacy, 191–192
Iris L., 38, 41, 83, 101, 145, 150
Iris T., 226
Irrigation, 213
Isaac, 115–116, 167–169
Isherwood, C., 14
Island, 215–218

James, W., 20, 142, 226
Jeep, 176
Jerusalem, 1, 14, 44, 69, 146
Jesus, 13, 16, 198
Jews, 122
Jnana-yoga, 139
Job coordinator, 56
John Deere, 182
Johnson, M., 21
Jolt, 171. *See also* shock
Jordan, 49
Judaism, 14
Juergensmeyer, M., 89–90

Kabbalah, 3, 189
Kabir, 3
Kafka, 84, 128
Kapferer, B., 213
Karma-yoga, 139
Kataphatic, 127
Katz, S.T., 123
Kehilah, 189
Kibbutz, 2, 4, 189–190
    Movement, 86–87
    And school, 59
    Yossef on, 79
Kitchen, 30–44

Knowledge, 135, 216
Kobi, 130, 145–147, 148
Kosher, 51
Krishna, 40, 155, 220
Krishnamurti, 14, 67–69, 155, 214, 221, 234–235
Kundera, Milan, 113
Kung, Dr. Michel, 69
Kurta, 40
Kvutzah, xii, 55, 189, 199, 232
Kwilecki, S., 16–17

Laborers, 35
Lake, 46, 47, 215–218
Lakoff, G., 21
Landscaping, 52, 67, 200–201
Language, 124
Laughter, 209
Laundry, 52
Leadership, 59, 60–61, 172–175
    Support, 174
Leary, T., 14
Library, 51
Lilly, J., 14, 214
Limud, xii, 69
Listening, 107, 113, 120, 175
Liza Minelli, 209
Lotus pond, 208
Love, 88, 188, 194, 217, 230
Lunch, 41–41

Machtesh Ramon, 12–13
MacIntyre, A., 28
Mahayana, 123–124
Majority vote, 91
Manitou forklift, 177, 183
Map, 19–20, 28, 106, 122–129
    Erasing, 21, 124, 135
    And scripture, 128
    Social role, 129
    And territory, 27
Marpa, 3, 142
Mary Magdalene, 126

Maya, 50, 165–167, 171
    And Dani, 206–207
Maya (concept), 130
Mazda, 178–179
McCutcheon, R., 18, 20
McGinn, B., 123, 195, 128, 236–237
The Meaning and End of Religion, ix
Meat, 51
Meditation, 62
Meir, 15, 51, 202, 209–210
Meister Eckhart, 18, 194–195
Memory, 86
Merakz meshek, 56
Merlot, 160, 163
Merton, T., 195
Metal shop, 52
Metaphors, 21–22
Milarepa, 142
Milk, 166, 170
Milking, 165–167
Miller, B., 236
Mind, 98
Mindfulness, 113, 159, 238
Miriam, 132
Mitzpe Ramon, 12
Monastery, 8, 64
Moral obligations, 26–27
Morality, 79
Morphium, 85
Mortifications, 127
Moses, 186, 198
Mourning, 88–89
Mt. Sinai, 186, 198
Mulamadhyamikakarika, 219–220
Murray repair kit, 177
Muscat, 159–160
Music room, 51
Muslims, 122
The Mystical Society, 193
Mysticism, 3, 4, 8–9, 121, 127, 193,
    195
    Forms of, 127
    And maps, 194
    As verbal performance, 121

Nagarjuna, 219–220, 236
Naïve, 26, 56
Narayan, K., xi
Narrative, 27–29
Natalia, 32, 36–38, 39, 42
Negev, 1, 12
Neot Smadar, 3, 14, 23, 54, 95 and
    passim
    Economy, 49–51
    As mystical community, 122
    Mysticism in, 129
    As new society, 142
New Age, 14
Newberg, A., 114
Nicholson set, 177
Nietzsche, F., 18, 19, 141
Nirvana, 124
Noam, 33, 34–35, 42–43, 49
Noam S., 101, 103
Non-intervention, 70, 117
Nonresponse, 113, 197–198
Noumena, 131–132
NRM (new religious movement),
    186–187
Numbers, 65, 99–103
    And ego, 101
    And relationship, 103
    Yossef on, 100

Obligation, 142, 152
Observer-participant, 9, 23
Office complex, 52
Ojai, 214
Old age, 216
Olive harvest, 46
Olive oil, 36–37
Omelet, 45
Omri, 91, 101, 186–187, 234
    On extended family, 196–199
    On identification, 154–155
    On Self-inquiry, 196–197
Orchards, 208
Orit, 97
Orsi, R., 27

Otto, R., 15, 18, 194–195
Ouspensky, P.D., 7, 14, 67–69, 149
Owen, H.P., 123
Oxford English Dictionary, 121

Pain, 16, 21–22, 211–212
Pajama, 40
Pandora Box, 73
Parody, 212
Pasture, 171
Patanjali's *Yoga Sutras*, 123, 125–126
Patenkin, A., 1
Paving, 200–201
Peacocks, 31, 45
Peak experience, 127
Perennial Philosophy, 18
Performance, 212, 218
Phenomena, 131
Photographs, 160
Piaget, J., 21
Pilgrims, 16
Pinker, S., 229
Pioneers, 15, 141
Pirsig, R., 14
Pistons, 177
Plans, 146–147
Plates, 34
Plovers, 46
Pomegranate, 46
Pool of Wolves, 47–48
Porcupines, 90, 94
Posture, 40
Power, 229
Prakriti, 125–126
Precast, 144, 147
Presence, 7, 67–68, 98, 185
Prince, 117
Principles, 93, 98
Project, 45, 105, 174–175
    Communal, 141–156, 199–205
    In Jerusalem, 69
    Organization, 147
    Planning, 200
Psychology, 237

Pundak, 51, 115–116, 163, 177
Purpose, 197–198
Purusha, 125

Qumran, 13

Rakefet, 97
Ramana Maharshi, 15, 126, 233
Rappaport, R., 212
Rawls, J., 7, 205
Reb Sanders, 234
Reeds, 46
Refrigerators, 160
Relationship, 140, 175
Religious dialogue, 106–109
Religious experience, 10, 12–29
    In Neot Smadar, 23
Report, 70, 117–118, 150
Resistance, 119–120, 168
Restaurant, 51
Retreat, 76, 109, 207
Ricoeur, P., 28
Rites of passage, 11, 211–212
Ritual, 208, 212, 213
Roberts, T., 230
Robinson, R.H., 124
Ronen, 152
Rony M., 38–39, 98
Rony, O., 69–70
Room 113, 146, 194
Ruffing, J., 194
Rules of conduct, 93, 96
Runners, 209–210
Russia, xii
Ruth B., 24, 57, 75–76, 83
    On deciding, 92–93
Ruusbroec, 127
Ryle, G., 228

Sabari Malai, 16–17
Sacred, 15
Safra, Y., 2. *See also* Yossef
Saint Basil, 158
Salad, 39–40

Salad oil, 36
Samadhi, 125
Sammy (Dr. Eitan), 84–85
Samsara, 124
Samuel, 52, 61, 176–185
San Francisco, 15
Sankhya, 125
Satire, 213
Sauvignon Blanc, 48, 160
Savion, 84, 133, 134
Schechter, Dr. Yossef, 68
Schemas, 21–22
Scholem, G., 14
School, 15, 63, 64–68, 75–81, 219–220
    And decision-making, 94
    As family, 54
    History of, 66–71
    And kibbutz, 54–55, 57
    Leadership, 57, 59
    Today, 95–99
    After Yossef, 82–88, 90
Schug, 36
Screams, 209–210
Scripture, 128
Secretary, 52, 56
Secularism, 4–5
Self, 23, 108–109, 195
Self-importance, 58, 80
Self-inquiry, xii, 1, 15, 65, 77–81, 98–98
    And art center, 152
    And attribution, 17–18, 235
    Beginning, 97–98, 109
    Conditions, 95–96, 220
    And conflict, 149
    And consciousness, 190
    And conversation, 106
    And cooperation, 54
    And death, 89
    And decision-making, 89
    Experiments, 70–71
    And goats, 167–168
    As *limud*, 225
    And morality, 79
    In Ouspensky, 68

    And relationships, 117, 188
    On time, 66
    On work, 157–158, 169, 237
    After Yossef, 82–88, 90–93
    Yossef on 24, passim
Self-restraint, 119
Self-sufficiency, 5
Seminar, 52, 60, 97, 109
Sewage, 231
Shabbat, 45, 100, 115, 191
Shachar, 206
Shankaracharya, 18, 129–130
Sharat, 57–58, 76, 87, 94–95, 108, 119,
    149, 232
    Role, 78
    Yossef on, 79
Shared view, 91–93
Shaul, 131
Shavuot, 53, 186, 187
Shay, 180–181
Shaykh, 8
Sheldrake, P., 195
Shepherding, 167, 171–172
Shimon, 25, 51
Shiraz, 48, 163, 164
Shiraz Merlot, 160
Shirley, 200, 204
Shiva, 16, 40
Shlomit, 40–41, 97, 101, 115–116
Shmuel, 49, 98, 159–165
    On time, 161–162
Shock, 129, 233
Shop Class as Soulcraft, 182
Shunyata, 123
Shvetaketu, 107
Sigal, 203
Sigal (wine), 163
Skillful means, 129
Smadar, 225
Smith, J. Z., 27, 106, 228
Smith, W.C., ix–x
Smoking shed, 37, 42, 104, 118
Social affairs, committee, 56
Social exchange, 218

Sociality, 4, 193–196
Solar plant, 52
Song, 6
Sorrow, 88, 198
Sri Caitanya, 196
St. Augustine, 226
St. Benedict, 64
Stanford Prison Experiment, 230
Staying in the Shadow, 117
Steiner, Rudolf, 65
Sticks, 208
Storytellers, Saints and Scoundrels, xi
Struggle, 145
Subaru, 181
Success, and failure, 181
Succession, of teacher, 89–90
Suffering, 24, 89, 95, 135–138
    Buddhism on, 124
    Overcome, 139
    Yoga and, 125
Sufis, 3
Sukkah, 59, 60, 77, 90, 104
    As sharat, 91
Sulfur dioxide, 163
Sun, 150
Superessential, 126–127
Suzuki, D.T., 14, 214
Swami Ramdas, 121–122
Swimming, 47

Tables, 33, 45
Tahini, 32, 42
Talmud, 107
Tamara, 7
Taves, A., 19–20, 228
Taylor, C., 19, 28
Tbilisi, 217
Tea, 31–32, 35, 37, 216
Teacher, 8, 233, 234
Tessa, 50, 97, 164
Thought, 24–25, 74–75, 87, 96, 99, 114,
    125, 230
    And consciousness, 77–78
    And empathy, 116

And experience, 133
And identification, 155
And numbers, 99–103
    Numerical, 102
    Temporal, 101
Time, 131, 137–138
Toilets, 34
Torah, 186
Tower, 141, 144–145, 147
Trappist monks, 161
Trust, 133, 205
Tsaddik, 107
Turak, A., 161
Turner, V., 189, 212, 242
Twilight, 74
Tyler, R., 27

UCLA, 214
Uddalaka Aruni, 107
Upanishads, 107
Uri, M. 47

Valantasis, R., 143, 156
Vedanta, 214, 237
Vegetable masala, 41
Vegetables, 32, 35–36
Vered, 98
Veterans, 40
Vimalakirti, 3, 220
Vimalakirti Sutra, 220
Vineyard, 48, 104
Vinters, 160
Vinter's Art, 161
Violence, 86
Vipassana, 15
Vision, 43, 94, 95
Volf, M., 158, 161
Volunteers, 31, 32, 41, 97
VW Minibus, 175
Vygotski, L., 21, 229

Waldman, M.R., 114
Walk, 40
Walls, 144

Water, 46–47
Watts, A., 214
Weber, M., 142, 187, 189, 205
Wedding, 206, 217–218
Wednesday, 97, 104–105
Wexler, P., 4, 193, 240
Whitehouse, H., 227
Willard, L.J., 124
Wimbush, V., 142
Wine, 159–165
Wine barrels, 163
Wine Bible, 161
Wine making, 157
Wine, tasting, 162
Winemaking chemistry, 164
Winery, 49–50, 159–165
Wittgenstein, L., 228
Wizard of Oz, 33
Words, 5–6, 43, 127
Words Can Change Your Brain, 114
Work, 38, 60, 157–159, 161, 232
    Crew, 61
    Defined, 157
    Sacred, 227
    And Self-inquiry, 9
    And suffering, 136
    And talk, 173–174
Workshops, 51

Yajnavalkya, 107
Yaqui, 214
Yehudit, 83, 202
Yodfat, 68
Yodfata, 52
Yoga, 15
Yogurt, 32, 39, 166
Yoram, 5, 74, 98, 103, 131, 141, 145–147, 149, 154
Yossef, xiii, 57, 71 and *passim*
    On asceticism, 142–143, 151
    Biography, 69
    On Buddhism and Hinduism, 221, 230
    Charisma, 187
    Death of, 82–88
    On desire, 107–108
    And Gurdjieff, 71
    And mysticism, 3–4, 122
    Planning art center, 146, 148
    On the Real, 130–135
    On school, 55
    As theater director, 207–208, 241
    On time, 137–138
Yuval, 61, 144

Za'atar, 35
Zen, 9, 29, 107, 124, 159, 161, 214
Zionists, 2, 15, 141